UNDERSTANDING HUMAN RIGHTS

UNDERSTANDING HUMAN RIGHTS
An Overview

O.P. Dhiman

KALPAZ

Understanding Human Rights

ISBN: 978-81-7835-880-2

Published in 2011 in India by
Kalpaz Publications
C-30, Satyawati Nagar,
Delhi-110052
E-mail: kalpaz@hotmail.com
Phone : 9212729499

Laser Type Setting : Quick Media, Delhi
Printed at : Chawla Offset Printers, Delhi

To

The Champions

of

Human Rights

Contents

Preface

Since my childhood, because of the influence of my great democrat mother, I have been a staunch believer in Individual Freedom and Dignity of Man, and hence Human Rights. During the period of emergency—enemy number one of Human Rights—I delivered lectures at several forums to make the people, especially the students, fight against emergency and for the safeguard of Human Rights. I am author of several books on Education and Philosophy, and this is my first humble attempt to write a book on Human Rights to make the people aware of Human Rights.

There are a number of books available on Human Rights and also some more books on this subject are coming out. All these books touch one or the other aspect of Human Rights. They do not give a complete picture of this subject.

The term 'Human Rights', these days, is much talked about, but little understood. That is why, I was tempted to author the book, 'Understanding Human Rights—An Overview'.

This book is a comprehensive but comprehensible treatise which gives an overview of Human Rights by touching all aspects of the subject—historical, philosophical and legal. Various International Charters have been discussed in detail and their relationship with Indian Constitution has been brought out.

I am sure, this compact book of seventeen chapters will give a full understanding of the term, 'Human Rights'. This book will be useful to the students of Political Science, Philosophy, History and Human Rights. It will also be of interest to general readers. Any suggestion for improvement in the next edition will be appreciated.

Ashiana
49, Raghbir Nagar
Patiala-147001

O.P. Dhiman
E-mail: profesor.dhiman@yahoo.com

Acknowledgements

Any accomplishment requires inspiration, help and guidance of many people and this book is not an exception. During its preparation, I have been inspired, helped and guided by a number of well-wishers.

I cannot but remember with feeling of piety and gratitude my mother, Late Mrs. Maya Dhiman, my first teacher, friend and philosopher, a straunch democrat who created in me a burning passion for democratic ideals, critical objective thinking and positive attitude.

Formal, though it may look, I must acknowledge my grateful appreciation to my wife, Mrs. Manorama Dhiman, former Head, Department of Home Science, Govt. College for Women, Patiala for her inspiration and devotion but for which the present work would have been impossible.

I must appreciate my 16 year old grand-son Anish Dhiman who helped me a lot working hard on computer.

I extend my thanks to my colleagues—Dr. C.P. Sharma Former Head, Deptt. of Economics and Dr. Harcharan Singh,

Associate Professor, Punjabi, Multani Mal Post-Graduate College, Patiala for reading the manuscript of this book and for their valuable suggestions.

I must be thankful to all authors on whose works I have drawn freely.

I also express my thanks to my publishers, Kalpaz Publications, Delhi for extending me full co-operation to publish this book in an elegant manner.

O.P. Dhiman

ONE

Prologue

Human Rights is a twentieth century name for what has been traditionally known as natural rights or, in more exhilarating phrase, the rights of man. Much has been said about them, and yet one may still be left wondering what they are?

Human Rights can be generally defined as those rights which are inherent in our nature and without which we cannot live as human beings. Human Rights and fundamental freedoms allow us to develop and use our human qualities, our intelligence, our talents and our conscience and to satisfy our spiritual and other needs. They are based on mankind's increasing demand for a life in which the inherent dignity and worth of each human being will receive respect and protection. Human Rights are sometimes called "fundamental rights" or "basic rights" or "natural rights". As fundamental or basic rights they are those which must not be taken away by any legislature or any act of government and which are often set out in the constitution. As natural rights they are seen as belonging to men and women by their very nature. Another way to describe them would be to call them 'Common Rights' for they are rights which all men or women in the world should share just as the Common Law in England, for example, was the body of rules and customs which, unlike local customs, governed the whole country.

Human Rights are not created by any Legislature, they assume the position of natural rights. Any civilized country or body like the UN must recognise them. They can not be subjected to the process of amendment even. The legal duty to protect human rights include the legal duty to respect them. Members of UN have committed themselves to promote respect for and observance of human rights and fundamental freedoms.

The concept of Human Rights is not entirely Western in origin. It is also not so modern. It is a crystallization of values that are the common heritage of mankind. As ideals, human rights define the community within which people want to live, but have their roots in the community in which they live. Based on our common humanity, human rights differ from rights grounded in domestic law, but in other respects they operate much like rights grounded in domestic law: violation of one of the enumerated human rights would serve as a predicate or justification within the legal system for exercises of the state's coercive power. Human rights might be better viewed more as Social Ideals than as Legal Claims.

The expression "human rights" denotes all those rights, which are inherent in our nature and without which we cannot live as human beings. In other words, human rights being eternal part of the nature of human beings are essential for individuals to develop their personality, their human qualities, their intelligence, talent and conscience and to enable them to satisfy their spiritual and other higher needs.

Further, it is described that the rights, which are natural and inherent for the life and happiness of every individual, are called human rights. These rights are indispensable for the maintenance of human dignity and the individual enjoys these rights from birth to death. In fact human rights are the very essence of a meaningful life, and human dignity is the ultimate purpose of the Government.

The purpose of securing human rights as such is to provide protection to these rights against the abuse of power committed by the organs of State; to establish institutions for the promotion of living condition of human beings and for the development of their personality; and at the same time, to provide effective remedial measures for obtaining redressal when these rights are violated. Karel Vasak has aptly remarked that the human rights are essentially individual in character. They are meant to be enjoyed by individuals and they constitute a social phenomenon by virtue of those for whom they are intended.

Lexicon's meaning of the term 'human rights' is: claims and assertions which are legally recognized and protected to secure for each individual the fullest development of personality and spiritual, moral and other independence. The Protection of Human Rights Act 1993 defines 'Human Rights' as the rights relating to life, liberty, equality and dignity of the individual. These rights are derived from the dignity and worth inherent in the human beings. The recognition of these rights has been a result of man's long struggle for the realization of his human values.

Human Rights are essentially a product of democracy. Man's struggle against tyranny has been long and sustained. Tyranny has surfaced in different forms and modes. Human beings have always tried to assert their rights.

"The primitive man had no notion of fundamental rights, though he did have a number of limitless freedoms which no civilized man can ever boast of. He had the freedom of movement, the absolute freedom of movement. In a world which had no national frontiers and consequently no system of passports, permits or visas, the man could move all over the world. He had the freedom of speech and expression. He could talk himself hoarse. But a period when man had not yet developed political institutions, this freedom had no real utility. He also had the absolute and anarchic freedom of sexual relationship. But in a society where refinement did not exist, this freedom merely indicated his closeness to other animals. Thus, he had all possible and conceivable freedoms, but in the primitive society these freedoms had no meaning, no relevance. Freedoms and liberty in an unorganized society are freedoms and liberty in wilderness. The fact of the matter is that in the society the social need for liberty and freedoms did not exist.

It is a unique feature of the history of the development of political institutions, that the progress towards organized society was not a movement towards the attainment of rights, fundamental or otherwise, but towards the suppression of the absolute and anarchic freedoms of the primitive man.

Thus, the rapid growth of Scientific Knowledge and thought; the deepest intellectual interest in every subject; and the wide spread tendencies in all parts of the world to reform or reconstruct the society, had the lasting effect on social, political and cultural development of mankind. Professor Hawkings goes on to say *"there are well defined laws that govern the universe and everything in it develops in time."*

One must undergo one's share of the experiences of the world. Men find themselves forced to reconsider current and inheriting beliefs and ideas to gain some harmony between present and past experiences to reach a position which satisfies demands of feeling and reflexion and new confidence for facing future.

CONCEPT OF HUMAN RIGHTS

The concept of Human Rights is not a recent phenomenon. It is as old as the human race. These rights have their roots in antiquity. The roots for the protection of the human rights may be traced as far back as in the *Bafilonian law*, Assyrian laws and in the *Dharam* of the Vedic period in India. Writings of Plato and other Greek and Roman philosophers also depict for the protection of human rights though they had a religious foundation. The city state of Greece gave equal freedom of speech, equality before law, right to vote, right to be elected to public office, right to trade and right of access to justice to their citizens. Similar rights were secure to the Romans by the *Jus Civil of Roman Law.*

The term human rights covers in its ambit those essential rights, defined or undefined which lead and contribute to the balanced development of Human beings. The concept of Human Rights in Modern times can be traced to Natural Law philosophers, who propounded these rights to protect individuals against the excesses of the State. However, the international concern with human rights as enshrined in the U.N. Charter is not a modern innovation. It is in fact heir to all the great historic movements for man's freedom to the enduring elements in the tradition of natural law and natural rights. The concept of Human Rights represents an attempt to protect the individual from oppression and injustice. They provide a human standard of achievement for all the people and all the nations. These rights are independent, inalienable and inviolable and hence universal.

HUMAN RIGHTS AND FUNDAMENTAL RIGHTS

Human Rights

Human Rights are essential for leading a decent and dignified life as human being. These are inalienable rights of all members of human family. These can be defined as the rights which every human-being is to enjoy and to have protected. These are those minimum rights which every individual must have against the State or other public authority by virtue of his being a human being. Human Rights can be termed as universal and politically identified human values. The contemporary conception of Human Rights, though rooted in the rich heritage of past, is of recent origin.

Fundamental Rights

Fundamental Rights are the modern name for what have been traditionally known as natural rights. So, the Human Rights and Fundamental Rights have sprung from the doctrine of natural rights. Natural rights are those minimal rights of an individual which must be guaranteed by every society which claims to be civilized. Natural Rights are considered to be superior and inviolable by any human authority. These are considered to exist independent of law of the land. When guaranteed by the constitution, fundamental laws of the land are called Fundamental Rights. Natural rights theory entered the realm of constitutional law with two important documents, viz.; American Declaration of Independence 1776 and French Declaration of Rights of Man 1791. French Declaration has proclaimed, "The end of all political association is the preservation of natural rights of man; and these rights are liberty, property, security and resistance of oppression." Jeffrson has explained the nature of these rights by saying, "A Bill of Rights is what the people are entitled to against every government on earth." Similarly Vienna Declaration proclaims, "Human Rights and Fundamental Freedoms are the birth-rights of all human beings; their protection and promotion is the first responsibility of Governments."

The Indian Constitution seeks to preserve these natural rights against State encroachment and constitute higher judiciary as the sentinel of the said rights. The Apex Court has not only protected the fundamental rights but also extended rights beyond the list provided in Part III of the Constitution. Applying the theory of emanation, the Supreme Court has evolved following unnumerated rights as Fundamental Rights. Rights to privacy, human dignity, traveling aboard, rights against torture and degrading treatment, speedy trial, free legal aid in criminal trial, health, pollution free environment, education, etc. These rights are not specifically guaranteed as fundamental rights by the Constitution, it is only by the interpretation given by the courts that these are elevated to the status of Fundamental Rights.

Distinction between Human Rights and Fundamental Rights

There is no basic or qualitative difference between human rights and fundamental rights. Both belong to same genus. The origin of both can be traced to the natural rights as stated above. Both aim at welfare, well - being and upliftment of human being. The term 'human rights' was mostly used to denote the rights to be promoted and protected by the international organs and agencies. Fundamental rights' is the nomenclature used by the Constitution of India for a group of rights listed in Part III.

Since the last decade this distinction has almost been blurred. Terminology of Human Rights is much more in vogue at the national level as well. The passing of the *Protection of Human Rights Act*1993 and the definition of "human rights given in it has almost liquidated to life, liberty, equality and dignity of the individual guaranteed by the Constitution or embodied in the International Covenant and enforceable by courts in India". The Constitution of India and Universal Declaration of Human Rights were drafted almost simultaneously. Framers of the Indian Constitution were influenced by the concept of human rights in the UN charter and also by the deliberation for the Universal Declaration. The Constitution incorporated most of the human rights which were later embodied in the International Covenants.

Human Rights	*Fundamental Rights*
1. Human Rights, as is evident from the nomenclature, are the rights of the human being only. These are inalienable rights of all the members of the human family.	1. All the fundamental rights contained in Part III except those mentioned in Articles 15,16,19,29, and 30 are available to natural as well as artificial persons.
2. Only natural persons are entitled to human rights.	2. The fundamental rights are basically available to the citizen.
3. The Human Rights were mostly used to denote the rights to be promoted and protected by the international organs and agencies.	3. Fundamental Rights is the term .used by the Constitution of India for a Group of rights listed in its Part III.
4. Human Rights is a broader term.	4. Fundamental Rights is a narrower term.
5. All the human rights are not fundamental rights.	5. All the fundamental rights are human rights.
6. Human rights are birth rights.	6. The fundamental rights are so called because these are secured not by the ordinary law of land but by the fundamental law which is usually embodied in a written constitution that cannot be altered by the ordinary process of legislation.

Human Rights	*Fundamental Rights*
7. Human Rights encompass fundamental rights, constitutional rights, directive principles and statutory rights.	7. These rights in India are confined to Part III of the Constitution and emanate from there as interpreted by the Supreme Court.
8. Human rights are understood in the global sense. These are available to one and all, nationals as well as aliens.	8. On the other hand, Constitution of India reserves some fundamental rights for the citizens alone e.g. discrimination in public places, rights to hold public office and employment and rights to freedom contained respectively in Articles 15,16,19 are available to the citizen alone while the remaining fundamental rights in Part III are available to all citizens as well as aliens.

It is clear from above distinction that there is only general difference. Thus human rights are called, Fundamental Rights or Basic Rights or Natural Rights. As fundamental or basic rights these are those rights which must not be taken away by any Act of legislature or government and which are often set out in the Fundamental law of the land, *i.e.* Constitution. Broadly speaking, human rights are the minimal rights which every individual must have against the State. They are Universal and Inalienable Rights.

TWO

Approaches to Explain the Nature and Meaning of Human Rights

There are two main approaches adopted to explain the nature and meaning of human rights : Philosophical or Theoretical Approach and The Pragmatic or Utilitarian Approach.

There are five following theories to explain the meanings of Human Rights as discussed below :

PHILOSOPHICAL OR THEORETICAL APPROACH

The Natural Rights Theory

The growth of the concept of the 'Rights of Man' has been closely associated with the traditional natural law theories. As a matter of fact the notion of individual rights has never been projected as special feature in these theories. Law as such "implies both duties and rights, and it is no doubt fair to say that the ancient and medieval theories of natural law were more concerned with the foundations of moral, legal and political duty than with the foundations of rights".

Rights, in the traditional doctrine of natural law, are rights against other people. These rights have corresponding duties in the sense that some other person is under a duty towards the holder of the right. For example, I have natural right to life. I hold this right against any other person and such in the sense that no one can deprive me of my life. Hence others are under corresponding duty not to kill me. Similarly, my natural right to liberty imposes duty upon others to leave me alone. Consequently, the rights and duties are co-related with each other. D.D. Raphael has rightly observed that :

"The Rights are rights against other people, and the duties are duties to other people. Thus, a system of natural law, is a system of duties which all men have to others and at the same time a system of rights which all men have against others."

Moreover, human rights are generally or at least at first stage, secured through political actions. In the contemporary sense of the term, human rights have been defined by Elaine Pagels as "The idea that the individual has right, claims upon society, or against society; that these rights which society must recognise, on which it is obliged to act, are intrinsic to human being." This definition of human rights is an improvement upon the traditional 18th century definition of the Right of Man since it recognises the human rights as a claim upon or against the society. It clearly implies following three characteristic features of human rights.

Human Rights are said to be Recognised

Human Rights are neither derived from the social order nor conferred upon the individual by the society. They reside inherently in the individual human being's independent of and even prior to his participation in the society. As such, they are the result of recognition by the State but they are logically independent of the legal system for their existence. For this reason, many thinkers have assigned the origin of human rights to natural law and not to positive law. In this sense, natural law is said to be "a normative system which is characterised by the fact that the criterion for the validity of its norms is based not on their enactment or recognition by certain individuals but on their intrinsic justification." In the same spirit, the human rights being derived from the principles of natural law do not depend for their validity on being formulated or accepted by any authority. Thus, a positive legal system 'which does not recognize human rights is not law'.

Human Rights are inalienable in the sense that a holder of these rights cannot divest himself of them. The reason is simple, for these rights are inherent in the very nature of human being. Jacques Martain has said that the "Human person possesses rights because of the very fact that it is a person, a whole, a master of itself and of its act...by natural law, the human person has the right to be respected, is the subject of rights, possesses rights. These are the things which are owed to a man because of the very fact that he is a man."

The inalienable or natural rights are not identified with the norms of positive law. They are independent of the positive law, as such, Human Rights are used as a reference to evaluate the rules of positive law, law enforcement machinery, legal institutions and performances of State. When a legal system does not recognize human rights it is criticized as being oppressive and persistent demand is made for upholding the value of human rights.

All human beings are said to be essentially equal

Now it is an established fact that human rights are derived directly or indirectly from the very nature of man. From this it may be argued that by virtue of being human, one inherits all those attributes which are inherent in human personality, and natural rights being one among those attributes are inherited naturally. Thus, the only condition necessary for enjoying natural basic rights is to be a human being. Apparently, this appears to be a very reasonable proposition because it lays down an objective equalitarian principle according to which a human being, by virtue of being human, can possess or enjoy all human rights without any distinction as to his colour, stature, wealth or to his nationality. From this Carlos Santiago Nino argues that, "If the only relevant condition for enjoying certain rights is being human and if this property does not admit of degrees, there can not be differences of degree in the extent to which the rights in question are held; this is, all human beings have them to the same degree."

This leads to inevitable conclusion that "all human beings are equal". It may be useful to quote Barnard Mayo also :

"Human Rights are the rights that a human being has by virtue of whatever characteristics he has that are both specifically and universally human."

The Legal Rights Theory

Jermy Bentham has criticized natural law theory as nonsense upon stilts. He has advocated in favour of legal rights theory. In the opinion of supporters of Legal Rights Theory rights are the creation of State. As such, they are neither absolute nor inherent in the nature of man. These rights, such as right to life, liberty or property are artificially created by the law of land.

Thomas Hobbes, one of the ardent supporters of the legal right theory holds the view that fundamental rights of individual are the right of self-preservation which can be protected by state in better manner than by any other means.

This theory can be upheld to the extent that the recognition of a right by state is necessary for its enforcement. If a state does not recognise a right, it can not be enforced, however, potential it may be. Even in democratic societies, where people's will reign supreme recognition of rights by state is essential for their enforcement against the state. Bosanquet has rightly noted that: "A right...has both a legal and moral reference. It is a claim which can be enforced at law, which no moral imperative can be; but it is also recognised to be a claim which ought to be capable of enforcement at law, and thus, it has a moral aspect... A typical 'right' unites the two sides. It is, and ought to be, capable of being enforced as law.

The Historical Theory of Rights

The historical theory of rights maintains that the rights are the creation of historical process. A long-standing custom in the course of time concretise in the specific form of right. A traditional example may be used here to explain the process in which rights generally concretise. A person who receives birthday presents from his friends and relatives regularly for a long time develops expectation to receive it as a matter of right. Indeed, there are rights which are created in this process more particularly, most of the prescriptive rights such as, right of way or right to light or air. In the same spirit many of the natural rights have "the sanction of the longest and the least broken custom," for example, the rights of Englishmen, which have found mention in the Magna Carta and the Petition of Right, these in fact have been enjoyed from very early days. This justifies the comment of Richies that "those rights which people think they ought to have are just those rights which they have been accustomed to have, or which they have a 'tradition' (whether true or false) of having once possessed. Custom is primitive law.

The Social Welfare Theory of Rights

The Social Welfare Theory is also known as the Social Expediency Theory. The advocates of this theory believe that law, custom and natural rights, all are conditioned by social expediency. For instance, right to freedom of speech is not absolute but rather regulated in accordance with the requirements of social expediency. Roscoe Pound and Prof. Chafee have supported this theory. The utilitarians like Bentham and Mill advocated the 'greatest happiness of the greatest number' as a principle on the basis of which all the social measures should be judged. Utility can be determined by means of reason and experience.

The Idealistic Theory of Rights

This theory is also known as Personality Theory. This theory insists upon the inner development of man and development of his full potentiality. Hence, it treats rights of personality as a supreme and absolute right. All other rights, such as right to life, liberty or property are derived from this fundamental right.

PRAGMATIC OR UTILITARIAN APPROACH

Besides philosophical and theoretical approach, the another way of looking at the meaning and nature of human rights is pragmatism. Every right, whether it has been perceived as inalienable or otherwise, can have validity and effectiveness only through some process or institution. Thus, it can not be defined without reference to some institutional structure. As a room cannot be defined without reference to the walls, so human rights, can not be defined without reference to institutional settings.

After 1950, the world has seen three different trends of approaches to the human rights followed by three different groups. Their growing influence effected the framing of human rights instruments. They were the approaches of Western, Socialist and Third World Countries. Some of the writers have, however, cautioned against such human rights approaches.

WESTERN COUNTRIES AND HUMAN RIGHTS

It is said that the concept of 'Human Rights' is an exclusively western concept. It is also said that its 'imposition' on the rest of the world constitutes a form of intellectual, political or legal neo-colonialism or neo-imperialism. But, this view seems to be quite fallacious. Concepts of legitimacy, the justice, the integrity and dignity of the individual, safeguards against arbitrary rule, freedom from oppression and persecution, individual participation in collective endeavours and the like are to be found in every civilization throughout the world. Besides, the international instruments in which these concepts have been included were freely negotiated, adopted and ratified by many existing nations in all parts of the world, covering the entire spectrum of different cultural, religious and political set up.

The concept of human rights varies with traditions and cultures even if a body of substantive human rights norms exist, its meaning may also vary from culture to culture. It was, therefore, argued that it may not be possible to impose western notions on non-western countries having different traditions and culture.

Vasak and Alston are also of the view that some persons will endeavour to demonstrate that this law is of western origin. In fact, human rights, by no means reflect the historic conditions of a particular society, for the values which they express are to be found in one form or another in all political, social and religious doctrines.

SOCIALIST COUNTRIES AND HUMAN RIGHTS

The socialist countries believed in the concept of absolute sovereignty of state and they refuse to admit any form of international control over their actions. Conflicts between individuals and state do exist, since the state covers the economic well being and the cultural development of the individuals. The individuals must, therefore, behave as required by the state.

THE THIRD WORLD COUNTRIES AND HUMAN RIGHTS

The human rights which are considered important in industrially developed countries are relatively less important in the Third World Countries. The reason being that the traditional approach of western countries has been principally concerned with civil and political rights and they give much less attention to economic, social and cultural rights. But there is now undesired recognition of the importance to economic, social and cultural rights. By September 1993, more than 120 states had ratified the two UN Conventions on Human Rights, half of them were from the Third World. Nevertheless many developing countries are more concerned with economic and social rights than with their civil and political rights.

The International Conference on Human Rights at Teharan in 1968 stated in its Resolution No. XVII that the enjoyment of economic and social rights is inherently linked with a meaningful enjoyment of civil and political rights and there is a profound interconnection between the realisation of human rights and economic development.

THREE

History of Human Rights

If Negro-slave trade in U.S.A. and colonization by European Powers constituted the greatest violations of human rights in the history of mankind, it was the Cyclonic Wave of freedom movement and decolonisation that had changed not only the entire political geography of the world radically, but also the fundamental law of mankind and revolutionized human thinking based on oneness of human race and solidarity of human rights. The liberation and independence of a large number of countries in the three continents of Asia, Africa and Latin America involved the freedom of more than half of human population and that did vitally alter the future of mankind for the betterment. The potency of human rights will have to be accepted as an acknowledged fact in the history of mankind.

Human Rights dates back to the very dawn of human civilization; It is the concept of non-discrimination. It was enshrined to almost all the great religions of the World. The concept of universal brotherhood and belonging to one family of the whole world (वसुधैव कटुम्बकम्) was preached by Hinduism from the dawn of civilization.

The Sanskrit text which embodies the concept of fraternity and humanity sums as under :

न त्वहं कामये राज्यं, न स्वर्ग नापुनर्भवम्।
कामये दुःखतप्तानां, प्राणिनां आर्तिनाशनम्।।

It says that "I seek no Kingdom, nor heavenly pleasure nor personal salvation - once to relieve humanity from its manifold pains and distress is the supreme objective of mankind." Other religious beliefs such as Buddhism, Jainism, Christianity, Islam and Hinduism also preached similar doctrines.

HUMAN RIGHTS IN ANCIENT LAWS

It will be clear from the following historical analysis of literature in different countries and religions that human rights always found a place of pride in all ages.

Provisions for the protection of basic rights of man can be found as far back as in the *Babylonian laws* which were promulgated in Reigns of Urukogina of Lagarh (3260 B.C.), Sargon of Akkad (2300 B.C.) and Hammuraki of Babylon. It would, perhaps, be somewhat far-fetched to look for elements of the protection of human rights in the code of Babylonian king Hammuraki (about 2130 to 2088 B.C.), the most ancient code of law at present known. However, the sanctions which it provides in trying to protect the human rights such as the administration of justice, marriage and the family are so disproportionately cruel that it is preferable to disregard them in our context.

The Assyrian Laws which were inscribed on the Nine Clay-Tablets in the Reign of Tiglath-Pileser I (1115-1077 B.C.) contain hints of such protection, so do those Hittite Laws ascribed in the reign of king Telepinus (1511 -1486 B.C.).

The *City-States of Greece* gave Ironomia (equality before law), Irotima (equal respect for all), Jus Action (The right of access to their citizens), Jsogoria (equal freedom of speech), Jus Sufragii (The right to vote) and Jus Comercii (the right to trade) to their citizens.

Similar rights were secured to the *Romans* by the jus civil of the Roman Law. Some of which were extended even to Non-Romans under the Jus gentium.

However, as Rudolf Von Ihering pointed out the law of ancient republican Rome guaranteed to the Roman citizen (jus civile) the right to take part in the government of their country by participating in the exercise of the power of legislation, in the administration of criminal justice, in electing public officials and even in having a share in the police power.

The Great Charter of Liberties of *England* known as the Magna Carta of 1215 was imposed on King John by Prelates, Earls and Barons of his Kingdom after his defeat by the King of France, in 1214. The King accepted the Magna Carta, though it was exacted by his feudal barons in their own selfish interest and was by no means intended to assert rights and liberties for all. Several of its provisions, among them the famous clause 39 stating that :

"No freeman shall be taken or imprisoned or exiled or in any way destroyed...except by lawful judgement of his peers or (and) the law of land", gave expression to the idea of individual freedom and became the symbol of freedom for centuries to come.

Edward I gave the Statutem tellagio non concedendo to the English people in 1297. In the 17th century the immemorial rights of English people were successfully fought and ultimately they were successful in achieving the famous "Petition of Rights" in 1628. More Rights were included in the instrument of Government of 1653 which made Oliver Cromwell the Lord Protector of England, Scotland and Ireland. The Habeas Corpus Act, officially entitled, "an Act for the Better Securing the Liberty of the Subject and for Prevention of Imprisonment Beyond the Seas", was enacted by Charles II in 1679. The Bill of Rights officially entitled "an Act for Declaring the Rights and Liberties of the subject and for settling the succession of the Crown", was enacted in 1688 on the occasion of the succession of William of Orange and Marry Stuart to the throne of England. The Plantation Covenants such as Fundamental orders of Connecticut of 1638, proclaimed freedom of religion.

In USA Human Rights were included in the Virginia Declaration of Rights in 1776. When the American Declaration of Independence was made in that year. The American Bill of Rights, 1791 carried the ideas of earlier English documents but in some respects it was different from the English Declaration of Rights. Not only England exported its doctrine of rights, the powerful influence of the French Philosophers was visible among all the American Revolutionaries when the Constitution was ready by the spring of 1791, the Declaration was connected there to and this completed one of the most crucial epochs in the development of the concept of human rights. Before the American and French revolution it had what was for all practical purposes only a philosophical appeal but after the declaration and the Constitutional Bill of Rights the concept assumed a positive importance. Human Rights were included in the Constitution of the United States of 1787, with Amendment of 1789 and 1865.

Lafayette, who had supported the cause of the American colonies for independence, introduced the declaration *des droits de La' Homme et du citoyen* in the French Assembly in 1789. The French Philosophers had helped the colonies with an ideology. The Revolution of the colonies, in its turn, gave the French an example to follow and an enormous impact on the events in *France.* The French Declaration of the Rights of Man and of Citizen(1789) was directly inspired by earlier American examples.

NATURAL LAW

There is a close connection between the idea of "natural law" and the idea of "natural rights of man". These ideas may be found in the works of the stories, both Greek and Roman and in the teachings of St. Thomas Aquinas and medieval English Scholars of Law. They are encountered in the writings of Spanish Theologian-Lawyers of the 16th and 17th centuries - in the works of the Dutch Hugo Grotius, the founder of the modern international law and of John Milton and John Locke, the ideological architects of the English revolution of that century.

The American and French Revolutions and the Declaration that expressed the principles inspired the natural rights philosophers of 18th century, which made them secular, rational, universal, individual, democratic and radical. Instead of divine foundations for the rights of man, they substituted a social contractual base.

The concept of natural rights has survived in its modern name, but not without vicissitudes. In the course of its long history it has been persistently assaulted from diverse quarters. Burke claimed that the French Declaration of Rights of Man had done great damage by proclaiming human equality which he characterized as a 'monstrous fiction'. Bentham maintained that natural right is simple nonsense. It was thus attacked by those who were frightened by the revolutionary movement which proclaimed the rights of man. Finally, it attracted the condemnation of the Idealist and Marxist Philosophers, who saw in the State the highest end and ultimate value.

Rationalism, secularism and humanism rejected natural law in the 19th century. The 20th Century added new and changing political contexts for human rights which transformed the Philosophical and ideological base. Second half of the 20th century could be seen as period of universal acceptance of human rights.

INDIAN LAW

The Indian Civilization was at its peak when the Vedas were written. During the period of Mahabharata (3100 B.C.) Maharishi Ved Vyas divided Vedas in four parts *i.e.*, Rigveda, Samveda, Atharvaveda and Yajurveda. The concept of Rit (ऋत) was given utmost importance. It says that in this world lay some automatic system. This concept gives a rare hope to the sufferers of injustice and maladministration that there is some automatic law in the Universe and, therefore, injustice and maladministration will be for a small period and temporary. The concept of Rit teaches us that the law of nature is under regular system which observes the law without any exception. This system gave birth to the binding force of law. Rit gives moral force to the concept of law and makes it a model rule based on truth and justice.

The Rit or the truth and justice regulates the conduct of human being. In ancient India the rights of people were protected. It was binding on the King to protect people against all kinds of offences and give justice to people. Narada Smriti classified the offences into 10 kinds and provided that it was mandatory for the king to initiate criminal trials and protect the rights of people.

Manu has also stated that the Punishment is the only weapon which protects the rights of the individuals in the society:

दण्डः शास्ति प्रजः सर्वा दण्ड एवाभिरक्षति।
दण्डः सुप्तेषु जार्गृत दण्डं धर्म विदुर्वध।।

Manu has stated that King should be impartial in protecting the rights of the people even if the offender is the father or teacher or friend or mother or wife or son or a domestic priest, the King should not leave him unpunished. This shows that principle of equality before law and equal protection of law was observed without any discrimination, he himself was liable to be punished one thousand times more :

पिता ऽचार्यसुहृन्माता भार्यर् पुत्रः पुरोहित।
ना दण्डयो राज्ञो ऽस्ति यः स्वधर्मे न तिष्ठति।
कार्षायणे भवे दण्डयो यत्रान्य प्राकृते जनः।
तत्र राजाभवेत्दण्डयः सहरत्रमिति धारणाः।।

The maximum sentences werc prescribed for different offences. The exact quantum of punishment was required to be decided by the judges. The discretion of a judge was limited only. The judge (or the king) was required to take into account the offender's age, physical strength, health, sex, etc. before exercising his discretion. Manu warned the judges (the king) against unjust, improper and inhuman punishments.

The scholars of Indian History have expressed the view that there was a rich jurisprudence in ancient India. The jurisprudence provided an adequate framework for the regulation of the behaviour of ordinary person as well as the king. Two norms viz. Dharma and Dandas, which were necessarily influenced by the theological tenets of the Vedic Aryans, contained several features of a regulation mechanism for religious practices. The king had the authority to implement this system and the laws under it. But he himself was bound to follow the law, the norms laid down by religious codes and commentaries. Referring to the social responsibility of the king, Nagendra Singh quotes a statement from Manu :

"To end lawlessness was created the institution of the king whose supreme duty was to protect his subjects against disorder and anarchy. Detailed rules were laid down for the guidance of the king. Besides these Vedic features, the Upanishads furnished philosophical foundations for subsequent social developments."

Kautilya, the author of the celebrated political treatise Arthashastra, not only affirmed and elaborated the civil and legal rights first formulated by Manu but also added a number of economic rights. While categorically asserting that an Arya can never be subjected to slavery, he ordains that the king provide the orphan, the aged, the infirm, the afflicted and helpless with maintenance; he shall also provide subsistence to the helpless expectant mothers and also to the children they give birth to.

ISLAMIC LAW

Muhammad, the prophet of Islam, while delivering his "Farewell Sarmon" to a mammoth gathering at Mecca a few months before his demise in the tenth year of Hijra era (632 A.D.) spoke :

> O mankind! The Arab is not superior to Non-Arab, nor Vice-versa; the white has no superiority over the black, nor vice-versa; and the rich has no superiority over the poor. All of you are Adam's descendants and Adam was made of earth.

With all the force at his command he made an important declaration. Declaration of the equity of mankind, trans-national racial and economic. Earlier the Divine Revolution that he had transmitted to man had spelt out all human rights. The Quran and Sunna carried whole character of human rights.

Discarding all discrimination between man on the ground of nationality, nobility and descent and racial distinction, The Quran proclaimed :

> O mankind! We created you from a single couple and made you into tribes and nation's (only) so that you may recognize each other. Very (otherwise) the most

> notable among you, in our sight is he who is most righteous in conduct.

The Quran provides human rights, specially, right to religious freedoms, right to life and its necessities, Right of personal liberty, mobility and freedom of speech, Right to respect and privacy, Right to justice and fair deal, Right to family and Right to personal earnings and property.

The operational ramifications of the Islamic norms can be glanced through the Mughal History of India. Though the Mughal Government introduced a centralised despotism, its judicial administration contained all the basic elements of the modern doctrines of due process of law, fair trial and independent judiciary. In one place, Akbar went to the extent of saying that if he was guilty of an unjust act, he would rise in judgement against himself. Various European travellers, who visited Akbar's empire, highly appreciated his regard for rights and justice. His justice-loving tradition was followed by his son Jahangir, too. There was a popular legend that Jahangir arranged a chain with bells to be hung outside the fort in order to enable petitioners to approach him for the redressal of their grievances. Was it not an easily accessible individual petition system in comparison to our modern, lengthy and expensive writ petition system?

The above mentioned historical account proves an important fact that human rights were very much visible in the ancient Hindu and Islamic civilizations, as in the European Christian civilization. In other words, the majority of the Third World Countries which inherited non-western civilization contributed to the origin and development of human rights and movement connected with human rights.

PERIOD OF RENAISSANCE AND INDUSTRIAL REVOLUTION

The concept of rights of man in the modern context emerged at a time when the roots of the medieval society were already shaken in the 16th century by the challenge posed by the renaissance. Under its impact, radical socio-economic transformation took place which resulted in the destabilization of the then existing political equation. It is important to note that the philosophical and ideological revolution of the 17th and 18th centuries regarding the nature of man and his inalienable rights were accompanied by radical socio-economic transformations and changing society values.

The medieval despotism and emergence of the new rich class as a result of the industrial revolution were two important factors that shaped the concept of the rights of man. Firstly, common suffering under despotic rulers necessitated the demand for some sort of freedom from such a situation. This has been well described by a 16 Century Venetian Ambassador to the Grand Turk :

"When someone dies, the Grand Signor, who is the real owner of everything, takes whatever he wants from the estate and considered it a favour if he leaves anything to the widow..and the children. He can easily find a pretext to make it appear that justice requires him to confiscate the goods. He often takes property from the wealthy, a thing he can easily do because no one would dare to speak out against him. The mere will of the Grand Signor is justification enough to do anything in the world.'

Under the above-mentioned circumstances, human rights were identified in the form of mere individual freedom and less Governmental interference. This freedom had a negative notion as it was a freedom from, not freedom for, a certain situation. The human rights, at that stage, were looked upon as something against the state authority. Secondly, the newly emerging industrial middle class which was bargaining under restrictions imposed by the monarchial political system of that time, demanded political rights and access to the political area. This class demanded political rights in the name of democracy in order to establish its own identity against the medieval feudal order, which were necessary to ensure the natural rights to freedom. Therefore, civil and political rights emerged as a theme for human rights philosophy in the west.

ERA OF COLONIALISM

The 17th, 18th and 19th centuries witnessed the era of colonization of European powers (English, French, Dutch, Germany, Portugal, Spain etc.) of vast areas comprising of number of countries in Africa, Latin America and Asia. In this era of colonization, there was large scale conversion of faith. The religious belief does not allow conversion of non-believers to the faith. The Negro Slavery almost world-wide was present with brutality and inhuman practices. The slave trading was practice of that period.

In the 19th and 20th centuries freedom movement developed in the countries of all the continents. Hundred and thousands of freedom fighters were killed by the colonial powers violating all human rights norms. In India, from 1857 and 1947 the freedom movement faced the atrocities at the hands of British Governments. Similar was the position in other colonies. Human Rights worth name, were not protected by European Colonial Powers.

The next phase in the development of human rights was marked by the rise and expansion of imperialism. Imperialism was nothing but a policy of political and economic expansion which was pursued by the industrialized Europe during the later 19th and earlier 20 centuries. As a result of that, for the first time in history, the bulk of the entire World belonged to Europe. The close relationship between political and economic leaderships, resulted in the total exploitation of the masses who were already economically hard pressed and the wear imposed by imperialist further aggravated their suffering and hardship.

SOCIALIST MOVEMENT AND ROLE OF HUMANITARIANISM

The socialist movement of the early 19th century made demands for economic security and social justice in addition to civil and political rights. The Bolshevik Revolution of 1917 in Russia was a step further in this direction. The foremost task to which these revolutionaries addressed themselves was the establishment of a new social order based on economic equality. It became obligatory on the part of the State to ensure the basic minimum economic and social rights to its citizens. Thus, under the socialist approach, the State was looked upon as the promoter and protector of economic and social well-being.

The socialist approach to human rights was based on the basic assumptions that the rights and freedoms of individuals in any state depend on socio-economic, political and other conditions of the society, its achievement and progress. For the realization of political and civil rights, first economic equality and social security be protected. That is why the socialists emphasized on economic and social rights.

The traditional Western concept of human rights was essentially political in nature. Many Western scholars are, therefore, critical of the socialist approach to human rights. In fact, one scholar, Maurice Cranston, has gone to the extent of refusing to accept economic and social rights as universal human rights at all. Macpherson, opposing the cranstonian stand, has said that there was a basic underlying commonality in the two apparently contradictory approaches to human rights. He argued that logical disparity between the traditional rights and the new human rights would disappear if one noticed that one of the essential traditional civil rights was the right to property, necessarily required by the right to life or by the right to a free or genuinely human life. All that had changed was the view of possible ways of securing individual right to the material means of a fully human life.

Another eminent scholar John Somerville has rightly observed that those two different approaches were not necessarily contradictory but could be viewed as supplementary. Analysing the contents and nature of the two approaches, he explained as under :

> The difference between the Soviet and Western democratic concepts are not of principle, but rather of problem area and method of implementation ... They may well be regarded as different phases or stages in the growth of human rights.

This has led to a demand by some activists for a new approach to problem of human rights. Pope John Paul II, in his address to a Conference of Latin American Bishops in Maxico in January 1979, declared that "the Church has no need to resort to systems and ideologies in order to love and defend man and contribute to his liberation."

Such a trend of an ideologically neutral approach to human rights was not acceptable to the socialists. They asserted that there was no concept of human rights outside an ideology, just as there can be no concrete ideology of human rights outside philosophical systems. It is true as well, no concept of human rights will survive long if it is not based on the philosophy of humanitarianism. Humanitarianism carries with it a force of universal conviction and, hence, it is acceptable to all.

Today's world is still faced with the problem of ever-increasing piles of nuclear arsenals and the threat of nuclear war. After the end of cold war the most urgent question before humanity is their own survival which is being threatened by so many things like uncontrolled arms race, ecological and environmental imbalance caused by the rapid modernization leading to want, hunger, disease and death. Any concept of human rights, which is not aimed at protecting and preserving the human race, will not be acceptable to anyone at all.

At the end of 20th century, the new emerging rights reflect the human needs of our times because they aim at solving our problems with a desire to make this world a better place to live in, not only for ourselves but for the future generations also. That is why these rights are sometimes called "Third generation or solidarity rights." These solidarity rights include the right to development, right to peace, right to clean and healthy environment, right to privacy, right to share in the common heritage of mankind, right to communication, right to food and right to shelter.

FOUR

Philosophy of Human Rights

Human rights are international norms that help to protect all people everywhere from severe political, legal, and social abuses. Examples of human rights are the right to freedom of religion, the right to a fair trial when charged with a crime, the right not to be tortured, and the right to engage in political activity. These rights exist in morality and in law at the national and international levels. They are addressed primarily to governments, requiring compliance and enforcement. The main sources of the contemporary conception of human rights are the *Universal Declaration of Human Rights* (United Nations, 1948) and the many human rights documents and treaties that followed in international organizations such as the United Nations, the Council of Europe, the Organization of American States, and the African Union.

The philosophy of human rights addresses questions about the existence, content, nature, universality, justification, and legal status of human rights. The strong claims made on behalf of human rights (for example, that they are universal, or that they exist independently of legal enactment as justified moral norms) frequently provoke skeptical doubts and countering philosophical defences. Reflection on these doubts and the responses that can be made to them has become a sub-field of political and legal philosophy with a substantial literature.

THE GENERAL IDEA OF HUMAN RIGHTS

The *Universal Declaration of Human Rights* (1948) sets out a list of over two dozen specific human rights that countries should respect and protect. These specific rights can be divided into six or more families: *security rights* that protect people against crimes such as murder, massacre, torture, and rape; *due process rights* that protect against abuses of the legal system such as imprisonment without trial, secret trials, and excessive punishments; *liberty rights* that protect freedoms in areas such as belief, expression, association, assembly, and movement; *political rights* that protect the liberty to participate in politics through actions such as communicating, assembling, protesting, voting, and serving in public office; *equality rights* that guarantee equal citizenship, equality before the law, and nondiscrimination; and *social* (or *"welfare") rights* that require provision of education to all children and protection against severe poverty and starvation. Another family that might be included is *group rights*. The Universal Declaration does not include group rights, but subsequent treaties do. Group rights include protections of ethnic groups against genocide and the ownership by countries of their national territories and resources.

In this section I try to explain the general idea of human rights by setting out some defining features. The goal here is to answer the question of what human rights are with a general description of the concept rather than a list of specific rights. Two people can have the same general idea of human rights even though they disagree about whether some particular rights are human rights.

Human rights are political norms dealing mainly with how people should be treated by their governments and institutions. They *are not ordinary moral norms applying mainly to interpersonal conduct* (such as prohibitions of lying and violence). As Thomas Pogge puts it, "to engage human rights, conduct must be in some sense official". But we must be careful here since some rights, such as rights against racial and sexual discrimination are primarily concerned to regulate private behavior. Still, governments are directed in two ways by rights against discrimination. They forbid governments to discriminate in their actions and policies, and they impose duties on governments to prohibit and discourage both private and public forms of discrimination.

Second, human rights *exist as moral and/or legal rights*. A human right can exist as a shared norm of actual human moralities, as a justified moral norm supported by strong reasons, as a legal right at the national level (here it might be referred to as a "civil" or "constitutional" right), or as a legal right within international law. The aspiration of the human rights movement is that human rights will come to exist in all four ways.

Third, human rights *are numerous (several dozen) rather than few*. John Locke's rights to life, liberty, and property were few and abstract, but human rights as we know them today address specific problems (e.g., guaranteeing fair trials, ending slavery, ensuring the availability of education, preventing genocide.) They are the rights of the lawyers rather than the abstract rights of the philosophers. Human rights protect people against familiar abuses of people's dignity and fundamental interests. Because many human rights deal with contemporary problems and institutions they are not trans-historical. One could formulate human rights abstractly or conditionally to make them trans-historical, but the fact remains that the formulations in contemporary human rights documents are neither abstract nor conditional. They presuppose criminal trials, governments funded by income taxes and formal systems of education.

Fourth, human rights *are minimal standards.* They are concerned with avoiding the terrible rather than with achieving the best. Their focus is protecting minimally good lives for all people. Henry Shue suggests that human rights concern the "lower limits on tolerable human conduct" rather than "great aspirations and exalted ideals". As minimal standards they leave most legal and policy matters open to democratic decision-making at the national and local levels. This allows them to accommodate a great deal of cultural and institutional variation and to leave a large space for democratic decision-making at the national level.

Fifth, human rights are *international norms* covering all countries and all people living today. International law plays a crucial role in giving human rights global reach. We can say that human rights *are universal* provided that we recognize that some rights, such as the right to vote, are held only by adult citizens; that some human rights documents focus on vulnerable groups such as children, women, and indigenous peoples; and that some rights, such as the right against genocide, are group rights.

Sixth, human rights *are high-priority norms.* Maurice Cranston held that human rights are matters of "paramount importance" and their violation "a grave affront to justice" (Cranston 1967). This does not mean, however, that we should take human rights to be absolute. As James Griffin says, human rights should be understood as "resistant to trade-offs, but not too resistant". The high priority of human rights needs support from a plausible connection with fundamental human interests or powerful normative considerations.

Seventh, human rights *require robust justifications that apply everywhere and support their high priority.* Without this they cannot withstand cultural diversity and national sovereignty. Robust justifications are powerful but need not be understood as ones that are irresistible.

Eighth, human rights *are rights, but not necessarily in a strict sense.* As rights they have several features. One is that they have rightholders — a person or agency having a particular right. Broadly, the rightholders of human rights are all people living today. More precisely, they are sometimes all people, sometimes all citizens of countries, sometimes all members of groups with particular vulnerabilities (women, children, racial and religious minorities, indigenous peoples), and sometimes all ethnic groups (as with rights against genocide.) Another feature of rights is that *they focus on a freedom, protection, status, or benefit for the rightholders.* When we talk about a right to freedom of speech, for example, the focus is on a generally beneficial freedom that the rightholders are to have available.

Rights also *have addressees* who are assigned duties or responsibilities. A person's human rights are not primarily rights against the United Nations or other international bodies; they primarily impose obligations on the government of the country in which the person resides or is located. The human rights of citizens of Belgium are mainly addressed to the Belgian government. International agencies, and the governments of countries other than one's own, are secondary or "backup" addressees. International human rights organizations provide encouragement, assistance, and sometimes criticism to states in order to assist them in fulfilling their duties. The duties associated with human rights typically require actions involving respect, protection, facilitation and provision. Finally, rights *are usually mandatory* in the sense of imposing duties on their addressees, but they sometimes do little more than declare high-priority goals and assign responsibility for their progressive realization. It is possible to argue, of course, that goal-like rights are not real rights, but it may be better simply to recognize that they comprise a weaker notion of a right.

Having set out a general idea of human rights with eight elements, it is useful to consider three other candidates which I think should be rejected. The first is the claim that all human rights *are negative rights,* in the sense that they only require governments to refrain from doing things. On this view, human rights never require governments to take positive steps such as protecting and providing. To refute this claim we do not need to appeal to social rights that require the provision of things like education and medical care. It is enough to note that this view is incompatible with the attractive position that one of the main jobs of governments is to protect people's rights by creating a system of criminal law and of legal property rights. The European Convention on Human Rights (Council of Europe 1950) incorporates this view when it says that "Everyone's right to life shall be protected by law" (article 2.1). And the UN Convention against Torture and Other Cruel, Inhuman or Degrading Treatment or Punishment (United Nations 1984) imposes the requirement that "Each State Party shall ensure that all acts of torture are offences under its criminal law" (article 4.1). Providing protections is providing services, not merely refraining

A second claim to be rejected is that all human rights *are inalienable.* Inalienability does not mean that rights are absolute or can never be overridden by other considerations. To say that a right is inalienable means that its holder cannot lose it temporarily or permanently by bad conduct or by voluntarily giving it up. I doubt that all human rights are inalienable in this sense. If we believe in imprisonment for serious crimes, then people's rights to freedom of movement can be forfeited temporarily or permanently by just convictions of serious crimes. And the right to freedom of movement can be voluntarily alienated by a person who makes a lifelong commitment to live in a monastery. Human rights are not inalienable but they are hard to lose (for a stronger view of inalienability).

Third, I think we should reject John Rawls' proposal in *The Law of Peoples* that *human rights define where legitimate toleration of other countries ends.* Rawls says that human rights "specify limits to a regime's internal autonomy" and that "their fulfillment is sufficient to exclude justified and forceful intervention by other peoples, for example, by diplomatic and economic sanctions, or in grave cases by military force".

It is a grave oversimplification to suggest that there is a line defined by human rights where national sovereignty ends. There is no need to deny that human rights are helpful in identifying the limits of justifiable toleration, but there are several reasons to doubt that they simply define that boundary. First, the "fulfillment" of human rights is a very vague idea. No country fully satisfies human rights; all countries have significant human rights problems. Some countries have large human rights problems, and many have massive problems ("gross violations of human rights"). Beyond this, the responsibility of the current government of a country for these problems also varies. The main responsibility may belong to the previous government and the current government may be taking reasonable steps to move towards greater compliance.

Further, defining human rights as norms that set the bounds of toleration requires restricting human rights to only a few fundamental rights. Rawls suggests the following list: "the right to life (to the means of subsistence and security); to liberty (to freedom from slavery, serfdom, and forced occupation, and to a sufficient measure of liberty of conscience to ensure freedom of religion and thought); to property (personal property); and to formal equality as pressed by the rules of natural justice (that is, that similar cases be treated similarly)". As Rawls recognizes this list leaves out most freedoms, rights of political participation, equality rights, and social rights. Leaving out any protection for equality and democracy is a high price to pay for assigning human rights the role of setting the bounds of tolerance, and we can accommodate Rawls' underlying idea without paying it. The intuitive idea that Rawls uses is that *countries engaging in massive violations of the most important human rights* are not to be tolerated — particularly when the notion of toleration implies, as Rawls thinks it does, full and equal membership in good standing in the community of nations. To use this intuitive idea we do not need to follow Rawls in equating human rights with some radically stripped down list of human rights. Instead we can work up a view — which is needed for other purposes anyway — of which human rights are the most important. Massive violations of the most fundamental rights can then be used as grounds for non-tolerance.

THE EXISTENCE OF HUMAN RIGHTS

The most obvious way in which human rights exist is as norms of national and international law created by enactment and judicial decisions. At the international level, human rights norms exist because of treaties that have turned them into international law. For example, the human right not to be held in slavery or servitude in article 4 of the European Convention and in article 8 of the International Covenant on Civil and Political Rights exists because these treaties establish it. At the national level, human rights norms exist because they have, through legislative enactment, judicial decision, or custom become part of a country's law. For example, the right against slavery exists in the United States because the *13th*

Amendment to the U.S. Constitution prohibits slavery and servitude. When rights are embedded in international law we speak of them as human rights; but when they are enacted in national law, we more frequently describe them as civil or constitutional rights. As this illustrates, it is possible for a right to exist within more than one normative systems at the same time.

Enactment in national and international law is one of the ways in which human rights exist. But many have suggested that this is not the only way. If human rights exist only because of enactment, their availability is contingent on domestic and international political developments. Many people have sought to find a way to support the idea that human rights have roots that are deeper and less subject to human decisions than legal enactment. One version of this idea is that people are born with rights, that human rights are somehow innate or inherent in human beings. One way that a normative status could be inherent in humans is by being God-given. The U.S. *Declaration of Independence* (1776) claims that people are "endowed by their Creator" with natural rights to "life, liberty, and the pursuit of happiness." On this view, God is the supreme lawmaker and enacted some basic human rights.

Rights plausibly attributed to divine decree must be very general and abstract (life, liberty etc.) so that they can apply to thousands of years of human history, not just to recent centuries. But contemporary human rights are numerous and specific (the right to a fair trial, the right to freedom of religion, the right to equality before the law etc.) Even if people are born with God-given natural rights, we need to explain how we get from those general and abstract rights to the specific rights found in contemporary declarations and treaties.

Attributing human rights to God's commands may give them a secure status at the metaphysical level, but in a very diverse world it does not make them practically secure. Billions of people do not believe in the God found in Christianity, Islam, and Judaism. If people do not believe in God, or in the sort of god that prescribes rights, then if you want to base human rights on theological beliefs you must persuade these people of a rights-supporting theological view. This is likely to be even harder than persuading them of human rights. Legal enactment at the national and international levels provides a far more secure status for practical purposes.

Human rights might also exist independent of legal enactment by being part of actual human moralities. It appears that all human groups have moralities, that is, imperative norms of behavior backed by reasons and values. These moralities contain specific norms (for example, a prohibition of the intentional murder of an innocent person) and specific values (for example, valuing human life.) One way in which human rights could exist apart from divine or human enactment is as norms accepted in all or almost all actual human moralities. If almost all human groups have moralities containing norms prohibiting murder, these norms could constitute the human right to life. Human rights can be seen as basic moral norms shared by all or almost all accepted human moralities.

This view is attractive but filled with difficulties. First, it seems unlikely that the moralities of almost all human groups agree in condemning, say, torture, unfair criminal trials, undemocratic institutions, and discrimination on the basis of race or sex. There is a lot of disagreement among countries and cultures about these matters. Human rights declarations and treaties are intended to change existing norms, not just describe the existing moral consensus. Second, it is far from clear that the shared norms that do exist support rights held by individuals. A group may think that torture is generally a bad thing without holding that all individuals have a high-priority right against being tortured. Third, human rights are mainly about the obligations of governments. Ordinary interpersonal moralities often have little to say about what governments should and should not do. This is a matter of political morality, and depends not just on moral principles but also on views of the dangers and capacities of the contemporary state.

Yet another way of explaining the existence of human rights is to say that they exist in true or justified moralities. On this account, to say that there is a human right against torture is just to say that there are strong reasons for believing that it is almost always wrong to engage in torture. This approach would view the Universal Declaration as attempting to formulate a justified political morality. It was not merely trying to identify a pre-existing moral consensus; it was also trying to create a consensus on how governments should behave that was supported by the most plausible moral and practical reasons. This approach requires commitment to the objectivity of moral and practical reasons. It holds that just as there are reliable ways of finding out how the physical world works, or what makes buildings sturdy and durable, there are ways of finding out what individuals may justifiably demand of governments. Even if there is little present agreement on political morality, rational agreement is available to humans if they will commit themselves to open-minded and serious moral and political inquiry. If moral reasons exist independent of human construction, they can, when combined with premises about current institutions, problems and resources, generate moral norms different from those currently accepted or enacted. The Universal Declaration seems to proceed on exactly this assumption. One problem with this view is that existence as good reasons seems a rather thin form of existence for human rights. But perhaps we can view this thinness as a practical rather than a theoretical problem, as something to be remedied by the formulation and enactment of legal norms. After all, the best form of existence for human rights would combine robust legal existence with the sort of moral existence that comes from being supported by strong moral and practical reasons.

WHICH RIGHTS ARE HUMAN RIGHTS?

This section discusses the question of which rights do belong to the list of human rights. Not every question of social justice or wise governance is a human rights issue. For example, a country could have too much income inequality, inadequate provision for higher education, or no national parks without violating any human rights. Deciding which norms should be counted as human rights is a matter of some difficulty. And there is continuing pressure to expand lists of human rights to include new areas. Many political movements would like to see their main concerns categorized as matters of human rights, since this would publicize, promote, and legitimize their concerns at the international level. A possible result of this is "human rights inflation," the devaluation of human rights caused by producing too much bad human rights currency.

One way to avoid rights inflation is to follow Cranston in insisting on the idea that human rights only deal with extremely important goods, protections and freedoms. A supplementary approach is to impose several justificatory tests for specific human rights. For example, it could be required that a proposed human right not only deals with some very important good but also responds to a common and serious threat to that good, imposes burdens on the addressees that are justifiable and no larger than necessary, and be feasible in most of the world's countries. This approach restrains rights' inflation with several tests, not just one master test.

Human rights are specific and problem-oriented. Historic bills of rights often begin with a list of complaints about the abuses of previous regimes or eras. Bills of rights may have preambles that speak grandly and abstractly of life, liberty and the inherent dignity of persons, but their lists of rights contain specific norms addressed to familiar political, legal or economic problems.

In deciding which specific rights are human rights, it is possible to make either too little or too much of international documents such as the Universal Declaration and the European Convention. One makes too little of them by proceeding as if drawing up a list of important rights were a new question, never before addressed, and as if there were no practical wisdom to be found in the choices of rights that went into the historic documents. And one makes too much of them by presuming that those documents tell us everything we need to know about human rights. This approach involves a kind of fundamentalism: it holds that if a right is on the official lists of human rights that settles its status as a human right ("If it's in the book that's all I need to know.") But the process of listing human rights in the United Nations and elsewhere was a political process with plenty of imperfections. There is little reason to take international diplomats as the most authoritative guides to which human rights there are. Further, even if a treaty could settle the issue of whether a certain right is a human right within international law, such a treaty cannot settle its weight. It may claim that the right is supported by weighty considerations, but it cannot make this so. If an international treaty enacted a right to visit national parks without charge as a human right, the ratification of that treaty would make free access to national parks a "human right" within international law. But it would not be able to make us believe that the right to visit national parks without charge was sufficiently important to be a real human right.

Once one takes seriously the question of whether some norms that are now counted as human rights do not merit that status and whether some norms that are not currently accepted as human rights should be upgraded, there are many possible ways to proceed. One approach that should be avoided puts a lot of weight on whether the norm in question really is, or could be, a right in a strict sense. This approach might yield arguments that human rights cannot include children's rights since young children cannot exercise their rights by invoking, claiming, or waiving (Hart 1955, Wellman 1995). This approach raises the question : whether human rights are rights in a strict sense rather than a fairly loose one. The human rights movement and its purposes are not well served by being forced into a narrow conceptual framework. The basic idea of the human rights movement is not that of a right, but the idea of regulating the behavior of governments through international norms. And when we look at human rights documents we find that they use a variety of normative concepts. Sometimes they speak of rights, as when the Universal Declaration says that "Everyone has the right to freedom of movement" (Article 13). Sometimes these documents issue prohibitions, as when the Universal Declaration says that "No one shall be subjected to arbitrary arrest, detention, or exile" (Article 9). And at other times they express general principles, as illustrated by the Universal Declaration's claim that "All are equal before the law" (Article 7).

A better way to evaluate a norm that is nominated for the status of human right is to consider whether it is compatible with the general idea of human rights that we find in international human rights documents. If the general idea of human rights suggested above is correct, it requires affirmative answers to questions such as whether this norm could have governments as its primary addressees, whether it ensures that people can have minimally good lives, whether it has high priority, and whether it can be supported by strong reasons that make plausible its universality and high priority.

Questions about which rights are human rights arise in regard to many families of human rights. Discussed below are (1) civil and political rights; (2) social rights; (3) minority and group rights; and (4) environmental rights.

CIVIL AND POLITICAL RIGHTS

These rights are familiar from historic bills of rights such as the *French Declaration of the Rights of Man and the Citizen* (1789) and the *U.S. Bill of Rights* (1791, with subsequent amendments). Contemporary sources include the first 21 articles of the *Universal Declaration,* and such treaties as the *European Convention,* the International Covenant on Civil and Political Rights, the American Convention on Human Rights, and the *African Charter on Human and People's Rights.* Some representative formulations follow: Everyone has the right to freedom of thought and expression. This right includes freedom to seek, receive and impart information and ideas of all kinds, regardless of frontiers, either orally, in writing, in print, in the form of art, or through any other medium of one's choice. (American Convention on Human Rights, Article 13.1)

Everyone has the right to freedom of peaceful assembly and to freedom of association with others, including the right to form and to join trade unions for the protection of his interests (European Convention, Article 11).

Every citizen shall have the right to participate freely in the government of his country, either directly or through freely chosen representatives in accordance with the provisions of the law. 2. Every citizen shall have the right of equal access to the public service of his country. 3. Every individual shall have the right of access to public property and services in strict equality of all persons before the law (African Charter, Article 13).

These rights fit the general idea of human rights suggested above (see 1. *The General Idea of Human Rights).* First, they are political norms that primarily impose responsibilities on governments and international organizations. Second, they are minimal norms in that they protect against the worst things that happen in political society rather than setting out standards of excellence in government. Third, they are international norms establishing standards for all countries — and that have been accepted by more than 150 of the world's countries. Finally, it is plausible to make claims of high priority on their behalf, and to support these claims of importance with strong reasons. Consider the right to freedom of movement. One approach to justifying this right and its high priority would argue the importance of free movement to being able to find the necessities of life, to pursuing plans, projects, and commitments, and to maintaining ties to family and friends. A related approach argues that it is impossible to make use of other human rights if one cannot move freely. The right to political participation is undermined if a person is not permitted to go to political rallies or to the polls.

Most civil and political rights are not absolute—they are in some cases overridden by other considerations and rightly set aside in those cases. For example, some civil and political rights can be restricted by public and private property rights, by restraining orders related to domestic violence, and by legal punishments. Further, after a disaster such as a hurricane or earthquake free movement is often appropriately suspended to keep out the curious, to permit access of emergency vehicles and equipment, and to prevent looting. The International Covenant on Civil and Political Rights permits rights to be suspended during times "of public emergency which threatens the life of the nation" (Article 4). But it excludes some rights from suspension including the right to life, the prohibition of torture, the prohibition of slavery, the prohibition of ex post facto criminal laws, and freedom of thought and religion.

SOCIAL RIGHTS

Besides the civil and political rights just discussed, the Universal Declaration includes social (or welfare) rights.

These include equality and nondiscrimination for women and minorities, access to employment opportunities, fair pay, safe and healthy working conditions, the right to form trade unions and bargain collectively, social security, an adequate standard of living (covering adequate food, clothing, and housing), health care, and education. These rights were made part of international law by treaties such as the *International Covenant on Economic, Social, and Cultural Rights, European Social Charter,* and the *Protocol of San Salvador* (1988), which amended the American Convention on Human Rights. Whether social rights are genuine human rights is discussed below: *(4. Are Social Rights Genuine Human Rights?).*

MINORITY AND GROUP RIGHTS

Concern for the equal rights of women and minorities is a longstanding concern of the human rights movement. Human rights documents emphasize that all people, including women and members of minority ethnic and religious groups, have the same basic rights and should be able to enjoy them without discrimination. The right to freedom from discrimination figures prominently in the Universal Declaration and subsequent treaties. The Civil and Political Covenant, for example, commits its participating states to respecting and protecting their people's rights "without distinction of any kind, such as race, color, sex, language, political or other opinion, national or social origin, property, birth or social status".

Some standard individual rights are especially important to ethnic and religious minorities, including rights to freedom of association, freedom of assembly, freedom of religion and freedom from discrimination. Human rights documents also include rights that refer to minorities explicitly and give them special protections. For example, the Civil and Political Covenant in Article 27 says that persons belonging to ethnic, religious, or linguistic minorities "shall not be denied the right, in community with other members of their group, to enjoy their own culture, to profess and practice their own religion, or to use their own language."

Since 1964 the United Nations has mainly dealt with the rights of women and minorities through specialized treaties such as the International Convention on the Elimination of All Forms of Racial Discrimination (1965); the Convention on the Elimination of All Forms of Discrimination Against Women (1979); and the Convention on the Rights of the Child (1989). Specialized treaties allow international norms to address unique problems of particular groups such as prostitution and trafficking in the case of women, custody issues in the case of children, and the loss of territory by indigenous peoples.

Minority groups are often targets of violence. Human rights norms call upon governments to refrain from such violence and to provide protections against it. This work is partly done by the right to life, which is a standard individual right. It is also done by the right against genocide which protects *groups* from attempts to destroy or decimate them. The *Genocide Convention* was one of the first human rights treaties after World War II. It gives the following definition of genocide:

...genocide means any of the following acts committed with intent to destroy, in whole or in part, a national, ethnical, racial, or religious group, as such: (a) Killing members of the group; (b) Causing serious bodily or mental harm to members of the group; (c) Deliberately inflicting on the group conditions of life calculated to bring about its physical destruction in whole or in part; (d) Imposing measures intended to prevent births within the group; (e) Forcibly transferring children of the group to another group.

The right against genocide seems to be a group right. It is held by groups and provides protection to groups as groups. It is largely negative in the sense that it requires governments and other agencies to refrain from destroying groups; but it also requires that legal and other protections be implemented for this purpose.

Can a group right fit the general idea of human rights proposed earlier? It can if we broaden the conception of who can hold human rights to include ethnic and religious groups. This can be made more palatable, perhaps, by recognizing that the beneficiaries of the right against genocide are individual humans who enjoy greater security against attempts to destroy the group to which they belong.

ENVIRONMENTAL RIGHTS

In spite of the danger of rights inflation, there are doubtless norms that should be counted as human rights but are not generally so treated. After all, there are lots of areas in which people's dignity and fundamental interests are threatened by governmental actions and omissions. Consider environmental rights, which are often defined as rights of animals or of nature itself. Conceived in this way they do not fit our general idea of human rights because the rightholders are not humans or human groups. But more modest formulations are possible; environmental rights can be understood as rights to an environment that is healthy and safe. Such a right is human-oriented: it does not cover directly issues such as the claims of animals, biodiversity, or sustainable development.

The right to a safe environment can be sculpted to fit the general idea of human rights suggested above by conceiving it as primarily imposing responsibilities on governments and international organizations. It calls on them to regulate the activities of both governmental and nongovernmental agents to ensure that environmental safety is maintained. Citizens are secondary addressees. This right sets out a minimal environmental standard, safety for humans, rather than calling for higher and broader standards of environmental protection. (Countries that are able to implement higher standards are of course free to enact those standards in their law or bill of rights.)

A justification for this right must show that environmental problems pose serious threats to fundamental human interests, values, or norms; that governments may appropriately be burdened with the responsibility of protecting people against these threats; and that most governments actually have the ability to do this. This last requirement — feasibility — may be the most difficult. Environmental protection is expensive and difficult, and many governments will be unable to do very much of it while meeting other important responsibilities. The problem of feasibility in poorer countries might be addressed here in the same way that it was in the Social Covenant. That treaty commits governments not to the immediate realization of social rights for all, but rather to making the realization of such rights a high-priority goal and beginning to take steps towards its fulfillment.

In thinking about adding new rights to the list of human rights it is important to recognize that implementing a right is an activity with opportunity costs. If no new resources are available, implementing a new right will mean that fewer resources are available for the implementation of existing rights. Rights are not magical sources of supply

ARE SOCIAL RIGHTS GENUINE HUMAN RIGHTS?

The Universal Declaration included social (or 'welfare' rights) that addressed matters such as education, food and employment. Their inclusion has been the source of much controversy (Beetham 1995). Social rights are often alleged to be statements of desirable goals but not really rights. The European Convention did not include them (although it was later amended to include the right to education). Instead they were put into a separate treaty, the *European Social Charter.* When the United Nations began the process of putting the rights of the Universal Declaration into international law, it followed the model of the European system by treating economic and social standards in a treaty separate from the one dealing with civil and political rights. This treaty, the International Covenant on Economic, Social, and Cultural Rights (the "Social Covenant," 1966), treated these standards as rights — albeit rights to be progressively realized.

A human rights treaty usually contains three parts: (1) a list of rights; (2) a specification of what the parties are agreeing to do in regard to this list; and (3) a system to monitor and promote compliance with the agreement. The Social Covenant's list of rights includes nondiscrimination and equality for women in the economic and social area (Articles 2 and 3), freedom to work and opportunities to work (Article 4), fair pay and decent conditions of work (Article 7), the right to form trade unions and to strike (Article 8), social security (Article 9), special protection for mothers and children (Article 10), the right to adequate food, clothing, and housing (Article 11), the right to basic health services (Article 12), the right to education (Article 13), and the right to participate in cultural life and scientific progress (Article 15).

Article 2.1 of the Social Covenant sets out what the parties commit themselves to do about this list, namely to "take steps, individually and through international assistance and co-operation.. .to the maximum of its available resources, with a view to achieving progressively the full realization of the rights recognized in the present Covenant." In contrast, the Civil and Political Covenant simply commits its signatories to "respect and to ensure to all individuals within its territory the rights recognized in the present Covenant" (Article 2.1). The contrast between these two levels of commitment is one of the things that has led some people to suspect that economic and social rights are really just goals.

The system to monitor and promote compliance with the Social Covenant is weak since it merely requires participating countries to make periodic reports on measures taken to comply with the treaty. Countries agree "to submit ... reports on the measures which they have adopted and the progress made in achieving the observance of the rights recognized herein" (Article 16). A committee of experts, created by the Economic and Social Council in 1987, is given the job of looking at the progress reports from the participating countries. This body, the Committee on Economic, Social and Cultural Rights, studies the reports, discusses them with representatives of the governments reporting, and issues interpretive statements (General Comments) on the requirements of the treaty. Since 1991 it has issued more than a dozen of these interpretative statements (United Nations 1991). The Social Covenant has no system for receiving complaints of violations of economic and social rights.

Why did the Social Covenant opt for progressive implementation and thereby treat its rights as being somewhat like goals? The main reason, I think, is that more than half of the world's countries were in no position, in terms of economic, institutional and human resources, to realize these standards fully or even largely. For many countries, noncompliance due to inability would have been certain if these standards had been treated as immediate binding. We return to this topic in the following paragraphs:

Opponents of social rights often deny them the status of human rights, restricting that standing to civil and political rights. Familiar objections to social rights include the following: (1) they do not serve truly fundamental interests; (2) they are too burdensome on governments and taxpayers; and (3) they are not feasible in less-developed countries.

Let's first address the issue of importance. Human rights, such as rights to freedom from torture or to fair trials in criminal and civil cases, set out minimal but extremely important standards that governments everywhere should meet. One might object that social rights do not meet this standard of great importance. Perhaps they identify valuable goods, but not extremely valuable goods. If this objection is that some formulations of social rights in international human rights documents are too expansive and go beyond what is necessary to a minimally good life, it can be conceded and those formulations rejected. For example, the Universal Declaration included a putative right to holidays with pay (Article 24), and such a right pertains to a good life, not to a minimally good life. It is far from the case, however, that all or most social rights pertain to superficial interests. To discuss the issue of importance I will use two social rights as examples: the right to an adequate standard of living, and the right to free public education. These rights require governments to try to remedy widespread and serious evils such as hunger and ignorance.

The importance of food and other basic material conditions of life is easy to show. These goods are essential to people's ability to live, function and flourish. Without adequate access to these goods, interests in life, health, and liberty are endangered and serious illness and death are probable. The connection between having the goods the right guarantees and having a minimally good life is direct and obvious — something that is not always true with other human rights.

In the contemporary world lack of access to educational opportunities typically limits (both absolutely and comparatively) people's abilities to participate fully and effectively in the political and economic life of their country. Lack of education increases the likelihood of unemployment and underemployment.

Another way to support the importance of social rights is to show their importance to the full implementation of civil and political rights. If a government succeeds in eliminating hunger and providing education to everyone this promotes people's abilities to know, use and enjoy their liberties, due process rights, and rights of political participation. This is easiest to see with regard to education. Ignorance is a barrier to the realization of civil and political rights because uneducated people often do not know what rights they have and what they can do to use and defend them. It is also easy to see in the area of democratic participation. Education and a minimum income make it easier for people at the bottom economically to follow politics, participate in political campaigns, and to spend the time and money needed to go to the polls and vote.

The second objection is that social rights are too burdensome. It is very expensive to guarantee to everyone basic education and minimal material conditions of life. Perhaps social rights are too expensive or burdensome to be justified even in rich countries. Frequently the claim that social rights are too burdensome uses other, less controversial human rights as a standard of comparison, and suggests that social rights are substantially more burdensome or expensive than liberty rights. These rights require both respect and protection from governments. And people cannot be adequately protected in their enjoyment of liberties such as these unless they also have security and due process rights. The costs of liberty, as it were, include the costs of law and criminal justice. Once we see this, liberties start to look a lot more costly. To provide effective liberties to communicate, associate, and move it is not enough for a society to make a prohibition of interference with these activities part of its law and accepted morality. An effective system of provision for these liberties will require a legal scheme that defines personal and property rights and protects these rights against invasions while ensuring due process to those accused of crimes. Providing such legal protection in the form of legislatures, police, courts and prisons is extremely expensive.

Further, we should not think of social rights as simply giving everyone a free supply of the goods these rights protect. Guarantees of things like food and housing will be intolerably expensive and will undermine productivity if everyone simply receives a free supply. A viable system of social rights will require most people to provide these goods for themselves and their families through work as long as they are given the necessary opportunities, education, and infrastructure. Government-implemented social rights provide guarantees of availability (or "secure access"), but governments should have to supply the requisite goods in only a small fraction of cases. Note that primary education is often an exception to this since many countries provide free public education irrespective of ability to pay.

Countries that do not accept and implement social rights still have to bear somehow the costs of providing for the needy since these countries — particularly if they recognize democratic rights of political participation — are unlikely to find it tolerable to allow sizeable parts of the population to starve and be homeless. If government does not supply food, clothing and shelter to those unable to provide for themselves, then families, friends and communities will have to shoulder this burden. It is only in the last century that government-sponsored social rights have taken over a substantial part of the burden of providing for the needy. The taxes associated with social rights are partial replacements for other burdensome duties, namely the duties of families and communities to provide adequate care for the unemployed, sick, disabled and the aged. Deciding whether to implement social rights is not a matter of deciding whether to bear such burdens, but rather of deciding whether to continue with total reliance on a system of informal provision that distributes benefits in a very spotty way and whose costs fall very unevenly on families, friends and communities.

Once we recognize that liberty rights also carry high costs, that intelligent systems of provision for social rights supply the requisite goods to people in only a small minority of cases, and that these systems are substitutes for other, more local ways of providing for the needy, the difference between the burdensomeness of liberty rights and the burdensomeness of social rights ceases to seem so large.

Even if the burdens imposed by social rights are not excessive, they might still be wrong to impose on individuals. Libertarians object to social rights as requiring impermissible taxation. Nozick, for example, says that "Taxation of earnings from labor is on a par with forced labor". This view is vulnerable to an attack asserting two things. First, taxation is permissible when used to discharge the duties of taxpayers, when, for example, it is used to support government-organized systems of humanitarian assistance that fulfill more effectively duties of assistance that all individuals have (Beetham 1995, 53). Second, property rights are not so strong that they can never be outweighed by the requirements of meeting other rights.

The third objection to social rights is that they are not feasible in many countries. It is very expensive to provide guarantees of subsistence, minimal public health measures and basic education. As we saw above, the Social Covenant dealt with the issue of feasibility by calling for progressive implementation, that is, implementation as financial and other resources permit. Does this view of implementation turn social rights into high-priority goals? If so, is that a bad thing?

Standards that outrun the abilities of many of their addressees are good candidates for normative treatment as goals. Treating such standards as goals, which allows us to view them as largely aspirational rather than as imposing immediate duties, avoids massive problems of inability-based noncompliance. One may worry, however, that this is too much of a demotion. Goals seem much weaker than rights. But goals can be formulated in ways that make them more like rights. Goals can be assigned addressees (the party who is to pursue the goal), beneficiaries, scopes that define the objective to be pursued, and a high level of priority. Strong reasons for the importance of these goals can be provided. And supervisory bodies can monitor levels of progress and pressure low-performing addressees to attend to and work on their goals.

Treating very demanding rights as goals has several advantages. One is that proposed goals that exceed one's abilities are not as farcical as proposed duties that exceed one's abilities. Creating grand lists of human rights that many countries cannot realize seems fraudulent to many people, and perhaps this fraudulence is reduced if we understand that these "rights" are really goals that countries should promote. Goals are inherently ability-calibrated. What you should do now about your goals depends on your abilities and other commitments. Goals coexist happily with low levels of ability to achieve them. Another advantage is that goals are flexible; addressees with different levels of ability can choose ways of pursuing the goals that suit their circumstances and means. Because of these attractions of goals, it will be worth exploring ways to transform very demanding human rights into goals. The transformation may be full or partial.

A right together with its supporting reasons might be divided into two parts. One part, call it the "demand side," sets out the rightholder's claim and the reasons why it is very valuable or important that this claim be fulfilled. If the right is the right to a fair trial when one is arrested and accused of a crime, the demand side would set out the rightholder's claim to a fair trial and the reasons why that claim is very valuable or important. The other part, the "supply side," would set out the addressees' responsibilities in regard to the rightholder's claim. It would explain why this claim to a fair trial is a matter of duty, what the duties are, and why it is these particular addressees rather than other possible addressees that have the duty.

A goal that is similar to a right could also be divided into these two parts. The demand side would set out the beneficiary's claim or demand and the reasons why it is very desirable or important that this demand be fulfilled. For example, the demand side might set out the reasons why it is desirable for the beneficiary to have access to employment. And the supply side would set out the addressee's responsibility in regard to the beneficiary's demand. It would explain why promoting access to employment for the beneficiary should be a goal for the addressee. It does not impose duties on the addressee, but it shows that the addressee has good reasons for acting to satisfy the demand.

Since even a goal that is supported by good reasons imposes no duties — that is, fails to be mandatory in character — we may think that such goals are poor substitutes for rights and should not be called "rights." But it is possible to create right-goal mixtures that contain some mandatory elements and that therefore seem more like real rights. A minimal right-goal mixture would include a duty *to try to realize the goal as quickly as possible.* Here the demand side would set out the beneficiary's demand or claim and the reasons why it is very desirable or important that this demand be fulfilled. And the supply side would explain not only why the addressee has good reasons to pursue this goal, but also explain why the addressee has a duty to try to realize this goal with all deliberate speed. The economic and social rights in the Social Covenant seem to fit this model. The countries ratifying the Covenant agree to make it a matter of government duty to realize the list of rights as soon as possible. As we saw earlier, the Social Covenant's signatories agree to "take steps, individually and through international assistance and co-operation to the maximum of its available resources, with a view to achieving progressively the full realization of the rights recognized in the present Covenant." The signatories agree, on this interpretation, to make it a matter of duty to realize the listed rights as soon and as far as resources permit.

A problem with such a right-goal mixture is that it allows the addressee great discretion concerning *when* to do something about the right and *how much* to do. A body supervising compliance with a human rights treaty may wish to remove some of this discretion by requiring that the addressees at least take some significant and good faith steps immediately and regularly and that these steps be documented. Duties to try are less vaporous if they are combined with duties that require immediate steps. Countries may be required to act in certain ways (e.g., make a good faith effort and be prepared to demonstrate that they have done so), set specific benchmarks and timetables, establish agencies to work on the goals, provide them with budgets, and use expert assistance from international agencies. To facilitate the monitoring of compliance the country may be required to collect data continuously concerning realization of the goals, make periodic reports, and allow its citizens to complain to the monitoring body about failures to pursue the goals energetically (United Nations 1991).

Article 14 of the Social Covenant imposes a conditional duty in regard to the right to education declared in article 13. It says that countries that "have not been able to secure" compulsory primary education, free of charge, "undertake, within two years, to work out and adopt a detailed plan of action for the progressive implementation, within a reasonable number of years, to be fixed in the plan, of the principle of compulsory education free of charge for all." Compliance with this requirement, which is only present for the right to education, involves planning and setting timetables. Instead of, or in addition to, requiring plans and timetables a goal-right mixture could require immediate compliance with minimal standards. The idea is that minimal provision might be within the capacity of all addressees. For example, countries could be required very soon to provide all children with reading and writing instruction.

These ways of creating right-goal mixtures allow us to see that some rights can be goals while still having enough mandatory elements to be counted as rights in a meaningful sense.

A complementary approach to implementing social rights (and other demanding rights as well) in developing countries emphasizes ability enhancement rather than burden reduction. It seeks to increase the ability of developing countries to implement rights effectively. Possible strategies include using aid to increase the resources available for this purpose, providing education to current and future officials, offering technical assistance concerning the mechanisms of implementation, and battling corruption. Human rights theory needs better accounts of how the rights, e.g., of a Haitian create (moral and legal) duties not just for the Haitian government but also for (1) other governments, (2) international organizations, (3) individuals resident in Haiti and (4) individual residents in other countries.

John Rawls has proposed a duty of liberal democratic countries to aid poor or "burdened" countries. Rawls defines "burdened societies" as ones that "lack the political and cultural traditions, the human capital and know-how and, often, the material and technological resources needed to be well-ordered". Rawls holds that well-off liberal countries have a moral duty to assist burdened societies. Unfortunately Rawls does not provide much justification for this claim. In particular he does not use his idea of an international "original position" to work out how the justification for such a duty would go and what objections it would need to overcome.

A good defense of a duty of well-off governments to assist poor countries in realizing human rights would not automatically impose that duty on the citizens of those well-off countries. But perhaps citizens should share somehow in duties of international aid. One approach to explaining how and why citizens share in these duties involves viewing the citizens of a democratic country as having ultimate responsibility for the human rights duties of their government. If their government has a duty to respect or implement the right to a fair trial, or a duty to aid poor countries, its citizens share in that duty. They are required as voters, political agents, and taxpayers to try to promote and support their government's compliance with its human rights duties. This principle of shared duty is particularly attractive in democratic societies where the citizens are the ultimate source of political authority. This view makes individuals back-up addressees for the duties of their governments.

Thomas Pogge has taken a related but slightly different approach to generating individual duties from human rights that have governments as their primary addressees. Pogge emphasizes the Universal Declaration's Article 28 which says that "Everyone is entitled to a social and international order in which the rights and freedoms set forth in this Declaration can be fully realized." Pogge sees in this article a plausible norm, namely that both countries and individuals have negative duties not to be complicit in an international order that unfairly disadvantages poor countries and the people in them. A coercive political order, whether national or international, "must not avoidably restrict the freedom of some so as to render their access to basic necessities insecure — especially through official denial or deprivation. If it does, then all human agents have a negative duty, correlative to the postulated social and economic human rights, not to cooperate in upholding it unless they compensate for their cooperation by protecting its victims or by working for its reform. Those violating this duty share responsibility for the harms (insecure access to basic necessities) produced by the unjust institutional order in question".

FIVE

Jurisprudence of Human Rights

The body of rules which lays down basic norms for the formulation of rights of human beings and provides the machinery for their application, implementation and recognition at the international and national level is known as "Science of Human Rights" or "Jurisprudence of Human Rights". In other words, jurisprudence of human rights requires the following things :

(i) Basic norms for the formulation of human rights.

(ii) Rights of human beings.

(iii) Machinery for the application, implementation and recognition of such rights.

BASIC NORMS FOR THE FORMULATION OF HUMAN RIGHTS

The UN Charter, after reaffirming in the Preamble, faith in (i) the fundamental human rights (ii) dignity and worth of the human person and (iii) equal rights of men and women, pronounced in Article 1(3) that one of its purposes is to promote and encourage respect for human rights and fundamental freedoms for all without distinction on account of sex or other ground.

The founding of the United Nations in 1945 with the signing of the UN Charter marked the first agreement among nations to promote and observe human rights and fundamental freedoms for all. The Universal Declaration of Human Rights was adopted on Dec. 10, 1948. It contained 30 Articles, the first 21 are generally identified as Civil and Political Rights which include prohibition of torture and arbitrary arrest, freedom of speech, assembly, religion and right to vote by secret ballot. The remaining articles contain the rights which are generally called Economic and Cultural Rights which include right to work, education and adequate standard of living, social security and valuations with pay.

The Universal Declaration is now acclaimed as the Magna Carta of humankind. This is to be complied with by all actors in the World arena. What earlier was a mere aspiration is now hailed both as an authoritative interpretation of the human rights provisions of the UN Charter and as established customary law having the attributes of *Jus Cogens* and constituting the heart of global Bill of Rights.

The adoption by UN General Assembly in 1966 of the Covenant on Economic, Social and Cultural Rights, the Covenant on Civil and Political Rights and the Optional Protocol to the Covenant on Civil and Political Rights transforming international concern for human rights into legally bound international obligations; the Covenant have laid groundwork for the erection of international institutions and procedures for giving concrete expression to these obligations.

The Principle of *Jus Cogens* restricts the freedom of States to make agreements at variance with these pre-emptory norms. The customary international law requiring the States to abstain from the violation of human rights constitute *Jus Cogens* and any agreement made in contravention of these rules is considered illegal.

A large number of States Parties to an international treaty provides some evidence of its universality or the acceptance of the norms in that treaty by the international community. As on 1st Sept. 1993, the UN Human Rights instruments which were ratified or acceded to by the following number of States prove the universality of human rights norms stated there in :

(i) The International Covenant on Economic, Social and Cultural Rights has been ratified by 124 States Parties.

(ii) The International Covenant on Civil and Political Rights (ICPR) has been ratified by 122 States.

(iii) The Optional Protocol to the Covenant on Civil and Political Rights (on the right of individual petition) has been ratified by 74 States Parties.

(iv) Second Optional Protocol to the International Covenant on Civil and Political Rights aiming at the Abolition of the Death Penalty, has been acceded by 19 States Parties.

(v) The International Convention on the Elimination of all Forms of Racial Discrimination has been ratified by 137 States Parties.

(vi) The International Convention on the Suppression and Punishment of the Crime of Apartheid has been ratified by 97 States Parties.

(vii) The Convention on the Elimination of All Forms of Discrimination Against Women has been ratified by 125 States Parties.

(viii) The Convention Against Torture and other Cruel, Inhuman or Degrading Treatment or Punishment, has been ratified by 76 States Parties.

(ix) The Convention on the Rights of the Child has been ratified by 196 States Parties.

The above list shows that the international consensus on the abolition of the death penalty is still quite limited.

The jurisprudence of human rights aims at realizing the common core of human rights as a condition essential for human living and development without the incidence of the forms of government. This can be done by bringing about technological and industrial development and also to make trade, commerce and business useful and fruitful for the community of nations. Apart from this, education and understanding of the basic human right is necessary so that all the people of the world may have a common course of development.

The catalyst to which we owe the Universal Declaration of Human Rights and indeed much of new international law of human rights which has so radically changed the theory and practice of the law of nations was the gross violations of human rights that were committed by certain countries during the Second World War.

RIGHTS OF HUMAN BEINGS

The term "Right" consists of five elements, *i.e.*, (i) a right-holder or the subject of a right, (ii) a claim of such right holder to some substance or the object of a right, (iii) he or she might assert, demand, enjoy or enforce such claim by exercising such a right, (iv) it must be against some individual or group who has committed a breach of co-relative duty, and (v) the right-holder must cite in support of his or her claim some particular ground or justification for such a right. According to Hohfeldian analysis, "right" sometimes is used in its strict sense of the right-holder being entitled to something with a correlative duty in another. Sometimes, right is used to indicate an immunity from having a legal status altered or indicates a privilege to do something or refers to a power to create a legal relationship.

Although all of these terms have sometimes been identified as rights, each concept invokes different protections and produces variant results. For example, some of human rights dealt with in the International Covenant on Civil and Political Rights, are in the nature of immunities, meaning thereby that Governments can not derogate them. But are there any absolute rights? Surely, the right to life guaranteed by Article 6(1) of the International Covenant on Civil and Political Rights would seem to be so basic as to be considered absolute. Yet Article 6(1) only offers protection against "arbitrary" deprivation of life. What is the effect of this qualification on the nature of the right involved?

If we classify a right as a claim against a Government to refrain from certain acts, such as not to torture its citizens or deny them freedom of speech, religion or emigration, then these complexities arise. Again, we need to understand the basis for asserting such claims. If a particular claim stems from a metaphysical concept such as the nature of humanity, or from a religious concept such as the divine will, or from some other prior concept, then the claim may really be an immunity, to which normative judgements should not apply.

What does the addition of word "human" to prefix "right" denote. It means, in the first place, that everybody has such right. The basic qualification for holding human rights is that this holder of rights belongs to the human race. Secondly, the objects of human rights are of great importance. They are the claims of the human being which may override other considerations. Thirdly, the exercise of human rights have a more definite range than that of civil rights. Fourthly, there is a necessity of location of the duties that correlate with human rights. For example, everyone has a right to life against everyone else, there is general duty to respect it. Fifthly, the characteristic of the justification for the human rights is not an appeal to this statute or that contract, for if the rights in question were written into statutes or contracts those provisions under Municipal Law would themselves be sufficient justification.

Human Rights are a check on public bodies and authorities as well as other institutions of society to ensure that they refrain from certain acts of commission, which would interfere with an individual's basic right to dignity. Modern international human rights jurisprudence adopts a simplistic philosophy that all human beings differ from each other and that each individual is unique, which underlies the concept of integrity and dignity of the individual person which human rights law is primarily concerned to protect. This does not require that all persons must be treated alike in all circumstances, but regardless of their many differences they are entitled to the protection. Thus regardless of their personal characteristics, they must not be tortured, enslaved or arbitrarily killed or imprisoned without a fair trial, nor must they be deprived of the opportunity of gaining their living by work of their choice, or of fair access to food, clothing, housing, education and health services. Equality of treatment is required only in respect of the rights and freedoms often called 'fundamental' which are inherent in their individual humanity and which are necessary to enable their personal diversity to develop and manifest itself.

The function of national government in relation to 'human rights' is different from its function in relation to 'ordinary rights'. The Government's only concerns are to provide an adequate framework of domestic law to define who has what rights, against whom and to what circumstances, to provide tribunal to apply and interpret those laws. But the claims of human rights are primary claims against the public authorities of the State itself, either to remain free from interference by them or to require them to act in some specific fashion. For any human right the correlative duty falls, in the first instance, on the authorities of the State and not on other members of the community. Many States have domestic laws and Constitutions which restrict and regulate the use of State's monopoly of force, and provide for independent tribunals in which the State itself is made answerable. In such States, human rights are to that extent already protected by national human rights law and the Constitution. It is important to note that protection must be effective, particularly, the obligation has been imposed on States by the international law.

The International Court of Justice and the National Courts have been able to develop a substantial body of jurisprudence in the field of international law of human rights through a number of decided cases.

MACHINERY FOR THE RECOGNITION, APPLICATION AND IMPLEMENTATION OF HUMAN RIGHTS

The major problem in the development of the human rights law is its enforcement that mainly depends upon the consent of nations. Currently, the implementation and enforcement of human rights law are largely dependent on voluntary compliance, normal pressures and other forms of influence. The vast body of human rights jurisprudence as is available today is the proof of the fact that Governments know that the demand of the human rights is universal.

The basic norms of human rights jurisprudence can be enforced by the Court when any matter concerning such rights are brought before them. The fundamental human rights have also been protected by the Constitutions of different nations. The international instruments relating to human rights lay down important guidance in cases concerning human rights and freedoms. Through the decisions of national and international Courts, an impressive body of jurisprudence concerning interpretation of particular human rights and their application have developed, which is of practical relevance to the judges and advocates of Common Law Countries.

The National Courts of Common Law Countries do not enforce directly the human rights norms included in the International Conventions, unless their provisions have been incorporated into the domestic law. But there is growing tendency amongst the judges of Supreme Court of India and other such higher courts of other countries to introduce basic principles of international instruments by interpreting the provisions of their Constitutions. Through such a tendency, judges do accept universal character of fundamental human rights and freedoms. In fact, judges and advocates are often unaware of the remarkable and comprehensive development of international human rights norms. At the judicial colloquium on the domestic application of international human rights norms held at Bangalore in 1988, it was recommended that appropriate courses in universities and colleges be introduced for lawyers and law-enforcement officers, so that they may be aware of the human rights norms and may foster respect for fundamental human rights and freedoms.

Application of Human Rights Norms by the International Court of Justice

The questions of human rights arose in a number of cases before the International Court of Justice, and the Court has rendered judgements or given advisory opinions which have significantly influenced international law relating to human rights. In *U.S.A. V. Iran,* the court dealing with the capture of U.S. hostage by Iran, observed as follows:

"Wrongly to deprive human beings of their freedom and to subject them to physical constraint in conditions of hardship is in itself manifestly incompatible with the principles of the charter of the United Nations, as well as with the fundamental principles enunciated in the Universal Declaration of Human Rights."

The point to emphasize was that apart from the obligations created by the United Nations Charter, the Court would not hesitate to emphasize the legal importance of the Universal Declaration of Human Rights 1948, when it specifically mentioned that the said Declaration enunciates "fundamental principle of international law." In *Barcelona Traction, Light and Power Company Limited Cases,* the Court recognised the rights of the human beings in categorical terms when it observed:

"Such obligations derive, for example, in contemporary international law, from the outlawing of acts of aggression, and of genocide, as also from the principles and rules concerning the basic rights of human person, including protection from slavery and racial discrimination, some of the corresponding rights of protection have entered into a body of general international law."

Further in Para 91 of the same judgement, The Court said that "Protection against denial justice" has also added to the aforesaid list of human rights. On the problem of enforcement of the human rights the Court stated that:

On the Universal level, the instruments which embody human rights do not confer on States the capacity to protect the victims of infringements of such rights irrespective of their nationality. It is therefore, still at regional level that a solution to this problem has had to be sought, within the Council of Europe, of which Spain is not a member. The problem of admissibility encountered by the claim in the present case has been resolved by the European Convention on Human Rights, which entitles each State which is a party to the Convention to lodge a complaint against any other contracting State for violation of the Convention, irrespective of the nationality of victim.

In case of *Military and Para Military Activities in and Against Nicaragua* the Court made several remarks of interest in the sphere of human rights. The Court persuasively held that "while the United States might form its own appraisal of the situation as to respect for human rights in Nicaragua, the use of force could not be appropriate method to monitor or ensure such respects." The Court concluded that protection of human rights cannot be compatible with the mining of ports, the destruction of oil installations and support for the contras. It, therefore, held that any argument derived from the protection of human rights of Nicaragua could not afford a legal justification for the conduct of United States.

The influence of the Court on the evolution of the International Law of Human Rights has been considerable and predominantly constructive. There is a ground for the expectations that the Court will continue to contribute to the progressive development of the human rights.

Implementation of International Human Rights Norms by the Machinery Provided under Different Treaties

As regards the application of the Principles of the International Covenants on Human Rights, it is important to note that the text of the treaties themselves provide for enforcement measures. State parties to such treaties undertake to respect and observe the Covenanted Rights and freedoms and also place them under international protection. The essence of international protection of human rights is the accountability of the State Parties for their international obligations.

Under the Helsinki Declaration adopted on 1st August, 1975, participating States re-affirmed in Part VII *inter alia,* a pledge to respect human rights and fundamental freedoms. One significant affirmation was contained in the Penultimate paragraph of Part VII by which the participating States confirmed the right of individual to know and act upon his rights and duties in this field.

Human Rights are clearly not without a proper legal binding force but the problem of enforcing them through a regular machinery is "vital for their effective functioning if they have to mould the future of mankind. Lauterpacht pointed out that "the practical unanimity of the members of the United Nations in stressing the importance of the Declaration was accompanied by an equally general repudiation of the idea that the Declaration imposed upon them a legal obligation in respect of the human rights and fundamental freedoms."

The Declaration has influenced certain international treaties and agreements. Many of the provisions of the Declaration are incorporated in the national Constitutions of member States. It has also been cited in the judicial decisions of International and National Courts.

Following Agencies working for the enforcement of human rights at the international level are :

(i) The Human Rights Committee.

(ii) UN Organs, such as Economic and Social Council, and General Assembly, and

(iii) Specialized Agencies of the UN.

The Human Rights are implemented through the following methods that have been contemplated under various Covenants :

(a) Adhoc study groups set up by UN Charter based Institution-Commission on Human Rights.

(b) Creation of Regional Human Rights Commissions such as, the European Commission of Human Rights, the Inter-American Commission on Human Rights and the African Commission on Human and Peoples' Rights.

(c) Domestic application of international human rights norms through national laws.

(d) High Commissioner for Human Rights, a newly created institution.

Growth and development of Non-Governmental Human Rights Organizations is also noteworthy for these organizations take responsibility to build public opinion against violations of human rights. The International Commission of Jurists and the Amnesty International have brought to the notice of World Community and UN Commissions and Committees on Human Rights many instances of violations of human rights.

SIX

Human Rights and the United Nations

The idea of human rights pre-dates the United Nations. Yet it was only with the setting up of this body that it finally achieved formal, universal recognition.

The international community has grown and changed enormously in the course of the twentieth century, but it was one event — the Second World War — that prompted the victors to try to assemble a forum, firstly to deal with some of the War's consequences, but foremost to help provide a way to prevent such appalling events in the future. This forum was the United Nations.

1945 HUMAN RIGHTS FOR ALL

The founders of the United Nations responded to the horrors of the Second World War by emphasizing human rights in the Organization's Charter. At the San Francisco Conference, where the Charter was adopted, some 40 non-governmental organizations successfully lobbied delegates for relatively strong language on human rights.

The Charter of the United Nations was signed on 26 June 1945. It states that the main objective of the new organization is 'to save succeeding generations from the scourge of war' and 'to reaffirm faith in fundamental human rights.' Article 1 of the Charter states that one of the aims of the United Nations is to achieve international co-operation in 'promoting and encouraging respect for human rights and for fundamental freedoms for all without distinction as to race, sex, language or religion.'

The Articles of the Charter have the force of positive international law because the Charter is a treaty and therefore, a legally binding document. All United Nations Member States must fulfill in good faith the obligations they have assumed under the Charter of the United Nations, including the obligations to promote and respect for human rights, to promote observance of human rights, and to cooperate with the United Nations and other nations to attain this aim. However the Charter does not specify human rights and does not establish any specific way to ensure their implementation in Member States.

U.N. COMMISSION ON HUMAN RIGHTS

In 1946, the UN established the Commission on Human Rights the principal policy-making body for human rights within the UN system.

Under the Chairmanship of Eleanor Roosevelt (USA), human rights activist and widow of former U.S. President Franklin Roosevelt, the Commission took up the job of defining basic rights and freedoms. Key contributors included Rene Cassin (France), Charles Malik (Lebanon),

Peng Chun Chang (China), Hernan Santa Cruz (Chile), Alexandre Bogomolov/Alexei Pavlov (Soviet Union), Lord Dukeston/Geoffrey Wilson (United Kingdom), William Hodgson (Australia) and John Humphrey (Canada).

Orignally composed of 18 members States, the Human Rights Commission now has now much more members who meet annually in Geneva to review human rights issues, develop and codify new international norms, and make recommendations to Governments. Non-governmental organizations play an active role.

ADOPTION OF THE UNIVERSAL DECLARATION OF HUMAN RIGHTS 1948

After thorough scrutiny and 1,400 rounds of voting on practically every word and every clause, the General Assembly adopted the Universal Declaration of Human Rights on 10 December 1948 in Paris at the newly built Palais de Chaillot.

Spelling out individual rights and freedoms for everyone, the Declaration was unprecedented. It remains the first pillar of twentieth-century human rights law and the cornerstone of the universal human rights movement.

The Universal Declaration is built on the fundamental principle that human rights are based on the inherent dignity of every person. This dignity, and the rights to freedom and equality which derive therefrom, are undeniable.

Although the Declaration does not have the binding force of a treaty, it has acquired universal acceptability. Many countries have cited the Declaration or included its provisions in their basic laws or constitutions. And many human rights covenants, conventions and treaties concluded since 1948 have been built on its principles.

INTERNATIONAL HUMAN RIGHTS 1948-1966

The United Nations strives to create a culture of human rights around the world. The broadest legally binding human rights agreements negotiated under UN auspices are the International Covenant on Civil and Political Rights and the International Covenant on Economic, Social and Cultural Rights.

Both were adopted in 1966 and came into force in 1976. They take the Universal Declaration a step further by making provisions legally binding. A majority of the world's countries are parties to the two Conventions, thereby opening the door to international monitoring of their human rights practices.

Along with the Universal Declaration, they comprise the International Bill of Rights.

The task of drawing up an International Bill of Human Rights defining human rights and freedoms referred to in the Charter, was charged upon the Commission on Human Rights, established in 1945. A major step in drafting the International Bill of Human Rights was realized on 10 December 1948, when the General Assembly adopted the Universal Declaration of Human Rights 'as a common standard of achievement for all people and nations'.

Since the Universal Declaration became international law, many other conventions have been convened and many specialized agencies have been set up to monitor, and enforce human rights standards that pertain to specific issues such as the rights of refugees, the rights of working people, and the special rights of children. Much of the work of the United Nations is built upon the basic principles of human rights set forth in the Universal Declaration of Human Rights.

One of the greatest achievements of the United Nations the creation of a comprehensive body of human rights legislation. For the first time in history, there eixsts a universal code of human rights one to which all nations can subscribe and to which all people can aspire.

Since 1948, some 60 human rights treaties and declarations have been negotiated at the United Nations. Some examples are :

1948 Convention on the Prevention and Punishment of the Crime of Genocide

1961 Convention Relating to the Status of Refugees

1965 International Convention on the Elimination of All Forms of Racial Discrimination

1979 Convention on the Elimination of All Forms of Discrimination Against Women

1984 Convention against Torture and Other Cruel, Inhuman or Degrading Treatment or Punishment

1989 Convention on the Rights of the Child

1990 International Convention on the Protection of the Rights of All Migrant Workers and Members of Their Families

HUMAN RIGHTS TREATY BODIES

Within the UN system, there are six committees that monitor compliance of States parties to specific treaties :

The Committee on the Elimination of Racial Discrimination

The Human Rights Committee

The Committee on Economic, Social and Cultural Rights

The Committee Against Torture

The Committee on the Elimination of Discrimination Against Women

The Committee on the Rights of the Child

U N COMMISION FOR HUMAN RIGHTS

On 20 December 1993, after nearly 50 years of alternate hope and disappointment, the General Assembly voted unanimously to create the post of UN High Commissioner for Human Rights. The High Commissioner coordinates the UN human rights programme and promotes universal respect for human rights. Appointed by the UN Secretary-General and approved by the General Assembly, the first High Commissioner was Jose Ayala-Lasso of Ecuador, who took up his duties on 5 April 1994. The current High Commissioner is South African lawyer Navanethen, whose four-year term began on 1 September 2008.

HUMAN RIGHTS IN THE FIELDS

During the 1990s, the United Nations witnessed a dramatic increase of human rights activities in field operations. Depending on the needs of the situation, these activities combine monitoring of human rights violations, education, training and other advisory services.

Currently, such operations exist in Abkhazia/Georgia, Burundi, Cambodia, Colombia, Gaza, Guatemala, Haiti, Malawi, Mongolia, the Democratic Republic of the Congo, Rwanda and the former Yugoslavia.

In 1968, the United Nations held the first International Conference on Human Rights in Tehran, Iran. The Proclamation of the Conference emphasized the link between civil and political rights and economic, social and cultural right.

Twenty-five years later, in 1993, the United Nations convened the World Conference on Human Rights in Vienna, Austria. The Vienna Declaration and Programme of Action stress the universal nature of human rights and the need to fight all forms of racism, discrimination, xenophobia and intolerance. It also places strong emphasis on the rights of women, children, minorities and indigenous people.

INTERNATIONAL CRIMINAL COURT

Hopes are high for a June 1998 conference in Rome to establish an international criminal court, which would form a vital part of an emerging system of international human rights protection.

For nearly half a century, the United Nations has recognized the need to establish an international criminal court to prosecute and punish persons responsible for crimes against humanity. In the absence of such a court, two ad-hoc criminal courts have been set up to judge war crimes in the former Yugoslavia and in Rwanda.

HUMAN RIGHTS IN THE 21ST CENTURY

General Assembly Resolution 49/184 of 23 December 1994 proclaims the ten-year period beginning on 1 January 1995 the United Nations Decade for Human Rights Education. The resolution states that "human rights education should involve more than the provision of information and should constitute a comprehensive life-long process by which people at all levels in development and in all strata of society learn respect for the dignity of others and the means and methods of ensuring that respect in all societies."

Growing international awareness, fostered by mass communications, has heightened the sense of urgency for respect of human rights. Thousands of individuals and citizens groups around the world are fighting for their rights and freedoms. United Nations action for human rights continues. Yet millions of people around the world suffer some serious violation or deprivation of their basic rights and freedoms — everything from torture, rape and corrupt judicial systems to bonded labour, hunger and lack of access to health services, housing, sanitation and water. Will there ever be a global culture of human rights?

The global quest for commitment to the Universal Declaration of Human Rights involves everyone. The campaign relies heavily on thousands of dedicated individuals and citizens' groups who often risk their lives for the cause. Increased involvement in the defense of human rights helps to build an environment where freedom and dignity are expected and respected. It is up to each and every one of us — from Presidents and Prime Ministers to business executives, farmers and students — to work toward this dream.

GLOBAL GATHERINGS FOR HUMAN RIGHTS

Since 1945, non-governmental organizations have contributed immensely to the work of the United Nations and Human Rights—as a source of information and a force for meaning ful change.

SEVEN

Universal Declaration of Human Rights

The *Universal Declaration of Human Rights (UDHR)* is a declaration adopted by the *United Nations General Assembly* on 10 December 1948 at the *Palais de Chaillot in Paris.* The Declaration has been translated into at least 375 languages and dialects, making it the most widely translated document in the world. The Declaration arose directly from the experience of the Second World War and represents the first global expression of rights to which all human beings are entitled. It consists of 30 articles which have been elaborated in subsequent international treaties, regional *human rights* instruments, national constitutions and laws. The *International Bill of Human Rights* consists of the Universal Declaration of Human Rights, the *International Covenant on Economic, Social and Cultural Rights,* and the *International Covenant on Civil and*

Political Rights and its two Optional Protocols. In 1966 the General Assembly adopted the two detailed Covenants, which complete the International Bill of Human Rights.

HISTORY OF UNIVERSAL DECLARATION OF HUMAN RIGHTS

The morals and values of human rights can be traced through the history of religious beliefs and cultures around the world. European philosophers of the *Age of Enlightenment* developed theories of natural law that influenced the adoption of documents such as the *Bill of Rights* of England, the *Bill of Rights* in the United States, and the *Declaration of the Rights of Man and of the Citizen* in France.

National and International pressure for an international bill of rights had been building throughout World War II. In his 1941 State of the Union address US president Franklin *Roosevelt* called for the protection of what he termed the "essential" *Four Freedoms: freedom of speech, freedom of conscience, freedom from fear* and *freedom from want* as its basic war aims. This has been seen as part of a movement of the 1940s that sought to make human rights part of the conditions for peace at the end of the war. The *United Nations Charter* "reaffirmed faith in fundamental human rights, and dignity and worth of the human person" and committed all member states to promote "universal respect for, and observance of, human rights and fundamental freedoms for all without distinction as to race, sex, language or religion".

When the atrocities committed by *Nazi Germany* became public knowledge around the world after World War II, the consensus within the world community was that the United Nations Charter did not sufficiently define the rights it referenced. A universal declaration that specified the rights of individuals was necessary to give effect to the Charter's provisions on human rights.

Drafting of the Universal Declaration of Human Rights

Canadian *John Peters Humphrey* was called upon by the United Nations Secretary-General to work on the project and became the Declaration's Principal Drafter. At the time Humphrey was newly appointed as Director of the Division of Human Rights within the United Nations Secretariat. The Commission on Human Rights, a standing body of the United Nations, was constituted to undertake the work of preparing what was initially conceived as an International Bill of Rights. The membership of the Commission was designed to be broadly representative of the global community with representatives of the following countries: Australia, Belgium, Byelorussian Soviet Socialist Republic, Chile, China, Cuba, Egypt, France, India, Iran, Lebanon, Panama, Philippines, United Kingdom, United States, Soviet Union, Uruguay and Yugoslavia.

Adoption of the Universal Declaration of Human Rights

The Universal Declaration was adopted by the General Assembly on 10 December 1948 by a vote of 48 in favour, 0 against, with 8 abstentions (Byelorussian SSR, Czechoslovakia, Poland, Ukrainian SSR, USSR, as well as Yugoslavia, South Africa and Saudi Arabia).

The following countries voted in favour of the Declaration: Afghanistan, Argentina, Australia, Belgium, Bolivia, Brazil, Burma, Canada, Chile, China, Colombia, Costa Rica, Cuba, Denmark, the Dominican Republic, Ecuador, Egypt; El Salvador, Ethiopia, France, Greece, Guatemala, Haiti, Iceland, India, Iran, Iraq, Lebanon, Liberia, Luxembourg, Mexico, Netherlands, New Zealand, Nicaragua, Norway, Pakistan, Panama, Paraguay, Peru, Philippines, Thailand, Sweden, Syria, Turkey, United Kingdom, United States, Uruguay and Venezuela.

Despite the central role played by Canadian John Humphrey, the Canadian Government at first abstained from voting on the Declaration's draft, but later voted in favour of the final draft in the General Assembly.

Structure of the Universal of Declaration of Human Rights

The underlying structure of the Universal Declaration was introduced in its second draft which was prepared by *Rene Cassin.* Cassin worked from a first draft prepared by *John Peters Humphrey.* The structure was influenced by the *Code Napoleon,* including a preamble and introductory general principles. Cassin compared the Declaration to the *portico* of a Greek temple, with a foundation, steps, four columns and a *pediment.* Articles 1 and 2 are the foundation blocks, with their principles of dignity, liberty, equality and brotherhood. The seven paragraphs of the preamble, setting out the reasons for the Declaration, are represented by the steps. The main body of the Declaration forms the four columns. The first column (articles 3-11) constitutes rights of the individual, such as the right to life and the prohibition of slavery. The second column (articles 12-17) constitutes the rights of the individual in civil and *political society.* The third column (articles 18-21) is concerned with spiritual, public and political freedoms such as freedom of religion and freedom of association. The fourth column (articles 22-27) sets out social, economic and cultural rights. In Cassin's model, the last three articles of the Declaration provide the pediment which binds the structure together. These articles are concerned with the duty of the individual to society and the prohibition of use of rights in contravention of the purposes of the United Nations. With regard to the Communist block's abstentions, the 9 December Velodrome d'Hiver meeting of 20,000 Parisiens at the invitation of World Citizen Garry Davis and his "Conseil de Solidarite" who had interrupted a General Assembly session on 22 November to call for a world government, provoked its abstention rather than voting against the human rights document. Eleanor Roosevelt in her column "My Day" wrote on 15 December that "Garry Davis, the young man who in Paris as a citizen of the world...has succeeded in getting the backing of a few intellectuals and even has received a cablegram from Albert Einstein telling him, from Professor Einstein's point of view, that the United Nations has not yet achieved peace. The United Nations, of course, is not set up to achieve peace. That the governments are supposed to do themselves. But it is expected to help preserve peace, and that I think, is it doing more effectively day by day...During a pleneary session in the General Assembly, this young man tried to make a speech from the balcony on the subject of how incompetent the United Nations is to deal with the questions before it. How much better it would be if Mr. Davis would .set up his own governmental organisation and start then and there a worldwide international government. All who would join him would learn that they had no nationality and, therefore, not being bothered by any special interest in any one country, everyone would develop...a completely cooperative feeling among all peoples and a willingness to accept any laws passes by this super government."

PREAMBLE OF THE UNIVERSAL DECLARATION OF HUMAN RIGHTS

The Universal Declaration begins with a preamble consisting of seven paragraphs followed by a statement "proclaiming" the Declaration.

Each paragraph of the preamble sets out a reason for the adoption of the Declaration. The first paragraph asserts that the recognition of human dignity of all people is the foundation of justice and peace in the world. The second paragraph observes that disregard and contempt for human rights have resulted in barbarous acts which have outraged the conscience of mankind and that the four freedoms: freedom of speech, belief, freedom from want, and freedom from fear - which is "proclaimed as the highest aspiration" of the people. The third paragraph states that so that people are not compelled to rebellion against tyranny, human rights should be protected by rule of law. The fourth paragraph relates human rights to the development of friendly relations between nations. The fifth paragraph links the Declaration back to the United Nations Charter which reaffirms faith in fundamental human rights and dignity and worth of the human person. The sixth paragraph notes that all members of the United Nations have pledged themselves to achieve, in cooperation with the United Nations, the promotion of universal respect for and observance of human rights and fundamental freedoms. The seventh paragraph observes that "a common understanding" of rights and freedoms is of "the greatest importance" for the full realisation of that pledged

These paragraphs are followed by the "proclamation" of the Declaration as a "common standard of achievement" for "all peoples and all nations", so that "all individuals" and "all organs of society" should by teaching and education, promote respect for these rights and freedoms and by progressive measures, national and international, secure their universal and effective recognition and observance.

The Preamble is

- **Whereas** recognition of the inherent dignity and of the equal and inalienable rights of all members of the human family is the foundation of freedom, justice and peace in the world,

- **Whereas** disregard and contempt for human rights have resulted in barbarous acts which have outraged the conscience of mankind, and the advent of a world in which human beings shall enjoy freedom of speech and belief and freedom from fear and want has been proclaimed as the highest aspiration of the common people,

- **Whereas** it is essential, if man is not to be compelled to have recourse, as a last resort, to rebellion against tyranny and oppression, that human rights should be protected by the rule of law,

• **Whereas** it is essential to promote the development of friendly relations between nations,

• **Whereas** the peoples of the United Nations have in the Charter reaffirmed their faith in fundamental human rights, in the dignity and worth of the human person and in the equal rights of men and women and have determined to promote social progress and better standards of life in larger freedom,

• **Whereas** Member States have pledged themselves to achieve, in co-operation with the United Nations, the promotion of universal respect for and observance of human rights and fundamental freedoms,

• **Whereas** a common understanding of these rights and freedoms is of the greatest importance for the full realization of this pledge.

• **Now, Therefore** The General Assembly proclaims This Universal Declaration of Human Rights as a common standard of achievement for all peoples and all nations, to the end that every individual and every organ of society, keeping this Declaration constantly in mind, shall strive by teaching and education to promote respect for these rights and freedoms and by progressive measures, national and international, to secure their universal and effective recognition and observance, both among the peoples of Member States themselves and among the peoples of territories under their jurisdiction.

UNIVERSAL DECLARATION OF HUMAN RIGHTS 1948

THE GENERAL ASSEMBLY

proclaims

THIS UNIVERSAL DECLARATION OF HUMAN RIGHTS as a common standard of achievement for all peoples and all nations, to the end that every individual and every organ of society, keeping this Declaration constantly in mind, shall strive by teaching and education to promote respect for these rights and freedoms and by progressive measures, national and international, to secure their universal and effective recognition and observance, both among the peoples of Member states themselves and among the peoples of territories under their jurisdiction.

Article 1

All human beings are born free and equal in dignity and rights. They are endowed with reason and conscience and should act towards one another in a spirit of brotherhood.

Article 2

Everyone is entitled to all the rights and freedoms set forth in this Declaration, without distinction of any kind, such as race, colour, sex, language, religion, political or other opinion, national or social origin, property, birth or other status. Further, no distinction shall be made on the basis of the political, jurisdictional or international status of the country or territory to which a person belongs, whether it is independent, trust, non-self-governing or under any other limitation of sovereignty.

Article 3

Everyone has the right of life, liberty and security of person.

Article 4

No one shall be held in slavery or servitude; slavery and the slave trade shall be prohibited in all their forms.

Article 5

No one shall be subjected to torture or to cruel, inhuman or degrading treatment or punishment.

Article 6

Everyone has the right to recognition everywhere as a person before the law.

Article 7

All are equal before the law and are entitled without any discrimination to equal protection of the law. All are entitled to equal protection against any discrimination in violation of this Declaration and against any incitement to such discrimination.

Article 8

Everyone has the right to an effective remedy by the competent national tribunals for acts violating the fundamental rights granted him by the constitution or by law.

Article 9

No one shall be subjected to arbitrary arrest, detention or exile.

Article 10

Everyone is entitled in full equality to a fair and public hearing by an independent and impartial tribunal, in the determination of his rights and obligations and of any criminal charge against him.

Article 11

1. Everyone charged with a penal offence has the right to be presumed innocent until proved guilty according to law in a public trial at which he has had all the guarantees necessary for his defence.

2. No one shall be held guilty of any penal offence on account of any act or omission, which did not constitute a penal offence, under national or international law, at the time when it was committed. Nor shall a heavier penalty be imposed then the one that was applicable at the time the penal offence was committed.

Article 12

No one shall be subjected to arbitrary interference with his privacy, family, home, or correspondence, or to attacks upon his honour and reputation. Everyone has the right to the protection of the law against such interference or attack.

Article 13

1. Everyone has the right to freedom of movement and residence within the borders of each state.

2. Everyone has the right to leave any country, including his own, and to return to his country.

Article 14

1. Everyone has the right to seek and to enjoy in other countries asylum from persecution.

2. This right may not be invoked in the case of prosecutions genuinely arising from non-political crimes or from acts contrary to the purposes and principles of the United Nations.

Article 15

1. Everyone has the right to nationality.

2. No one shall be arbitrarily deprived of his nationality nor denied the right to change his nationality.

Article 16

1. Men and women of full age, without limitation due to race, nationality or religion, have the right to marry and to found a family. They are entitled to equal rights as to marriage, during marriage and at its dissolution.

2. Marriage shall be entered into only with the free and full consent of the intending spouses.

3. The family is the natural and fundamental group unit of society and is entitled to protection by society and the state.

Article 17

1. Everyone has the right to own property alone as well as in association with others.

2. No one shall be arbitrarily deprived of his property.

Article 18

Everyone has the right to freedom of thought, conscience and religion; this rights includes freedom to change his religion or belief, and freedom, either alone or in community with others and in public or private, to manifest his religion or belief in teaching, practice, worship and observance.

Article 19

Everyone has the right to freedom of opinion and expression; this right includes freedom to hold opinions without interference and to seek, receive and impart information and ideas through any media regardless of frontiers.

Article 20

1. Everyone has the right to freedom of peaceful association.

2. No one may be compelled to belong to an association.

Article 21

1. Every one has right to take part in the government of his country, directly or through freely chosen representatives.

2. Everyone has the right of equal access to public service in his country.

3. The will of the people shall be the basis of the authority of government; this will, shall be expressed in periodic and genuine election, which shall be by universal and equal suffrage and shall be held by secret vote or by equivalent free voting procedures.

Article 22

Everyone, as a member of society, has the right to social security and is entitled to realisation through national effort and international co-operation and in accordance with the organisation and resources of each state, of the economic, social and cultural rights indispensable for his dignity and the free development of his personality.

Article 23

1. Everyone has the right to work, to free choice of employment, to just and favourable conditions of work to protection against unemployment.

2. Everyone, without any discrimination, has the right to equal pay for equal work.

3. Everyone who works has the right to just and favourable remuneration ensuring for himself and his family an existence worthy of human dignity, if necessary, by other means of social protection.

4. Everyone has the right to form and to join trade unions for the protection of his interests.

Article 24

Everyone has the right to rest and leisure including reasonable limitation of working hours and periodic holidays with pay.

Article 25

1. Everyone has the right to a standard of living adequate for the health and well-being of himself and his family, including food, clothing, housing and medical care and necessary social service, and the right to security in the event of unemployment, sickness, disability, widowhood, old age or other lack of livelihood in circumstances beyond his control.

2. Motherhood and childhood are entitled to special care and assistance. All children, whether born in or out of wedlock, shall enjoy the equal social protection.

Article 26

1. Everyone has the right to education. Education shall be free, at least in the elementary and fundamental stages.

Elementary education shall be compulsory. Technical and professional education shall be made generally available and higher education shall be equally accessible to all on the basis of merit.

2. Education shall be protected to the full development of the human personality and to the strengthening of respect for human rights and fundamental freedoms. It shall promote understanding, tolerance and friendship among all nations, racial or religious groups, and shall further the activities of the United Nations for the maintenance of peace.

3. Parents have a prior right to choose the kind of education that shall be given to their children.

Article 27

1. Everyone has the right to freely participate in the cultural life of the community, to enjoy the arts and to share in scientific advancement and its benefits.

2. Everyone has the right to protection of the moral and material interests resulting from any scientific, literary or artistic protection of which he is the author.

Article 28

Everyone is entitled to social and international order in which the rights and freedoms set forth in the Declaration can be fully realized.

Article 29

1. Everyone has duties to the community in which alone the free and full development of his personality is possible.

2. In the exercise of his rights and freedoms, every one shall be subject only to such limitations as are determined by law solely for the purpose of securing due to such limitations as are determined by law solely for the purpose of securing due recognition and respect for the rights and freedoms of others and of meeting the just requirements of

morality, public order and the general welfare in the democratic society.

3. These rights and freedoms may in no case be exercised contrary to the purposes and principles of the United Nations.

Article 30

Nothing in this Declaration may be interpreted as implying for any state, group of person any right to engage in any activity or to perform any act aimed at the destruction of any of the rights and freedoms set forth herein.

SIGNIFICANCE AND LEGAL EFFECTS

Significance

In the preamble, governments commit themselves and their peoples to measures to secure the universal and effective recognition and observance of the human rights set out in the Declaration. Eleanor Roosevelt supported the adoption of the UDHR as a declaration, rather than as a treaty, because she believed that it would have the same kind of influence on global society as the United States Declaration of Independence had within the United States. In this view, she proved to be correct. Even though not formally legally binding, the Declaration has been adopted in or influenced most national constitutions since 1948. It also serves as the foundation for a growing number of international treaties and national laws and international, regional, national and sub-national institutions protecting and promoting human rights.

Legal Effect

While not a treaty itself, the Declaration was explicitly adopted for the purpose of defining the meaning of the words "fundamental freedoms" and "human rights" appearing in the United Nations Charter, which is binding on all member states. For this reason, the Universal Declaration is a fundamental constitutive document of the United Nations. International lawyers, in addition, believe that the Declaration forms part *of customary international law* and is a powerful tool in applying diplomatic and moral pressure to governments that violate any of its articles. The 1968 United Nations International Conference on Human Rights advised that it "constitutes an obligation for the members of the international community" to all persons. The declaration has served as the foundation for two binding UN human rights covenants, the International Covenant on Civil and Political Rights and the International Covenant on Economic, Social and Cultural Rights and the principles of the Declaration are elaborated in international treaties such as the International Convention on the Elimination of All Forms of Racial Discrimination, the International Convention on the Elimination of Discrimination Against Women, the United Nations Convention on the Rights of the Child, the United Nations Convention Against Torture and many more. The Declaration continues to be widely cited by governments, academics, advocates and constitutional courts and individual human beings who appeal to its principles for the protection of their recognised human rights.

A BRIEF ANALYSIS OF THE UNIVERSAL DECLARATION OF HUMAN RIGHTS

The outstanding feature of the Universal Declaration of Human Rights is that it is a simple resolution of the General Assembly in the sense that it does't create binding obligation on the part of State to carry out its enforcement, yet it constitutes a "common standard of achievement for all peoples and all nations." As such it has normative value.

"The repeated invocation of the Universal Declaration over more than forty-five years by the United Nations and other international organizations, its use in diplomatic exchange between governments, its incorporation into treaties and national constitutions, and its application by international and national tribunals have given at least some of its rights binding characters custom."

The adoption of Declaration without dissent was considered a remarkable achievement since it was supported by overwhelming consensus of international community as represented in the General Assembly. It has defined and provided contents to the term "human rights and fundamental freedoms" as used in the United Nations Charter. The Declaration consists of a preamble and 30 articles incorporating civil, political, economic, social and cultural rights.

The preamble clearly states that "recognition of the inherent dignity and of the equal and inalienable rights of all members of the human family is the foundation of freedom, justice and peace in the world." Thus, the question of maintenance of international peace and security is interlinked with the recognition and protection of human rights.

The first two articles are general in nature providing philosophical assumptions upon which the Declaration is founded. They run as

Article 1

"All human beings are born free and equal in dignity and rights. They are endowed with reason and conscience and should act towards one another in a spirit of brotherhood."

Article 2

"Everyone is entitled to all the rights and freedoms set forth in this declaration, without distinction of any kind."

Article 3 to 21

The right to life, liberty and security of person; prohibition of slavery, of torture and cruel, inhuman or degrading treatment; the right to recognition every where as a person before the law; the right to effective judicial remedy; freedom from arbitrary arrest, detention; the right to a fair trial and public hearing by an independent and impartial tribunal; the right to be presumed innocent until provide guilty; freedom from arbitrary interference with privacy, family, home or correspondence; freedom of movement; the right of asylum; the right to nationality; freedom of opinion and expression; freedom of peaceful assembly and to form association; freedom of thought, conscience and religion; right to take part in Government of one's own country; and the right of equal access to public service.

Article 22 to 27

The economic, social and cultural rights, described in Article 22 to 27, are right to education, to social security, to work, to rest and leisure, to an adequate standard of living, and to participate in the cultural life of the community.

Above all the Declaration has realized that everyone is entitled to a social and international order in which the rights and freedom set forth in the Declaration can be fully realized. However, the rights recognized in the Declaration are not absolute. Such limitation as determined by law may be imposed for the purpose of securing due recognition and respect for the rights and freedom of others and of meeting the just requirements of morality, public order and general welfare in a democratic society. These rights and freedoms may in no case be exercised by a State, group or individual contrary to the purposes and principles of the United Nations.

Mary Ann Glendon situates the universal Declaration of Human Rights in this context as follows:

In 1948 the framers of the Universal Declaration achieved a distinctive synthesis of previous thinking about rights and duties. After canvassing sources from North and South, East and West, they believed they had found a core principle so basic that no nation would wish openly to disavow them. They wove those principles into a unified document that quickly displaced all antecedents as the Principal model for the rights instruments in force in the world today.

RIGHT TO INFORMATION AS PART OF THE UDHR

The Jurisprudence of democracy has been elaborately dealt in Articles 23 and 25 of the UDHR, 1948 and in Part-III and IV of the Constitution of India, 1950. It states that every one should be able to enjoy freedom of opinion and expression including the right to "seek, receive and impart information and ideas". This guarantee is now widely understood as including openness on the part of governments and right to access to information in possession of Government. Commenting on the significance of Right to Information once Justice Bhagabati said, "No democratic government can survive without accountability and the basic postulate of accountability that the people should have information about the functioning of the Government. It is only when people know how Government is functioning that they can fulfil the role which democracy assigns to them and make democracy a really effective participatory democracy".

Over fifty countries have adopted comprehensive Right to Information laws, and many other countries are seriously considering having such laws. The countries are not limited to the advanced western democracies only; but include a wide spectrum ranging from the emerging nation states of Africa through the developing countries of Asia, and Latin

America to the recent democracies of Eastern Europe. Countries like South Africa, Mexico and Bulgaria are quite advanced in respect of access to information. India is relatively a latecomer in this respect.

Right to information laws reflect the basic premise that Government is meant to serve the people; and are based on the notion that public bodies hold information not for themselves, but as custodian of public good and that this information must be available to the general public. Access to government recedes and information is a necessary pre-requisite for enhancing transparency. Good governance is only possible where there is transparency and accountability. Access facilitates public knowledge and discussion, and thereby enhances responsiveness in public policy-making and service delivery. It provides an important safeguard against abuses, mismanagement and corruption; it enhances openness and responsiveness in the decision-making process and thereby increases credibility and legitimacy of Government actions essential for a civil and democratic society.

Right to Information Act of India, which has become operational since 12th October 2005, is a milestone in the history of our democracy. The detail provisions of the Act have been referred in Appendix: Two.

EIGHT

International Covenant on Civil and Political Rights

The International Covenant on Civil and Political Rights (ICCPR) is a multilateral treaty adopted by the United Nations General Assembly on December 16, 1966, and in force from March 23, 1976. It commits its parties to respect the civil and political rights of individuals, including the right to life, freedom of religion, freedom of speech, freedom of assembly, electoral rights and rights to due process and a fair trial. As of October 2009, the Covenant had 72 signatories and 165 parties.

The ICCPR is part of the International Bill of Human Rights, along with the Universal Declaration of Human Rights (UDHR) and the International Covenant on Economic, Social and Cultural Rights (ICESCR).

The International Covenant on Civil and Political Rights is monitored by the *Human Rights Committee* (a separate body to the *Human Rights Council* which replaced the *Commission on Human Rights,* under the *UN Charter* in 2006) with permanent standing, to consider periodic reports submitted by member States on their compliance with the treaty. Members of the Human Rights Committee are elected by member states, but do not represent any State.

GENESIS OF THE COVENANT

The ICCPR has its roots in the same process that led to the *Universal Declaration of Human Rights.* A "Declaration on the Essential Rights of Man" had been proposed at the *1945 San Francisco Conference* which led to the founding of the *United Nations,* and the *Economic and Social Council* was given the task of drafting it. Early in the process, the document was split into a declaration setting forth general principles of human rights, and a convention or covenant containing binding commitments. The former evolved into the UDHR and was adopted on December 10, 1948.

Drafting continued on the convention, but there remained significant differences between UN members on the relative importance of negative Civil and Political versus *positive* Economic, Social and Cultural rights. These eventually caused the convention to be split into two separate covenants, "one to contain civil and political rights and the other to contain economic, social and cultural rights." The two covenants were to contain as many similar provisions as possible, and be opened for signature simultaneously. Each would also contain an article on the right of all peoples to self-determination.

The first document became the International Covenant on Civil and Political Rights, and the second the *International Covenant on Economic, Social and Cultural*

Rights. The drafts were presented to the UN General Assembly for discussion in 1954, and adopted in 1966.

SUMMARY OF THE COVENANT

The Covenant follows the structure of the UDHR and ICESCR, with a preamble and fifty-three articles, divided into six parts.

Part 1 (Article 1) recognises the right of all peoples to self-determination, including the right to "freely determine their political status", pursue their economic, social and cultural goals, and manage and dispose of their own resources. It recognises a *negative right* of a people not to be deprived of its means of subsistence, and imposes an obligation on those parties still responsible for non-self governing and trust territories (colonies) to encourage and respect their self-determination.

Part 2 (Articles 2-5) obliges parties to legislate where necessary to give effect to the rights recognised in the Covenant, and to provide an effective *legal remedy* for any violation of those rights. It also requires the rights be recognised "without distinction of any kind, such as race, colour, sex, language, religion, political or other opinion, national or social origin, property, birth or other status," and to ensure that they are enjoyed equally by women. The rights can only be limited "in time of public emergency which threatens the life of the nation," and even then no derogation is permitted from the rights to life, freedom from *torture* and *slavery,* the freedom from *retrospective law,* the right to personhood, and freedom of thought, conscience and religion.

Part 3 (Articles 6 - 27) lists the rights themselves. These include rights to

• physical integrity, in the form of the right to life and freedom from arbitrary *execution,* torture, and slavery (Articles 6, 7, and 8);

• liberty and security of the person, in the form of freedom from *arbitrary arrest and detention* and the right to *habeas corpus* (Article 9);

• procedural fairness in law, in the form of rights to due process, a *fair and impartial trial,* the *presumption of innocence,* and recognition as a person before the law (Articles 10, 11, 14, 15, and 16);

• individual liberty, in the form of the freedoms of movement, thought, conscience and religion, speech, association and assembly, *family* rights, the right to a nationality, and the right to *privacy* (Articles 12, 13, 17 - 24);

• political participation, including the right to join a political party and the *right to vote* (Article 25);

• Non-discrimination and equality before the law (Articles 26 and 27).

Many of these rights include specific actions which must be undertaken to realise them.

Part 4 (Articles 28 - 45) governs the establishment and operation of the *Human Rights Committee* and the reporting and monitoring of the Covenant. It also allows parties to recognise the competence of the Committee to resolve disputes between parties on the implementation of the Covenant (Articles 41 and 42).

Part 5 (Articles 46 - 47) clarifies that the Covenant shall not be interpreted as interfering with the operation of the United Nations or "the inherent right of all peoples to enjoy and utilize fully and freely their natural wealth and resources".

Part 6 (Articles 48 - 53) governs ratification, entry into force, and amendment of the Covenant.

CORE PROVISIONS OF THE COVENANT

Rights to Physical Integrity

Article 6 of the Covenant recognises the "inherent right of the individual to life" Article 6 has been criticised by some human rights organisations for specifically excluding the death penalty from its scope. This was a pragmatic move to ensure wide adoption of the convention in states such as the *United States.* The abolition of the death penalty is instead optional. The *Second Optional Protocol* commits its signatories to the abolition of the death penalty within their borders,

Article 7 prohibits torture and cruel, inhuman or degrading punishment, in response to *Nazi Human Experimentation* during second world war this article explicitly includes a prohibition on medical and scientific experimentation without consent,

Articles 8.1 and 8.2 represent a total prohibition of slavery and forced servitude in all situations, this can be contrasted with *Article* 8.3 the prohibition on forced labour, which includes several exceptions for criminal punishment, military service and civil obligations.

Political Rights

Article 3 provides an accessory non-discrimination principle. Accessory in the way that it cannot be used independently and can only be relied upon in relation to another right protected by the ICCPR.

In contrast, *Article 26* contains a revolutionary and unique norm by providing an autonomous equality principle which is not dependant upon another right under the convention being infringed. This has the effect of widening the scope of the non-discrimination principle beyond the scope of ICCPR.

OPTIONAL PROTOCOLS

There are two Optional Protocols to the Covenant. The *First Optional Protocol* establishes an individual complaints mechanism, allowing individuals to complain to the Human

Rights Committee about violations of the Covenant. This has led to the creation of a complex jurisprudence on the interpretation and implementation of the Covenant. As of September 2009, the First Optional Protocol has 113 parties.

The *Second Optional Protocol* abolishes the death penalty; however, countries were permitted to make a reservation allowing for use of death penalty for the most serious crimes of a military nature, committed during wartime. As of October 2009, the Second Optional Protocol had 72 parties.

Reservations

This section requires *expansion.*

A number of parties have made reservations and interpretative declarations to their application of the Covenant.

Argentina will apply the fair trial rights guaranteed in its *constitution* to the prosecution of those accused of violating the general law of nations.

Australia reserves the right to progressively implement the prison standards of Article 10, to compensate for miscarriages of justice by administrative means rather than through the courts, and interprets the prohibition on racial incitement as being subject to the freedoms of expression, association and assembly. It also declares that its implementation will be effected at each level of its federal system.

Austria reserves the right to continue to exile members of the *House of Habsburg,* and limits the rights of the accused and the right to a fair trial to those already existing in its legal system.

The *Bahamas* due to problems with implementation reserves the right not to compensate for miscarriages of justice.

Bahrain interprets Articles 3 (no sexual discrimination), 18 (freedom of religion) and 23 (family rights) within the context of Islamic Sharia law.

Bangladesh reserves the right to try people in absentia where they are fugitives from justice and declares that resource constraints mean that it cannot necessarily segregate prisons or provide counsel for accused persons.

Barbados reserves the right not to provide free counsel for accused persons due to resource constraints.

Belgium interprets the freedoms of speech, assembly and association in a manner consistent with the *European Convention on Human Rights.* It does not consider itself obliged to ban war propaganda as required by Article 20, and interprets that article in light of the freedom of expression in the UDHR.

NATIONAL IMPLEMENTATION AND EFFECTS

The International Covenant on Civil and Political Rights has been signed by 174 states, 8 of which have yet to ratify the treaty.

UNITED STATES' RESERVATIONS

Reservations, Understandings, and Declarations

The *United States Senate* ratified the ICCPR in 1992, with five *reservations,* five understandings, and four declarations. Some have noted that with so many reservations, its implementation has little domestic effect. Included in the Senate's ratification was the declaration that "the provisions of Article 1 through 27 of the Covenant are not self-executing", and in a *Senate Executive Report* stated that the declaration was meant to "clarify that the Covenant will not create a private cause of action in U.S. Courts.

Effect on Domestic Law

Where a treaty or covenant is not self-executing, and where Congress has not acted to implement the agreement with legislation, no private right of action is created by ratification. *Set Fujii v. State* 38 Cal.2d 718, 242 P.2d 617 (1952); also see *Buell v. Mitchell* 274 F.3d 337 (6th Cir., 2001) (discussing ICCPR's relationship to *death penalty* cases, citing to other ICCPR cases). Thus while the ICCPR is *ostensibly* binding upon the United States as a matter of international law, it does not form part of the domestic law of the nation.

International Law

Prominent critics in the human rights community, such as Prof. Louis Henkin (non-self-execution declaration incompatible with the Supremacy Clause) and Prof. *Jordan Paust* (Rarely has a treaty been so abused.) have denounced the United States' ratification subject to the non-self-execution declaration as a blatant fraud upon the international community, especially in light of its subsequent failure to conform domestic law to the minimum human rights standards as established in the Covenant over the last fifteen years. In 1994, the United Nations' *Human Rights Committee* expressed similar concerns:

Of particular concern are widely formulated reservations which essentially render ineffective all Covenant rights which would require any change in national law to ensure compliance with Covenant obligations. No real international rights or obligations have thus been accepted. And when there is an absence of provisions to ensure that Covenant rights may be sued on in domestic courts, and, further, a failure to allow individual complaints to be brought to the

Committee under the first Optional Protocol, all the essential elements of the Covenant guarantees have been removed.

Indeed, the United States has not accepted a single international obligation required under the Covenant. It has not changed its domestic law to conform with the strictures of the Covenant. See *Hain v. Gibson, 287 F.3d 1224* (10th Cir. 2002) (noting that Congress has not done so). Its subjects are not permitted to sue to enforce their basic human rights under the Covenant, as noted above. It has not ratified the *Optional Protocol.* As such, the Covenant has been rendered ineffective, with the bone of contention being United States officials' insistence upon preserving a vast web of sovereign, judicial, prosecutorial, and executive branch *immunities* that often deprives its subjects of the "effective remedy" under law the Covenant is intended to guarantee. In 2006, the Human Rights Committee expressed concern over what it interprets as material non-compliance, exhorting the United States to take immediate corrective action:

> The Committee notes with concern the restrictive interpretation made by the State party of its obligations under the Covenant, as a result in particular of... (b) its failure to take fully into consideration its obligation under the Covenant not only to respect, but also to ensure the rights prescribed by the Covenant; and (c) its restrictive approach to some substantive provisions of the Covenant, which is not in conformity with the interpretation made by the Committee before and after the State party's ratification of the Covenant.
>
> The State party should review its approach and interpret the Covenant in good faith, in accordance with the ordinary meaning to be given to its terms in their context, including subsequent practice, and in the light of its object and purpose. The State party should in particular ... (b) take positive steps, when necessary, to ensure the full

implementation of all rights prescribed by the Covenant; and (c) consider in good faith the interpretation of the Covenant provided by the Committee pursuant to its mandate.

As a reservation that is "incompatible with the object and purpose" of a treaty is void as a matter of international law, Vienna Convention on the Law of Treaties, Art. 19, 1155 U.N.T.S. 331 (entered into force Jan. 27, 1980) (specifying conditions under which signatory States can offer "reservations"), there is some issue as to whether the non-self-execution declaration is even legal under domestic law.

STATES NOT MEMBER OF THE COVENANT

The majority of states in the world are parties to the ICCPR. As of September 2009 the following 29 states have either not yet signed the convention, or have signed but have not yet ratified the convention.

Signed but not Ratified

1. *People's Republic of China (1998-10-05)*
2. *Comoros (2008-09-25)*
3. *Cuba (2008-02-28)*
4. *Guinea-Bissau (2000-09-12)*
5. *Laos (2000-12-07)*
6. *Nauru (2001-11-12)*
7. *Pakistan (2008-04-17)*
8. *Sao Tome and Principe (1995-10-31)*

Neither signed nor ratified

1. *Antigua and Barbuda*
2. *Bhutan*

3. *Brunei*
4. *Burma (Myanmar)*
5. *Fiji*
6. *Kiribati*
7. *Malaysia*
8. *Marshall Islands*
9. *Micronesia*
10. *Oman*
11. *Palau*
12. *Qatar*
13. *Saint Kitts and Nevis*
14. *Saint Lucia*
15. *Saudi Arabia*
16. *Singapore*
17. *Solomon Islands*
18. *Tonga*
19. *Tuvalu*
20. *United Arab Emirates*
21. *Vatican City (through the Holy See)*

Signed, non Membership

1. *Taiwan (Republic of China)*

INTERNATIONAL COVENANT ON CIVIL AND POLITICAL RIGHTS, 1966

(Adopted by General Assembly resolution 2200 AC (XXI) of 16 December 1966)

Preamble

The States Parties to the present Covenant,

Considering that, in accordance with the principles proclaimed in the Charter of the United Nations, recognition of the inherent dignity and of the equal and inalienable rights of all members of the human family is the foundation of freedom, justice and peace in the world,

Recognizing that these rights derive from the inherent dignity of the human person,

Recognizing that, in accordance with the Universal Declaration of Human Rights, the ideal of free human beings enjoying freedom from fear and want can only be achieved if conditions are created whereby everyone may enjoy his economic, social and cultural rights, as well as his civil and political rights,

Considering the obligation of States under the Charter of the United Nations to promote universal respect for, and observance of, human rights and freedoms,

Realizing that the individual, having duties to other individuals and to the community to which he belongs, is under a responsibility to strive for the promotion and observance of the rights recognized in the present Covenant,

PART-I

Article 1

1. All people have the right of self-determination. By virtue of that right they freely determine their political status and freely pursue their economic, social and cultural development.

2. All peoples may, for their own ends, freely dispose of their natural wealth and resources without prejudice to any obligations arising out of international economic co-operation, based upon the principle of mutual benefit, and international law. In no case may a people be deprived of its own means of subsistence.

3. The parties to the present covenant, including those having responsibility for the administration of Non-self-Governing and Trust Territories, shall promote the realisation of the right of self-determination, and shall respect that right, in conformity with the provisions of the charter of the United Nations.

PART-II

Article 2

1. Each state party to the present covenant undertakes to respect and to ensure to all individuals within its territory and subject to its jurisdiction the rights recognised in the present covenant, without distinction of any kind, such as race, colour, sex, language, religion, political or other opinion, national, or social origin, property, birth or other status.

2. Where not already provided for by existing legislative or other measures, each state party to the present covenant undertakes to take the necessary steps, in accordance with its constitutional processes and with the provisions of the present covenant, to adopt such legislative or other measures as may be necessary to give effect to the rights recognised in the present covenant.

3. Each state party to the present covenant undertakes:

(a) To ensure that any person whose rights or freedoms as herein recognised are violated shall have an effective remedy, notwithstanding that the violation has been committed by persons acting in an official capacity;

(b) To ensure that any person claiming such a remedy shall have his right thereto determined by competent judicial, administrative or legislative authorities, or by any other competent authority provided for by the legal system of the state, and to develop the possibilities of judicial remedy;

(c) To ensure that the competent authorities shall enforce such remedies when granted.

Article 3

The states parties to the present covenant undertake to ensure the equal right of men and women to the enjoyment of all civil and political rights set forth in the present Covenant.

Article 4

1. In time of public emergency which threatens the life of the nation and the existence of which is officially proclaimed, the state parties to the present Covenant many take measures derogating from their obligations under the present Covenant to the extent strictly required by the exigencies of the situation, provide that such measures are not inconsistent with their other obligations under international law and do not involve discrimination solely on the ground of race, colour, sex, language, religion or social origin

Article 5

1. Nothing in the present Covenant may be interpreted as employing for any State, group or person any right to engage in any activity or perform any act aimed at the destruction of any of the rights and freedoms recognised herein or at their limitation to a greater extent than is provided for in the present Covenant.

There shall be on restriction upon or derogation from any of the fundamental human rights recognised or existing in any State Party to the present Covenant pursuant to law, conventions, regulations or custom on the pretext that the present Covenant does not recognise such rights or that it recognises them to a lesser extent.

PART-III

Article 6

1. Every human being has the inherent right to life. This right shall be protected by law. No one shall be arbitrarily deprived of his life.

2. In countries which have not abolished death penalty, sentence of death may be imposed only for the most serious crimes in accordance with the law in force at the time of the commission of the crime and not contrary to the provisions of the present Covenant and to the Convention on the Prevention Punishment of the Crime of Genocide. This penalty can only be carried out pursuant to a final judgement rendered by a competent Court.

3. When deprivation of life constitutes the crime of genocide, it is understood that nothing in this Article shall authorise any State Party to the present Covenant to derogate in any way from any obligation assumed under the provisions of the Convention on the Prevention and Punishment of the Crime of Genocide.

4. Anyone sentenced to death shall have the right to seek pardon or commutation of the sentence. Amnesty, pardon or commutation of the sentence of death may be granted in all cases.

5. Sentence of death shall not be imposed for crimes committed by persons below 18 years of age and shall not be carried out on pregnant women.

6. Nothing in this Article shall be invoked to delay or to prevent the abolition of capital punishment by any state Party to the present Covenant.

Article 7

No one shall be subjected to torture or to cruel, inhuman or degrading treatment or punishment. In particular, no one shall be subjected without his free consent to medical or scientific experimentation.

Article 8

1. No one shall be held in slavery; slavery and the slave trade in all their forms shall be prohibited.

2. No one shall be held in servitude.

3. (a) No one shall be required to perform forced or compulsory labour;

(b) Paragraph 3(a) shall not be held to preclude, in countries where imprisonment with hard labour may be imposed as a punishment for a crime, the performance of hard labour in pursuance of a sentence to such punishment by a competent Court;

(c) For the purpose of this paragraph the term "forced or compulsory labour" shall not included:

(i) And work or service, not referred to in sub -paragraph (b), normally required of a person who is under detention in consequence of a lawful order of a Court, or of a person during conditional release from such detention;

(ii) Any service of a military character and, in countries where conscientious objection is recognised, any national service required by law of conscientious objects;

(iii) Any service exacted in cases of emergency or calamity threatening the life or well-being of the community;

(iv) Any work or service which forms part of normal civil obligations.

Article 9

1. Everyone has the right to liberty and security of person. No one shall be subjected to arbitrary arrest or detention. No one shall be deprived of his liberty except on

such grounds and in accordance with such procedure as are established by law.

2. Anyone who is arrested shall be informed, at the time of arrest, of the reasons for his arrest and shall be promptly informed of any charges against him.

3. Anyone arrested or detained on a criminal charge shall be brought promptly before a grudge or other officer authorised by law to exercise judicial power and shall be entitled to trial within a responsible time or to realise. It shall not be the general rule that persons awaiting trial shall be determined in custody, but release may be subject to guarantees to appear for trial, at any other stage of the judicial proceedings, and, should occasion arise, for execution of the judgement.

4. Anyone who is deprived of his liberty by arrest or detention shall be entitled to take proceedings before a Court, in order that Court may decide without delay on the lawfulness of his detention and order his release if the detention is not lawful.

5. Anyone who has been the victim of unlawful arrest or detention shall have an enforceable right to compensation.

Article 10

1. All persons deprived of their liberty shall be treated with humanity and with respect for the inherent dignity of the human person.

2. (a) Accused persons shall, save in exceptional circumstances, be segregated from convicted persons and shall be subject to separate treatment appropriate to their status as unconvicted persons;

(b) Accused juvenile persons shall be separated from adults and brought as speedily as possible for adjudication.

3. The penitentiary system shall comprise treatment of prisoners the essential aim of which shall be their reformation and social rehabilitation. Juvenile offenders shall be segregated from adults and be accorded treatment appropriate to their age and legal status.

Article 11

No one shall be imposed merely on the ground of inability to fulfil a contractual obligation.

Article 12

1. Everyone lawfully within the territory of a state shall, within that territory, have the right to liberty of movement and freedom to choose his residence.

2. Everyone shall be free to leave any country, including his own.

3. The above mentioned rights shall not be subject to any restrictions except those which are provided by law, are necessary to protect national security public order (order public), public health or morals or the rights and freedoms of others, and are consistent with the other rights recognised in the present Covenant.

4. No one shall be arbitrarily deprived of the right to enter his own country.

Article 13

An alien lawfully in the territory of a State Party to the present Covenant may be expelled there from only in pursuance of a decision reached in accordance with law and shall, except where compelling reasons of national security otherwise require, be allowed to submit the reasons against his expulsion and to have his case reviewed by, and be represented for the purpose before, the competent authority or a person or persons especially designated by the competent authority.

Article 14

1. All persons shall be equal before the Court and tribunals. In the determination of any criminal charge against him, or of this rights and obligations in a suit of law, everyone shall be entitled to a fair and public hearing of a competent, independent and impartial tribunal established by law. The Press and the public may be excluded from all or part of a trial for the reasons of morals, public order (order public) or national security in a democratic society, or where the interest of the private lives of the parties so requires, or the extent strictly necessary in the opinion of the Court in special circumstances where publicity would prejudice the interests of justice; but any judgement rendered in a criminal case or in a suit at law shall be made public except where the interest of juvenile persons otherwise requires or the proceedings concern matrimonial disputes or the guardianship of children.

2. Everyone charged with a criminal offence shall have the right to be presumed innocent until prove guilty according to law.

3. In the determination of any criminal charge against him, everyone shall be entitled to the following minimum guarantees, in full equality :

(a) To be informed promptly and, in detail, in a language which he understands of the nature and cause of the charge against him;

(b) To have adequate time and facilities for the preparation of his defence and to communicate with counsel of his own choosing;

(c) To be tried without undue delay;

(d) To be tried in his presence, and to defend himself in person or through legal assistance of his own choosing; to be informed, if he does not have legal assistance, of this right; and to have legal assistance assigned to him, in any case where the interests of justice so required, and without payment by him in any such case if he does not have sufficient means to pay for it;

(e) To examine, or have examined the witnesses against him and to obtain the attendance and examination of witnesses on the behalf under the same conditions as witnesses against him;

(f) To have the free assistance of an interpreter if he cannot understand or speak the language used in Court;

(g) Not to be compelled to testify against him or to confess guilt.

4. In the case of juvenile persons, the procedure shall be such as will take account of their age and the desirability of promoting their rehabilitation.

5. Everyone convicted of a crime shall have the right to his conviction and sentence being reviewed by a higher tribunal according to law.

6. When a person has by a final decision been convicted of a criminal offence and when subsequently his conviction has been reversed or he has been pardoned on the ground that a new or newly discovered fact shows conclusively that there has been a miscarriage of justice, the person who has suffered punishment as a result of such conviction shall be compensated according to law, unless it is proved that the non-disclosure of the unknown fact in time is wholly or partly attributable to him.

7. No one shall be liable to be tried or punished again for an offence for which he has already been finally convicted or acquitted in accordance with each country.

Article 15

1. No one shall be held guilty of any criminal offence on account of any act or omission, which did not constitute

a criminal offence, under national or internal law, at the time when it was committed. Nor shall a heavier penalty be imposed then the one that was applicable at the time when the criminal offence was committed. If, subsequent to the commission of the offence, provision is made by law for imposition of a lighter penalty, the offender shall benefit thereby.

2. Nothing in this Article shall prejudice the trial and punishment of any person for any act or omission, which, at the time when it was committed, was criminal according to the general principle of law, recognised by the community of nations.

Article 16

Everyone shall have the right to recognition everywhere as a person before the law.

Article 17

1. No one shall be subjected to arbitrary or unlawful interference with his privacy, family, home or correspondence, or to unlawful attacks on his honour and reputation.

2. Every one has the right to the protection of the law against such interference or attacks.

Article 18

1. Everyone shall have the right to freedom of thought, conscience and religion. This right shall include freedom to have or adopt a religion or belief of his choice, and freedom, either individually or in community with others and in public or private, to manifest his religion or belief in worship, observance, practice and teaching.

2. No one shall be subject to coercion which would impair his freedom to have or to adopt a religion or belief of his choice.

3. Freedom to manifest one's religion or beliefs may be subject only to such limitations as are prescribed by law and are necessary to protect public safety, order, health, or morals or the fundamental rights and freedoms of others.

4. The States Parties to the present Covenant undertake to have respect for the liberty of parents and, when applicable, legal guardians to ensure the religious and moral education of their children in conformity with their own convictions.

Article 19

1. Every one shall have the right to hold opinions without interference.

2. Everyone shall have the right to freedom of expression; this right shall include freedom to seek, receive and impart information and idea of all kinds, regardless of frontiers, either orally, in writing or in paint, in the form of art, or through any other media of his choice.

3. The exercise of the rights provided for in paragraph 2 of his Article carries with it special duties and responsibilities. It may therefore be subject to certain restrictions, but these shall only be such as are provided by law and are necessary :

(a) for respect of the rights or reputation of others;

(b) for the protection of national security or of public order (order public), or the public health or morals

Article 20

1. Any propaganda for war shall be prohibited by law.

2. Any advocacy of national, racial or religious hated that constitutes incitement to discrimination, hostility or violence shall be prohibited by law.

Article 21

The right of peaceful assembly shall be recognised. No restrictions may be placed on the exercise of this right other than those imposed in conformity with the law and which are necessary in a democratic society in the interest of national security or public safety, public order (order public), the protection of public health or morals or the protection of the rights and freedoms of others.

Article 22

1. Everyone shall have the right to freedom of association with others, including the right to form and join trade unions for the protection of his interests.

2. No restrictions may be placed on the exercise of this right other than those which are prescribed by law and which are in a democratic society in the interests of national security or public safety, public order (order public), the protection of public health or morals or the protection of rights and freedoms of others. This article shall not prevent the imposition of lawful restrictions on members of the armed forces and the police in their exercise of this right.

3. Nothing in this Article shall authorise State Parties to the international Labour Organisation Convention of 1948 concerning Freedom of Association and Protection of the Right to Organize to take legislative measures which would prejudice, the guarantees provided for in that Covenant.

Article 23

1. The family is the natural and fundamental group unit of society and is entitled to protection by society and state.

2. The rights of mens and womens of marriageable age to marry and to found a family shall be recognised.

3. No marriage shall be entered in to without the free and full consent of the intending spouses.

4. State parties of the present Covenant shall take appropriate steps to ensure equality of rights and responsibilities of spouses as to mariage, during marriage and at its dissolution. In the case of dissolution, provision shall be made for the necessary protection of any children.

Article 24

1. Every child shall have, without any discrimination as to race or birth the rights to such measures of protection as are required by his status as a minor, on the part of his family, society and the state.

2. Every child shall be registered immediately after birth and shall nave a name.

3. Every child has the right to acquire a nationality.

Article 25

Every citizen shall have the right and opportunity, without any of the distinctionmention in article 2 and without unreasonable restriction :

(a) to take part in Public affairs, directly or through freely chosen representatives;

(b) to vote and to be elected at genuine periodic elections which shall be by universal and equal suffrage and shall be held by secret ballot, guaranteeing the free expression expression of the will of the electors;

(c) to have access, on general terms of equality, to public service in his country.

Article 26

All persons are equal before the law and are entitled without any discrimination to the equal protection of law. In this respect, the law shall prohibit any discrimination and guarantee to all person equal and effective protection against discrimination on any ground such as race, colour, sex, language, political or other opinion, national or social origin, property or birth or other status.

Article 27

In those States in which ethnic, religious or linguistic minorities exists, persons belonging to such minorities shall not be denied the right, in community with the other members of their group, to enjoy their other group, to enjoy their own culture, to profess and practice their own religion, or to use there own language.

PART-IV

Article 28

1. There shall be established a Human Rights Committee (hereinafter referred to in the present Covenant as the committee). It shall consist of eighteen members and shall carry out the functions hereinafter provided.

2. The committee shall be composed of nationals of the State Parties to the present to the present Covenant who shall be persons of rights moral character and recognized competence in the field of human rights, consideration being given to the usefulness of the participation of some persons having legal experience.

3. The members of the Committee shall be elected and shall serve in their personal capacity.

Article 29

1. The members of the committee shall be elected by secret ballot from a list of persons possessing the qualifications prescribed in Article 28 and nominated for the purpose by the States Parties to the present Covenant.

2. Each State Party to the present Covenant may nominate not more than persons. These persons shall be nationals of the nominating State.

Article 30

1. The initial election shall be held later than six months after the date of the entry into force of the present Covenant.

2. At least four months before the date of each election to the Committee, other than an election to fill a vacancy

declared in accordance with Article 34, the Secretary General of the United Nations shall address a written invitation to the State Parties to the present Covenant to submit their nominations for membership of the Committee within three months.

3. The Secretary-General of the United Nations shall separate a list in alphabetical order of all the persons thus nominated, with an indication of the State Parties which have nominated them, and shall submit it to the State Parties to the present Covenant or later than one month before the date of each election.

4. Elections of the members of the Committee shall be held at the meeting of the State Parties to the present Covenant convened by the Secretary-General of the United Nations at the Headquarters of the United Nations. At the meeting, for which two-thirds of the State Parties to the present Covenant shall constitute a quorum, the persons elected to the committee shall be those nominees who obtain the largest number of votes and an absolute majority of the votes of the representatives of State Parties present and voting.

Article 31

1. The Committee may not include more than one national of the same state.

2. In the election of the committee, consideration shall be given to equitable geographical distribution of membership and to the presentation of the deferent forms of civilization and of the principal legal systems.

Article 32

1. The members of the Committee shall be elected for a term of four years. They shall be eligible for re-election if renominated. However the terms of nine of the members elected at the first election shall expire at the end of two years; immediately after the first election, lot by the

Chairman of the meeting referred to in Article 30, paragraph 4, shall choose the names of these nine members.

2. Election at the expiry of office shall hold in accordance with the preceding Articles of this part of the present covenant.

Article 33

1. If, in the unanimous opinion of the other members, a member of the Committee has ceased to carry out his functions for any cause other than absence of a temporary character, the Chairman of the committee shall notify the Secretary-General of the United Nations, who shall then declare the seat of that member to be vacant.

2. In the event of the death or the resignation of a member of the Committee, the Chairman shall immediately notify the Secretary-General of the United Nations, who shall declare the seat vacant from the date of death or the date on which the resignation takes effect.

Article 34

1. When a vacancy is declared in accordance with Article 33 and if the term of office of the member to be replaced does not expire within six months of the declaration of the vacancy, the Secretary-General of the United Nations shall notify each of the State Parties to the present Covenant, which may, within two months, submit nominations in accordance with Article 29 for the purpose of filling the vacancy.

2. The Secretary-General of the United Nations shall prepare a list in alphabetical order of the persons thus nominated and shall submit it to the States Parties to the present Covenant. The election to fill the vacancy shall then take place in accordance with the relevant provisions of this part of the present Covenant.

3. A member of the Committee elected to fill a vacancy declared in accordance with Article 33 shall hold office for

the remainder of the term of the member of the vacated the seat on the Committee under the provisions of that Article.

Article 35

The member of the Committee shall, with the approval of the General Assembly of the United Nations, receive emoluments from United Nations resources on such terms and conditions as the General Assembly may decide, having regard to the importance of the Committee's responsibilities.

Article 36

The Secretary-General of the United Nations shall provide the necessary staif ind facilities for the effective performance of the functions of the Committee of the present Covenant.

Article 37

1. The Secretary-General of the United Nations shall convene the initial meeting of the Committee at the Headquarter of the United Nations.

2. After its initial meeting, the Committee shall meet at such times as shall be provided in its rules of producer.

3. The Committee shall normally meet at the Headquarters of the United Nations or at the United Nations Office at Geneva.

Article 38

Every member of the Committee shall, before taking up his duties, make a solemn declaration in open committee that he will perform his functions impartially and conscientiously.

Article 39

1. The Committee shall elect its officers for a tern of two years. They may be re-elected.

2. The Committee shall establish its own rules of producer, but these rules shall provide, inter alia, that

(a) Twelve members shall constitute a quorum;

(b) Decisions of the Committee shall be made by majority vote of the members present.

Article 40

1. The State Parties to the present Covenant undertake to submit reports on the measures they have adopted which give effect to the rights recognized herein and on the progress made in the enjoyment of those rights:

(a) Within one year of the entry into force of the present Covenant for the State Parties ccncerned;

(b) Thereafter whenever the committee so requests.

2. All reports shall be submitted to the Secretary-General of the United Nations, who shall transmit then to the Committee for the consideration Reports shall indicate factors and difficulties, if any, affecting the implementation of the present Covenant.

3. The Secretary-General of the United Nations may, after consultation with the Committee, transmit to the specialized agency concerned, copies of such parts of the reports as may fall within their field of competence.

4. The Committee shall study the reports submitted by the State Parties to the present Covenant. It shall transmit its reports, and such general comments, as it may consider appropriate, to the State Parties. The Committee may also transmit to Economic and Social council these comments along with the copies of the reports it has received from State Parties to the present covenant.

5. The State Parties to the present Covenant may submit to the Committee observations on many comments that may be made in accordance with paragraph 4 of this Article.

Article 41

1. A State Party to the present Covenant may at any time declare under this Article that it recognizes the

competence of the Committee to receive and consider communications to the effect that a State Party claims that under State Party claims that another State Party is not fulfilling its obligations under the present Covenant. Communications under this Article may be received and considered only if submitted by the State Parties which has made a declaration recognizing in regard to itself the competence of the Committee. No communication shall be received by the Committee if it concerns a State Party which has not made such a declaration. Communications received under this Article shall be dealt with in accordance with the following procedure :

(a) If a State Party to the present Covenant considers that another State Party is not given effect to the provisions of the present Covenant, it may, by written communication, bring the matter to the attention of that State Party. Within three months after the receipt of the communication, the receiving State shall afford the state which sent the communication an explanation, or any other statement in writing clarifying the matter which should include, to the extent possible and pertinent, reference to domestic procedures and remedies taken, pending or available in the matter;

(b) If the matter is not adjust to the satisfaction of both State Parties concerned, within six month after the receipt by the receiving State of the initial communication, either State shall have the right to refer the matter to the Committee, by notice given to the Committee and to the other State;

(c) The Committee shall deal with a matter referred to it only after it has ascertained that all available domestic remedies have been invoked and exhausted in the matter, in conformity with the generally recognized principles of international law. This shall not be the rule where the application of the remedies is unreasonably prolonged.

(d) The committee shall hold closed meetings when examining communication under this Article.

(e) Subject to the provisions of sub-paragraph (c), the Committee shall make available its good office to the State Parties concerned with a view to friendly solution of the matter on the basis of respect for human rights and fundamental freedoms as recognized in the present Covenant;

(f) In any matter referred to it, the Committee call upon the State Parties concerned, referred to in sub-paragraph (b), to supply any relevant information;

(g) The State Parties concerned, referred to in sub-paragraph (b), shall have the right to be represented when the matter is being considered in the Committee and to make submissions orally and/or in writing;

(h) The Committee shall, within twelve months after the date of receipt of notice under sub-paragraph (b), submit a report;

(i) If a solution within the terms of sub-paragraph(e) is received, the Committee shall confine its report to a brief statement of the facts and the solution reached;

(ii) If a solution within the terms of sub-paragraph (e) is not reached, the Committee shall confine its report to brief statement of the facts; the written submission and record of the oral submission made by the State Parties concerned shall be attached to the report.

In every matter, the report shall be communicated to the State Parties concerned.

2. The provisions of this Article shall come into force when ten States parties to the present Covenant have made declarations under paragraph I of this Article. The State Parties with the Secretary-General of the United Nations, who shall transmit copies thereof to the other States Parties, shall deposit such declarations. A declaration may be withdrawn at any time by notification to the Secretary-General. Such a withdrawal shall not prejudice the consideration of any matter which is the subject of a

communication already submitted under this Article; no further communication by any State Party shall be received after the notification of withdrawal of the declaration has been received by the Secretary-General, unless the State Party concerned has made a new declaration.

Article 42

1. (a) If a matter referred to the Committee in accordance with Article 41 is not resolved to the satisfaction of the States Parties concerned, the Committee may, with the prior consent of the States Parties concerned, appoint an adhoc Conciliation Communication (hereinafter referred to as the Commission). The good office of the Commission shall be made available to the States Parties concerned with a view to an amicable solution of the matter on the basis of respect for the present Covenant.

(b) The Commission shall consist of five persons acceptable to the States Parties concerned. If State Parties concerned fail to reach agreement within three months on all parts of the composition of the Commission, the member of the Commission concerning whom no agreement has been reached shall be elected by secret ballot by a two-thirds majority vote of the committee from among its members.

2. The members of the Commission shall serve in their personal capacity. They shall not be nationals of the States Parties concerned, or of a state not party to the present Covenant, or of a State party which has not made a declaration under Article 41.

3. The Commission shall elect its own chairman and adopt its own rulers of procedure.

4. The meetings of the Commission shall normally be held at the Headquarters of the United Nations or at the United Nations Office at Geneva. However, they may be held at such convenient places as the Commission may determine in consultation with the Secretary-General of the United Nations and the States Parties concerned.

5. The Secretariat provided in accordance with Article 36 shall also service the commissions appointed under this Article.

6. The information received and collated by the Committee shall be made available to the Commission and the Commission call upon the States Parties concerned to supply any other relevant information.

7. When the Commission has fully considered the matter, but in any event not later than twelve months after having been seized of the matter, it shall submit to the Chairman of the Committee a report for communication to the States Parties concerned:

(a) If the Commission is unable to complete its consideration of the matter within twelve months, it shall confine its report to a brief statement of the status of its consideration of the matter.

(b) If an amicable solution to the matter on the basis of respect for human rights as recognized in the present Covenant is reached, the Commission shall confine its report to a brief statement of the facts and of the solution reached;

(c) If a solution within the terms of sub-paragraph (b) is not reached, the Commission's report shall embody its findings on all questions of fact relevant to the issues between the States Parties concerned, and its views on the possibilities of an amicable solution of the matter. This report shall also contain the written submissions and a record of the oral submissions made by the States Parties concerned;

(d) If the Commission's report is submitted under sub-paragraph (c), the States Parties concerned shall, within three months of the receipt of the report, notify the Chairman of the committee whether or not they accept the contents of the report of the Commission.

8. The provisions of this Article are without prejudice to the responsibilities of the committee under Article 41.

9. The States Parties concerned shall share equally all

the expenses of the members of the Commission in accordance with estimates to be provided by the Secretary -General of the United Nations.

10. The Secretary-General of the United Nations shall be empowered to pay the expenses of the members of the Commission, if necessary, before reimbursement by the States Parties concerned, in accordance with paragraph 9 of this Article.

Article 43

The members of the Commission, and of the adhoc conciliation commissions which may be appointed under Article 42, shall be entitled to the facilities, privileges and immunities of exports on mission for the United Nations as laid down in the relevant sections of the Convention on the Privileges and immunities of the United Nations.

Article 44

The provisions for the implementation of the present Covenant shall apply without prejudice to the procedures prescribed in the field of human rights by or under the constituent instruments and the conventions of the United Nations and of the specialized agencies and shall not prevent the States Parties to the present Covenant from having recourse to other producers for setting a dispute in accordance with general or special international agreements in force between them.

Article 45

The Committees shall submit to the General Assembly of the United Nations, through the Economic and Social Council, an annual report on its activities.

PART V

Article 46

Nothing in the present Covenant shall be interpreted as impairing the provisions of the Charter of the United

Nations and of the constitutions of the specialized agencies which define the respective responsibilities of the various organs of the United Nations and of the specialized agencies in regard to the matters dealt with in the present Covenant.

Article 47

Nothing in the present Covenant shall be interpreted as impairing the inherent right of all peoples to enjoy and utilise fully and freely their natural wealth and resources.

PART VI

Article 48

1. The present Covenant is open for signature by the State Members of the United Nations or members of any of its specialized agencies, by any State party to the Statute of the International Court of Justice, and by any other State which has been invited by the General Assembly of the United Nations to become a Party to the present Covenant.

2. The present Covenant is subject to ratification. Instruments of ratification shall be deposited with the Secretary-General of the United Nations.

3. The present Covenant shall be open to accession by any state referred to in paragraph 1 of this Article.

4. Accession shall be effected by the deposit of an instrument of accession with the Secretary-General of the United Nations.

5. The Secretary-General of the United Nations shall inform all States which have signed this Covenant or acceded to it of the deposit of each instrument of ratification or accession.

Article 49

1. The present Covenant shall come into force three months after the date of the deposit with the Secretary-General of the United Nations of the thirty-fifth instrument of ratification or instrument of Accession.

2. For each State ratifying the present Covenant or according to it after the deposit of the thirty-fifth instrument of ratification or instrument of accession, the present Covenant shall come into force three months after the date of the deposit of its own instrument of ratification or instrument of accession.

Article 50

The provisions of the present Covenant shall extend to all parts of federal States without any limitations or exceptions.

Article 51

1. Any State party to the present Covenant may propose an amendment and file it with the Secretary-General of the United Nations. The Secretary-General of the United Nations shall thereupon communicate favours such a conference, under the auspices of the United Nations. Any amendment adopted by a majority of the State Parties present and voting at the conference shall be submitted to the General Assembly of any proposed amendments to the State Parties to the present Covenant with a request that they notify him whether they favour a conference of state parties for the porpose of considering and voting upon the proposals. In the event that at least one-third of the State Parties the United Nations for approval.

2. Amendments shall come into force when they have been approved by the General Assembly of the United Nations and accepted by a two-thirds majority of the State Parties to the present Covenant in accordance with their respective constitutional processes.

3. When amendments come into force, they shall be binding on those State Parties which have accepted them, other State Parties still being bound by the provisions of the present Covenant and any earlier amendment which they have accepted.

Article 52

Irrespective of the notification made under Article 48, paragraph 5, the Secretary-General of the United Nations shall inform all States referred to in paragraph 1 of the same article of the following particulars :

(a) Signatures, ratifications made accessions under Article 48;

(b) The date of the entry into force of the present Covenant under Article 49 and the date of the entry into force of any amendment under Article 51.

Article 53

1. The present Covenant, of which the Chinese, English, French, Russian and Spanish texts are equally authentic, shall be deposited in the archives of the United Nations.

2. The Secretary-General of the United Nations shall transmit certified copies of the present Covenant to all States referred to in Article 48.

A BRIEF ANALYSIS THE INTERNATIONAL COVENANT ON CIVIL AND POLITICAL RIGHTS

The distinctive feature of this Covenant as described under Article 2 and 4 are:

1. Each State party undertakes to ensure to all individuals within its territory the rights recognized, in this Covenant without distinction of any kind, such as race, colour, sex, language, religion, political or other opinion, national or social origin, property, birth or other status;

2. Each State party undertakes to ensure that any person whose rights or freedoms are violated shall have an effective remedy;

3. Each State party undertakes to ensure that such effective remedy shall be determined by competent judicial,

administrative, legislative or any other competent authority provided for by the legal system of the State; and

4. That such remedies when granted should be enforced by the competent authority.

However, the State parties may take measures derogating form this obligation under the Covenant when the public emergency threatening the life of a nation exist and the existence of which is officially proclaimed. Such measures should be exercised to the extent strictly required by the exigencies of the situation provided they are not inconsistent with State's other obligations or other international law and do not involve discrimination solely on the ground of race, colour, sex, language, religion or social origin.

The rights which are included in this category are; the rights of life; prohibition of torture, cruel, inhuman or degrading treatment or punishment; prohibition of slavery, slave trade, servitude and forced labour; the right to liberty and security of person, freedom from arbitrary arrest and detention; prohibition of imprisonment on the ground of inability to fulfil contractual obligation; the right to liberty of movement and freedom to choose residence; right to equality before law and courts and tribunals; freedom from *ex-post facto* laws; the right to recognition as person; prohibition of arbitrary or unlawful interference with a person's privacy, family, home or correspondence; the right to freedom of thought, conscience and religion; right to hold opinion without interference; prohibition of propaganda for war; the right to peaceful assembly and freedom of association; the right to marry and protection of family; the right to the child to acquire nationality; the right to opportunity to take part in the conduct of public affairs, right to vote and right to be elected by the secret-ballot, the right to equality before law and equal protection of law; and the right of minorities to enjoy their culture, to profess their religion and to use their language.

NINE

International Covenant on Economic, Social and Cultural Rights

The *International Covenant on Economic, Social and Cultural Rights* (ICESCR) is a multilateral treaty adopted by the *United Nations General Assembly* on December 16, 1966, and in force from January 3, 1976. It commits its parties to work toward the granting *of economic, social, and cultural rights* (ESCR) to individuals, including *labour rights* and rights to health, education, and an adequate standard of living. As of December, 2008, the Covenant had 160 parties. A further six countries had signed, but not yet ratified the Covenant.

The ICESCR is part of the International Bill of Human Rights, along with the Universal Declaration of Human

Rights (UDHR) and the International Covenant on Civil and Political Rights (ICCPR), including the latter's first and second Optional Protocols.

The Covenant is monitored by the UN *Committee on Economic. Social and Cultural Rights.*

GENESIS OF THE COVENANT

The ICESCR has its roots in the same process that led to the *Universal Declaration of Human Rights.* A "Declaration on the Essential Rights of Man" had been proposed at the *1945 San Francisco Conference* which led to the founding of the *United Nations* and the *Economic and Social Council* was given the task of drafting it. Early in the process, the document was split into a declaration setting forth general principles of human rights, and a convention or covenant containing binding commitments. The former evolved into the UDHR and was adopted on December 10, 1948.

Drafting continued on the convention, but there remained significant differences between UN members on the relative importance of *negative* Civil and Political versus positive Economic, Social and Cultural rights. These eventually caused the convention to be split into two separate covenants, "one to contain civil and political rights and the other to contain economic, social and cultural rights." The two covenants were to contain as many similar provisions as possible, and be opened for signature simultaneously. Each would also contain an article on the right of all peoples to self-determination.

The first document became the *International Covenant on Civil and Political Rights,* and the second the International Covenant on Economic, Social and Cultural Rights. The drafts were presented to the UN General Assembly for discussion in 1954, and adopted in 1966.

SUMMARY OF THE COVENANT

The Covenant follows the structure of the UDHR and ICCPR, with a preamble and thirty-one articles, divided into five parts.

***Part* 1 (Article 1)** recognises the right of all peoples to *self-determination,* including the right to "freely determine their political status", pursue their economic, social and cultural goals, and manage and dispose of their own resources. It recognises a *negative right* of a people not to be deprived of its means of subsistence, and imposes an obligation on those parties still responsible for non-self governing and trust territories (colonies) to encourage and respect their self-determination.

***Part* 2 (Articles 2-5)** establishes the principle of "progressive realisation" - see below. It also requires the rights be recognised "without discrimination of any kind as to race, colour, sex, language, religion, political or other opinion, national or social origin, property, birth or other status". The rights can only be limited by law, in a manner compatible with the nature of the rights, and only for the purpose of "promoting the general welfare in a democratic society".

***Part* 3 (Articles 6-15)** lists the rights themselves. These include rights to

• work, under "just and favourable conditions", with the right to form and join *trade unions* (Articles 6, 7, and 8);

• social security, including social insurance (Article 9);

• family life, including paid parental leave and the protection of children (Article 10);

• an adequate standard of living, including adequate food, clothing and housing, and the "continuous improvement of living conditions" (Article 12);

• health, specifically "the highest attainable standard of physical and mental health" (Article 12);

• education, including free universal primary education, generally available secondary education, and equally accessible higher education. This should be directed to "the full development of the human personality and the sense of its dignity", and enable all persons to participate effectively in society (Articles 13 and 14);

• participation in cultural life (Article 15).

Many of these rights include specific actions which must be undertaken to realise them.

Part 4 (Articles 16 - 25) governs reporting and monitoring of the Covenant and the steps taken by the parties to implement it. It also allows the monitoring body - originally the *United Nations Economic and Social Council* - now the Committee on Economic, Social and Cultural Rights to make general recommendations to the *UN General Assembly* on appropriate measures to realise the rights (Article 21).

***Part* 5 (Articles 26-31)** governs ratification, entry into force, and amendment of the Covenant.

CORE PROVISIONS OF THE COVENANT

Principle of progressive realisation Article

Article 2 of the Covenant imposes a duty on all parties to

take steps... to the maximum of its available resources, with a view to achieving progressively the full realization of the rights recognized in the present Covenant by all appropriate means, including particularly the adoption of legislative measures.

This is known as the principle of "progressive realisation". It acknowledges that some of the rights (for example, the right to health) may be difficult in practice to achieve in a short period of time, and that states may be subject to resource constraints, but requires them to act as best they can within their means.

The principle differs from that of the ICCPR, which obliges parties to "respect and to ensure to all individuals within its territory and subject to its jurisdiction" the rights in that Convention. However, it does not render the Covenant meaningless. The requirement to "take steps" imposes a continuing obligation to work towards the realisation of the rights. It also rules out deliberately regressive measures which impede that goal. The Committee on Economic, Social and Cultural Rights also interprets the principle as imposing minimum core obligations to provide, at the least, minimum essential levels of each of the rights. If resources are highly constrained, this should include the use of targeted programmes aimed at the vulnerable.

The Committee on Economic, Social and Cultural Rights regards legislation as an indispensable means for realising the rights which is unlikely to be limited by resource constraints. The enacting of anti-discrimination provisions and the establishment of enforceable rights with judicial remedies within national legal systems are considered to be appropriate means. Some provisions, such as anti-discrimination laws, are already required under other human rights instruments, such as the ICCPR.

Labour Rights

Article 6 of the Covenant recognises the *right to work,* defined as the opportunity of everyone to gain their living by freely chosen or accepted work. Parties are required to take "appropriate steps" to safeguard this right, including technical and vocational training and economic policies aimed at steady economic development and ultimately full employment. The right implies parties must guarantee equal access to employment and protect workers from being unfairly deprived of employment. They must prevent discrimination in the workplace and ensure access for the disadvantaged. The fact that work must be freely chosen or accepted means parties must prohibit forced or child labour.

The work referred to in Article 6 must be *decent work. This* is effectively defined by *Article* 7 of the Covenant, which recognises the right of everyone to "just and favourable" working conditions. These are in turn defined as fair wages with equal pay for equal work, sufficient to provide a decent living for workers and their dependants; safe working conditions; equal opportunity in the workplace; and sufficient rest and leisure, including limited working hours and regular, paid holidays.

Article 8 recognises the right of workers to form or join *trade unions* and protects the right to strike. It allows these rights to be restricted for members of the armed forces, police, or government administrators. Several parties have placed reservations on this clause, allowing it to be interpreted in a manner consistent with their constitutions (China, Mexico), or extending the restriction of union rights to groups such as fire-fighters (Japan).

The Right to Social Security

Main article: Social security

Article 9 of the Covenant recognizes "the right of everyone to social security, including social insurance." It requires parties to provide some form of social insurance scheme to protect people against the risks of sickness, disability, maternity, employment injury, unemployment or old age; to provide for survivors, orphans, and those who cannot afford health care; and to ensure that families are adequately supported. Benefits from such a scheme must be adequate, accessible to all, and provided without discrimination. The Covenant does not restrict the form of the scheme, and both contributory and non-contributory schemes are permissible (as are community-based and mutual schemes).

The Committee on Economic, Social and Cultural Rights has noted persistent problems with the implementation of this right, with very low levels of access.

Several parties, including France and Monaco, have reservations allowing them to set residence requirements in order to qualify for social benefits. The Committee on Economic, Social and Cultural Rights permits such restrictions, provided they are proportionate and reasonable.

The right to family life

Main articles: *Children's rights, Fathers' rights, Mothers' rights,* and *Reproductive rights.*

Article 10 of the Covenant recognises the family as "the natural and fundamental group unit of society", and requires parties to accord it "the widest possible protection and assistance." Parties must ensure that their citizens are free to establish families and that marriages are freely contracted and not forced. Parties must also provide *paid leave* or adequate social security to mothers before and after childbirth, an obligation which overlaps with that of Article 9. Finally, parties must take "special measures" to protect children from economic or social exploitation, including setting a minimum age of employment and barring children from dangerous and harmful occupations.

The Right to an Adequate Standard of Living

Main articles : Right to food, Right to water, and Right to housing

Article 11 recognises the right of everyone to an adequate standard of living. This includes, but is not limited to, the right to adequate food, clothing, housing, and "the continuous improvement of living conditions." It also creat an obligation on parties to work together to eliminate w hunger. it

The right to adequate food, also referred to as ood to food is interpreted as requiring "the availabi etary in a quantity and quality sufficient to satisfy es, and needs of individuals, free from adverse su accessible acceptable within a given culture. This m to all, implying an obligation to provide special programmes for the vulnerable. The right to adequate food also implies a *right to water*.

The right to adequate housing, also referred to as the right to housing, is "the right to live somewhere in security, peace and dignity." It requires "adequate privacy, adequate space, adequate security, adequate lighting and ventilation, adequate basic infrastructure and adequate location with regard to work and basic facilities — all at a reasonable cost." Parties must ensure security of tenure and that access is free of discrimination, and progressively work to eliminate homelessness. Forced evictions, defined as "the permanent or temporary removal against their will of individuals, families and/or communities from the homes and/or land which they occupy, without the provision of, and access to, appropriate forms of legal or other protection", are a prima facie violation of the Covenant.

The Right to Health

Main article: Right to health

Article 12 of the Covenant recognises the right of everyone to "the enjoyment of the highest attainable standard of physical and mental health." "Health" is understood not just as a right to be healthy, but as a right to control ones own health and body (including reproduction), and be free from interference such as torture or medical experimentation. States must protect this right by ensuring that everyone within their jurisdiction has access to the underlying determinants of health, such as lean water, sanitation, food, nutrition and housing, and rough a comprehensive system of healthcare, which is lable to everyone without discrimination, and nically accessible to all.

impr *e 12.2* requires parties to take specific steps to
infant e health of their citizens, including reducing
lity and improving child health, improving

environmental and workplace health, preventing, controlling and treating epidemic diseases, and creating conditions to ensure equal and timely access to medical services for all. These are considered to be "illustrative, non-exhaustive examples", rather than a complete statement of parties' obligations.

The right to health is interpreted as requiring parties to respect women's reproductive rights, by not limiting access to *contraception* or "censoring, withholding or intentionally misrepresenting" information about sexual health. They must also ensure that women are protected from harmful traditional practices such as female genital mutilation.

The Right to Education

Article 13 of the Covenant recognises the right of everyone to education. This is to be directed towards "the full development of the human personality and the sense of its dignity", and enable all persons to participate effectively in society. Education is seen both as a human right and as "an indispensable means of realizing other human rights", and so this is one of the longest and most important articles of the Covenant.

Article 13.2 lists a number of specific steps parties are required to pursue to realise the right of education. These include the provision of free, universal and compulsory primary education, "generally available and accessible" secondary education in various forms (including technical and vocational training), and equally accessible *higher education.* All of these must be available to all without discrimination. Parties must also develop a school system (though it may be public, private, or mixed), encourage or provide scholarships for disadvantaged groups, and are encouraged to make education free at all levels.

Articles 13.3 and 13.4 require parties to respect the educational freedom of parents by allowing them to choose and establish private educational institutions for their children, also referred to as Freedom of education. It also recognises the right of parents to "ensure the religious and moral education of their children in conformity with their own convictions". This is interpreted as requiring public schools to respect the freedom of religion and conscience of their students, and as forbidding instruction in a particular religion or belief system unless non-discriminatory exemptions and alternatives are available.

The Committee on Economic, Social and Cultural Rights interpret the Covenant as also requiring states to respect the *academic freedom* of staff and students, as this is vital for the educational process. It also considers *corporal punishment* in schools to be inconsistent with the Covenant's underlying principle of the dignity of the individual.

Article 14 of the Covenant requires those parties which have not yet established a system of free compulsory primary education, to rapidly adopt a detailed plan of action for its introduction "within a reasonable number of years.

The Right to Participation in Cultural Life

Main article: Right to science and culture

Main article: Right to development

Article 15 of the Covenant recognises the right of everyone to participate in cultural life, enjoy the benefits of scientific progress, and to benefit from the protection of the moral and material rights to any scientific discovery or artistic work they have created. The latter clause is sometimes seen as requiring the protection of intellectual property, but the Committee on Economic, Social and Cultural Rights interprets it as primarily protecting the *moral rights* of authors and "proclaim[ing] the intrinsically personal character of every creation of the human mind and the ensuing durable link between creators and their *creations.* It thus requires parties to respect the right of authors to be recognised as the creator of a work. The material rights are interpreted as being part of the right to an adequate standard of living, and "need not extend over the entire lifespan of an author."

Parties must also work to promote the conservation, development and diffusion of science and culture, "respect the freedom indispensable for scientific research and creative activity", and encourage international contacts and cooperation in these fields.

RESERVATIONS

A number of parties have made reservations and interpretative declarations to their application of the Covenant.

Algeria interprets parts of Article 13, protecting the liberty of parents to freely choose or establish suitable educational institutions, so as not to "impair its right freely to organize its educational system."

Bangladesh interprets the self-determination clause in Article 1 as applying in the historical context of colonialism. It also reserves the right to interpret the labour rights in Articles 7 and 8 and the non-discrimination clauses of Articles 2 and 3 within the context of its constitution and domestic law.

Belgium interprets non-discrimination as to national origin as "not necessarily implying an obligation on States automatically to guarantee to foreigners the same rights as to their nationals. The term should be understood to refer to the elimination of any arbitrary behaviour but not of differences in treatment based on objective and reasonable considerations, in conformity with the principles prevailing in democratic societies."

China prohibits labour rights in Article 8 in a manner consistent with its constitution and domestic law.

Egypt accepts the Covenant only to the extent it does not conflict with Islamic Sharia law.

France views the Covenant as subservient to the *UN Charter*. It also reserves the right to govern the access of aliens to employment, social security, and other benefits.

India interprets the right of self-determination as applying "only to the peoples under foreign domination" and not to apply to peoples within sovereign nation-states. It also interprets the limitation of rights clause and the rights of equal opportunity in the workplace within the context of its constitution.

Indonesia interprets the self-determination clause (Article 1) within the context of other international law and as not applying to peoples within a sovereign nation-state.

Ireland reserves the right to promote the *Irish language*.

Japan reserved the right not to be bound to progressively introduce free secondary and higher education.

Kuwait interprets the non-discrimination clauses of Articles 2 and 3 within its constitution and laws, and reserves the right to social security to apply only to Kuwaitis. It also reserves the right to forbid strikes.

Mexico interprets the labour rights in Article 8 within the context of its constitution and laws.

Monaco interprets the principle of non-discrimination on the grounds of national origin as "not necessarily implying an automatic obligation on the part of States to guarantee foreigners the same rights as their nationals", and reserves the right to set residence requirements on the rights to work, health, education, and social security.

New Zealand reserved the right not to apply Article 8 (the right to form and join trade unions) insofar as existing measures (which at the time included compulsory unionism and encouraged arbitration of disputes) were incompatible with it.

Norway reserves the right to strike so as to allow for compulsory arbitration of some labour disputes.

Pakistan has a general reservation to interpret the Covenant within the framework of its constitution.

Thailand interprets the right to self-determination within the framework of other international law.

Trinidad and Tobago reserves the right to restrict the right to strike of those engaged in essential occupations.

Turkey will implement the Covenant subject to the UN Charter. It also reserves the right to interpret and implement the right of parents to choose and establish educational institutions in a manner compatible with its constitution.

The United Kingdom views the Covenant as subservient to the UN Charter. It made several reservations regarding its overseas territories.

United States - *Amnesty International* writes that "The United States signed the Covenant in 1979 under the Carter administration but is not fully bound by it until it is ratified. For political reasons, the Carter administration did not push for the necessary review of the Covenant by the Senate, which must give its "advice and consent" before the US can ratify a treaty. The Reagan and George H.W. Bush administrations took the view that economic, social, and cultural rights were not really rights but merely desirable social goals and therefore should not be the object of binding treaties. The Clinton Administration did not deny the nature of these rights but did not find it politically expedient to engage in a battle with Congress over the Covenant. The George W. Bush administration followed in line with the view of the previous Bush administration." The *Heritage Foundation,* a critical conservative think tank, argues that signing it would obligate the introduction of policies that it opposes such as universal health care.

Optional Protocol

The Optional Protocol to the International Covenant on Economic, Social and Cultural Rights is a side-agreement to the Covenant which allows its parties to recognise the competence of the Committee on Economic, Social and Cultural Rights to consider complaints from individuals.

The Optional Protocol was adopted by the UN General Assembly on 10 December 2008. It was opened for signature on 24 September 2009, and as of July 2010 has been signed by 32 parties and ratified by 2. It will enter into force when ratified by 10 parties.

The Committee on Economic, Social and Cultural Rights

The Committee on Economic, Social and Cultural Rights is a body of human rights experts tasked with monitoring the implementation of the Covenant. It consists of 18 independent human rights experts, elected for four-year terms, with half the members elected every two years.

Unlike other human rights monitoring bodies, the Committee was not established by the treaty it oversees. Rather, it was established by the Economic and Social Council following the failure of two previous monitoring bodies.

All states parties are required to submit regular reports to the committee outlining the legislative, judicial, policy and other measures they have taken to implement the rights affirmed in the Covenant. The first report is due within two years of ratifying the Covenant; thereafter reports are due every five years. The Committee examines each report and addresses its concerns and recommendations to the State party in the form of "oncluding observations".

The Committee typically meets every May and November in *Geneva*.

INTERNATIONAL COVENANT ON ECONOMIC, SOCIAL AND CULTURAL RIGHTS, 1966

PART-I

Article 1

1. All peoples have the right of self-determination. By virtue of that right they freely determine their political status and freely pursue their economic, social and cultural development.

2. All peoples may, for their own ends, freely dispose of their natural wealth and resources without prejudice to any obligations arising out of international economic co-operation, based upon the principle of mutual benefit, and international law. In no case may a people be deprived of its own means of subsistence.

3. The State Parties to the present Covenant, including those having responsibility for the administration of Non-Self-Governing and Trust Territories, shall promote the realisation of self-determination, and shall respect that right, in conformity with the provisions of the Charter of the United Nations.

PART-II

Article 2

1. Each State Party to the present Covenant undertakes to take steps, individually and through international assistance and co-operation, especially economic and technical, to the maximum of its available resources, with a view to achieving progressively of full realisation of the rights recognised in the present Covenant by all appropriate means, including particularly the adoption of legislative measures.

2. The State Parties to the Covenant undertake to guarantee that the rights enunciated in the present

Covenant will be exercised without discrimination of any kind as to race, colour, sex, language, religion, political or other opinion, national or social origin, property, birth or other status.

3. Developing countries, with due regard to human rights and their national economy may determine to what extent they would guarantee the economic rights recognised in the present Covenant to non-nationals.

Article 3

The State Parties to the present Covenant undertake to ensure the equal right of men and women to the enjoyment of all economic, social and cultural rights set forth in the present Covenant.

Article 4

The State Parties to the present Covenant recognise that, in the enjoyment of those rights provided by the State in conformity with the present Covenant, the State may subject such rights only to such limitations as are determined by law only in so far as this may be compatible with the nature of these rights solely for the purpose of promoting the general welfare in a democratic society.

Article 5

1. Nothing in the present Covenant may be interpreted as implying for any State, group or person any right to engage in any activity or to perform any act aimed at the destruction of any of the rights or freedoms recognised herein, or at their limitation to a greater extent than is provided for in the present Covenant.

2. No restriction upon or derogation from any of the fundamental human rights recognised or existing in any country in virtue of law, conventions, regulations or custom shall be admitted on the pretext that the present Covenant does not recognise such rights or existing in any country in virtue of law, conventions regulations or custom shall be

admitted on the pretext that the present Covenant does not recognise such rights or that it recognises them to a lesser extent.

PART-III

Article 6

1. The states Parties to the present Covenant recognise the right to work, which includes the rights of everyone to the opportunity to gain his living by work which he freely chooses or accepts, and will take appropriate steps to safeguard this right.

2. The steps to be taken by the State Party to the present Covenant to achieve the full realisation of this right shall include technical and vocational guidance and training programmes, policies and techniques to achieve steady economic, social and cultural development and full and productive employment under conditions safeguarding fundamental political and economic freedoms to the individual.

Article 7

The State Parties to the present Covenant recognise the right of everyone to the enjoyment of just and favourable conditions of work, which ensure, in particular :

(a) Remuneration which provides all workers, as a minimum, with:

(i) Fair wages and equal remuneration for work of equal value without distinction of any kind, in particular women being guaranteed conditions of work not inferior to those enjoyed by men, with equal pay for equal work;

(ii) a decent living for themselves and their families in accordance with the provisions of the present Covenant;

(b) Safe and healthy working conditions;

(c) Equal opportunity for every one to be promoted in his employment to an appropriate higher level, subject to considerations other than those of seniority and competence;

(d) Rest, leisure and reasonable limitation of working hours and periodic holidays with pay, as well as remuneration for public holidays.

Article 8

1. The State Parties to the present Covenant undertake to ensure :

(a) The right of everyone to form trade unions and join the trade union of his choice, subject only to the rules of the organisation concerned, for the promotion and protection of his economic and social interest. No restrictions may be placed on the exercise of this right other than those prescribed by law and which are necessary in a democratic society in the interest of national security or public order or for the protection of the rights and freedom of others;

(b) The right of trade unions to establish national federations or confederations and the right of the latter to form or join international trade-union organisations;

(c) The right of trade unions to function freely subject to no limitations other than those prescribed by law and which are necessary in a democratic society in the interest of national security or public order or for the protection of the rights and freedom of others;

(d) The right to strike provided that it is exercised in conformity with the law of the particular country.

2. This Article shall not prevent the composition of lawful restrictions on the exercise of these rights by members of the armed forces or of the police or of the administration of the state.

3. Nothing in this Article shall authorise State Parties to the International Labour Organisation Convention of 1948 concerning freedom of association and Protection of the Right to Organise to take legislative measures which without prejudice, to apply the law in such a manner as would prejudice, guarantees provided for in that Covenant.

Articles 9

The state parties to the present Covenant recognised the right of everyone to social security, including social insurance.

Article 10

The State Parties to the present Covenant recognise that:

1. The widest possible protection and assistance should be accorded to the family, which is the natural and fundamental group unit of society, particularly for its establishment and while it responsible for the care and education of dependent children. Marriage must be entered in to with the free consent of the intending spouses.

2. Special protection should be accorded to mother during a responsible period before and after childbirth. During such period working mother should be accorded paid leave or leave with adequate social security benefits.

3. Special measures of protection and assistance should be taken on behalf of all children and young persons without any discrimination for reasons of parentage or other conditions. Children and young persons should be protected from economic and social exploitation. Their employment in work harmful to their morals or health or dangerous to life or likely to hamper their normal development should be punishable by law. State should also set as limits below which the paid employment of child labour should be prohibited and punishable by law.

Article 11

1. The States Parties to the present Covenant recognise the right of everyone to an adequate standard of living for himself and his family, including adequate food, clothing and housing, and to the continuous improvement of living conditions. The State Parties will take appropriate steps to ensure the realisation of this right, recognising to this effect

the essential importance of international co-operation based on free consent.

2. The State Parties to the present covenant, recognising the fundamental rights of everyone to be free from hunger, shall take, individually and through international co-operation, the measures, including specific programmes, which are needed:

(a) to improve method of production, conservation of food by making full use of technical and scientific knowledge by disseminating of the principles of nutrition and by developing or reforming agrarian systems in such a way as to achieve the most efficient development and utilisation of natural resources;

(b) taking into account the problems of both food-importing and food-exporting countries, to ensure an equitable distribution of world food supplies in relation to need.

Article 12

1. The State Parties to the present Covenant recognise the right of everyone to the enjoyment of the highest attainable stand of physical and mental health.

2. The steps to be taken by the State Parties to the present Covenant to achieve the full realisation of this right shall include those necessary for :

(a) the provision for the reduction of the stillbirth-rate and of infant mortality and for the healthy development of the child;

(b) the improvement of all aspects of environmental and industrial hygiene;

(c) the prevention, treatment and control of epidemic, endemic, occupational and other diseases;

(d) the creation of conditions which would assure to all medical service and attention in the event of sickness.

Article 13

1. The State Parties of the present Covenant recognise the right of everyone to education. They agree that education shall be directed to the full development of the human personality and the sense of its dignity, and shall strengthen the respect for human rights and fundamental freedoms. They further agree that education shall enable all persons to participate effectively in a free society, promote understanding, tolerance and friendship among all nations and all racial, ethnic or religious groups, and further the activities of the United Nations for the maintenance of peace.

2. The State Parties of the present Covenant recognise that, with a view to achieving the full realisation of this right :

(a) Primary education shall be compulsory and available free to all;

(b) Secondary education in its different forms, including technical and vocational secondary education, shall be made generally available and accessible to all by every appropriate means, and in particular by the progressive introduction of free education;

(c) Higher education shall be made equally accessible to all, on the basis of capacity, by every appropriate means, and in particular by the progressive introduction of free education;

(d) Fundamental education shall be encouraged or intensified as far as possible for those persons who have not received or completed the whole period of their primary education;

(e) The development of a system of school at all levels shall be actively pursued, an adequate fellowship system shall be established, and the material conditions of teaching staff shall be continuously improved.

3. The State Party to the present Covenant undertake to have respect for the liberty of parents and, when applicable legal guardians, to choose for their children schools, other than those established by the public authorities, which conform to such minimum educational standards as may be laid down or approved by the State and to ensure the religious and moral education of their children in conformity with their own convictions.

4. No part of this Article shall be constructed so as to interfere with the liberty of individuals and bodies to establish and direct educational institutions, subject always to the observance of the principles set forth in paragraph 1 of this Article and to the requirement that the education given in such institutions shall conform to such minimum standards as may be laid down by the State.

Article 14

Each State Party, to the present Covenant which, at the time of becoming a Party, has not been able to secure in its metropolitan territory or other territories under its jurisdiction compulsory primary education, free of charge, undertakes, within two years, to work out and adopt a detailed plan of action for the progressive implementation, within a reasonable number of years, to be fixed in the plan, of the principle of compulsory education free of charge for all.

Article 15

1. The State Parties of the present Covenant recognise the right of every one :

(a) To take part in cultural life;

(b) To enjoy the benefits of scientific progress and its applications;

(c) To benefit from the protection of the moral and material interests resulting from any scientific, literary or artistic production of which he is the author.

2. The steps to be taken by the State Parties to the present Covenant to achieve the full realisation of this right shall include those necessary for the conservation, the development and the diffusion of science and culture.

3. The State Parties to the present Covenant undertake to respect the freedom indispensable for the scientific research and creative activity.

4. The State Party to the present Covenant recognise the benefits to be derived from the encouragement and development of international contacts and co-operation in scientific and cultural fields.

PART IV

Article 16

1. The State Parties of the present Covenant undertake to submit, in conformity with this part of the Covenant, reports on the measures which they have adopted and the progress made in achieving the observance of the rights recognized herein.

2. (a) All reports shall be submitted to the Secretary-General of the United Nations, who shall transmit copies to the Economic and Social Council for consideration in accordance with the provisions of the present Covenant;

(b) The Secretary-General of the United Nations shall also transmit to the specialized agencies copies of the reports, or any relevant parts there from, from State Parties to the present Covenant which are also members of these specialized agencies in so far as these reports, or part there form, related to any matter which falls within the responsibilities of the said agencies in accordance with their constitutional instruments.

Article 17

1. The State Parties of the present Covenant shall furnish their reports in stages, in, accordance with a

programme to be established by the Economic and Social Council within one year of the entry into the force of the present Covenant after consultation with the States Parties and the specialized agencies concerned.

2. Reports may indicate factors and difficulties affecting the degree of fulfilment of obligations under the present Covenant.

3. Where relevant information has previously been furnished to the United Nations or to any specialized agency by any State Party to the present Covenant, it will not be necessary to reproduce that information, but a precise reference to the information so furnished will suffice.

Article 18

Pursuant to its responsibilities under the Charter of the United Nations in the field of human right and fundamental freedoms, the Economic and Social Council may take arrangements with the specialized agencies in respect of their reports to it on the progress made in achieving the observance of the provisions of the present Covenant falling within the scope of their activities. These reports may include particulars of decisions and recommendations on such implementation adopted by their competent organs.

Article 19

The Economic and Social Council may transmit to the Commission on Human Rights for study and general recommendation or, as appropriate, for information the reports concerning human rights submitted by States in accordance with Article 16 and 17, and those concerning human rights submitted by the specialized agencies in accordance with Article 18.

Article 20

The States Parties to the present Covenant and the specialized agencies concerned may submit comments to the Economic and Social Council on any general recommendation under Article 19 or reference to such general recommendation in any report of the Commission on Human Rights or any documentation referred to therein.

Article 21

The Economic and Social Council may submit from time to time to the General Assembly reports with recommendations of a general nature and a summary of the information received from the States Parties to the present Covenant and the specialized agencies on the measures taken and the progress made in achieving general observance of the rights recognized in the present Covenant.

Article 22

The Economic and Social Council may bring to the attention of other organs of the United Nations, their subsidiary organs and specialized agencies concerned with furnishing technical assistance, any matter arising out of the reports referred to in this part of the present Covenant which may assist such bodies in deciding, each within its field of competence, on the advisability of international measures likely to contribute to the effective progressive implementation of the present Covenant.

Article 23

The State Party of the present Covenant agree that international action for the achievement of the rights recognised in the present Covenant includes such methods as the conclusion of conventions, the adoption of recommendations, the furnishing of technical assistance and the holding of regional meetings and technical meetings for the purpose of consultation and study organised in conjunction with the Governments concerned.

Article 24

Nothing in the present Covenant shall be interpreted as impairing the provisions of the Charter of the United Nations and of the constitutions of the specialised agencies which define the respective responsibilities of the various organs of the United Nations and of the specialised agencies in regard to the matters dealt with in the present Covenant.

Article 25

Every citizen shall have the right and the opportunity, without any of the distinctions mentioned in Article 2 and without unreasonable restrictions:

(a) To take part in the conduct of public affairs, directly or through freely chosen representatives;

(b) To vote and to be elected at genuine periodic elections which shall be by universal and equal suffrage and shall be held by secret ballot, guaranteeing the free expression of the will of the electors;

(c) To have access, on general terms of equality, to public service in his country.

PART V

Article 26

1. The present Covenant is open for signature by any State Member of the United Nations or member of any of its specialised agencies, by any State Party to the Statute of the International Court of Justice, and by any other State which has been invited by the General Assembly of the United Nations to become a party to the present Covenant.

2. The present Covenant is subject to ratification. Instruments of ratification shall be deposited with the Secretary-General of the United Nations.

3. The present Covenant shall be open to accession by any State referred to in paragraph 1 of this article.

4. Accession shall be affected by the deposit of an instrument of accession with the Secretary-General of the United Nations.

5. The Secretary-General of the United Nations shall inform all States, which have signed the present Covenant

and acceded to it of the deposit of each instrument of ratification or accession.

Article 27

1. The present Covenant shall enter into force three months after the date of the deposit with the Secretary-General of the United Nations of the thirty-fifth instrument of ratification or instrument of accession.

2. For each State ratifying the present Covenant or accessing to it after the deposit of the thirty-fifth instrument of ratification or instrument of accession, the present Covenant shall enter into force three months after the date of the deposit of its own instrument of accession.

Article 28

The provision of the present Covenant shall extend to all parts of federal States without any limitations or exceptions.

Article 29

1. Any State Party to the present Covenant may propose an amendment and file it with the Secretary-General of the United Nations. The Secretary-General shall thereupon communicate any proposed amendments to the States Parties to the present Covenant with a request that they notify him whether they favour a conference of States Parties for the purpose of considering and voting upon the proposals. In the event that at least one third of the States Parties favours such a conference, the Secretary-General shall convene the conference under the auspices of the United Nations. Any amendment adopted by a majority of the State Parties present and voting at the conference shall be submitted to the General Assembly of the United Nations for approval.

2. Amendments shall come into force when they have been approved by the General Assembly of the United Nations and accepted by a two-third majority of the States Parties to the present covenant in accordance with their respective constitutional processes.

3. When amendments come into force they shall be binding on those States Parties, which have accepted them, other State Parties still being bound by the provisions of the present, Covenant and any earlier amendment which they have accepted.

Article 30

Irrespective of the notifications made under Article 26, paragraph 5, the Secretary-General of the United Nations shall inform all States referred to in paragraph 1 of the some Article of the following particulars:

(a) Signatures, ratifications and accessions under Article 26;

(b) the date of the entry into force of the present Covenant under Article 27 and the date of the entry into force of any amendments under Article 29.

Article 31

1. The present Covenant, of which the Chinese, English, French, Russian and Spanish texts are equally authentic, shall be deposit in the archives of the United Nations.

2. The Secretary-General of the United Nations shall transmit certified copies of present Covenant to all States referred to in Article 26.

A BRIEF ANALYSIS OF THE INTERNATIONAL COVENANT ON ECONOMIC, SOCIAL AND CULTURAL RIGHTS

The distinctive features of this covenant as described under Article 2 are that each State party undertake to take step, to the maximum of its available resources, to achieve progressively the full realization of these rights by all appropriate means including the legislation;

that State parties undertake to guarantee that these rights will be exercised without discrimination of any kind as to race, colour, sex, language, religion, political or other opinion, national or social origin, property, birth or other status; and Developing countries may determine with due regard to human rights and their national economy as to what extent they would guarantee the economic rights to the non-nationals.

Following rights are included in the list of economic, social and cultural rights; the right to work; the right to the enjoyment of just and favourable condition of work; the right to form and join trade union of one's own choice; the right to social security including social insurance; the right to protection to family, special protection to motherhood and childhood; the right to adequate standard of living and freedom from hunger; the right to the enjoyment of the highest attainable standard of physical and mental health; the right to education; and the right to take part in cultural life and to enjoy the benefits of scientific progress.

The Rights Contained in the Covenants are not Identical to those Contained in the Universal Declaration

As compared to the Universal Declaration of Human Rights, the Covenant on Civil and Political Rights incorporates certain rights which do not found mention in the Universal Declaration, such as, prohibition of imprisonment merely on the ground of inability to fulfil a contractual obligation; human treatment detainees and, certain rights of the child not mentioned the Universal Declaration. At the same time the Covenant on Civil and Political Rights do not contain the right to own property, the right to seek and enjoy asylum and the right to nationality. The Covenant on Civil and Political Rights contains the provisions under which State parties may suspend many of the rights "in time of public emergency that threatens the life of the nation."

On the other hand Covenant of Economic, Social and Cultural rights are drafted in broader, and detailed manner. The list of the rights is long and more comprehensive.

Instrumentality of Enforcement of two Covenants

The Human Rights Committee has been established to supervise the State compliance with the provision of the covenant on Civil and Political rights by reviewing and commenting on the periodic reports submitted by the State parties. The committee receives and considers communication to the effect that a State party claims that another State parties are not fulfilling its obligations under the present Covenant. It also considers petition submitted by individuals under the First Optional Protocol to the Covenant on Civil and Political Rights. The Protocol enables the Human Rights Committee to receive and consider petitions from individual claiming to be victims of violations of any of the rights set forth in the Covenant.

The enforcement of the rights contained in the Covenant on Economic, Social and Cultural Rights depend upon the economic viability of the State parties and international economic and technical assistance, particularly to the developing and non-development States.

TEN

Declaration on the Right to Development

The General Assembly

Bearing in mind the purposes and principles of the charter of the United Nations relating to the achievement of international co-operation in solving international problems of economic, social, cultural or humanitarian nature, and in promoting and encouraging respect for human rights and fundamental freedoms for all without distinction as to race, sex, language or religion;

Recognizing that development is a comprehensive economic, social, cultural and political process, which aims at the constant improvement of the well-being of the entire population and of all individuals on the basis of their active, free and meaningful participation in development and in the fair distribution of benefits resulting there from;

Considering that under the provisions of the Universal Declaration of human rights everyone is entitled to a social and international order in which the rights and freedoms set forth in that Declaration can be fully realized;

Recalling the provisions of the International Covenant of Economic, Social and Cultural Rights and of the International Covenant on Civil and Political Rights;

Recalling further the relevant agreements, conventions, resolutions, recommendations and other instruments of the United Nations and its specialized agencies concerning the integral development of the human being, economic and social progress and development of all peoples, including those instruments concerning decolonisation, the prevention of discrimination, respect for and observance of human rights and fundamental freedoms, the maintenance of international peace and security and the further promotion of friendly relations and cooperation among states in accordance with the charter,

Recalling the right of peoples to self-determination, by virtue of which they have the right freely to determine their political status and to pursue their economic, social and cultural development;

Recalling also the right of peoples to exercise, subject to the relevant provisions of both International Covenants on Human Rights, full and complete sovereignty over all their natural wealth and resources;

Mindful of the obligation of states under the charter to promote universal respect for and observance of human rights and fundamental freedoms for all without distinction of any kind such as race, colour, sex language, religion, political or other opinion, national or social origin, property, birth or other status;

Considering that the elimination of the massive and flagrant violations of the human rights of the peoples and individuals affected by situations such as those resulting from colonialism, neo-colonialism, apartheid, all forms of racism and racial discrimination, foreign domination and occupation, aggression and threats against national sovereignty, national unity and territorial integrity and threats of war would contribute to the establishment of circumstances propitious to the development of a great part of mankind;

Concerned at the existence of serious obstacles to development, as well as to the complete fulfilment of human being and of peoples, constituted, inter alias, by the denial of civil, political, economic, social and cultural rights, and considering that all human rights and fundamental freedoms are indivisible and interdependent and that, in order to promote development, equal attention and urgent consideration should be given to the implementation, promotion and protection of civil, political economic, social and cultural rights and that accordingly, the promotion of, respect for and enjoyment of certain human right and fundamental freedoms cannot justify the denial of other human rights and fundamental freedoms;

Considering that international peace and security are essential elements for the realization of the right to development;

Reaffirming that there is a close relationship between disarmament and development and that progress in the field of disarmament would considerably promote progress in the field of development and that resources released through disarmament measures should be devoted to the economic and social development and well-being of all peoples and, in particular, those of the developing countries;

Recognizing that the human person is the central subject of the development process and that development policy should therefore make the human being the main participant and beneficiary of development;

Recognizing that the creation of conditions favourable to the development of peoples and individuals is the primary responsibility of their states;

Aware that efforts at the international level to promote and protect human rights should be accompanied by efforts to establish a new international economic order;

Confirming that the right to development is an inalienable human right and that equality of opportunity for development is a prerogative both of nations and of individuals, who make up nations;

Proclaims the following Declaration on the Right to Development :

Article 1

1. The right to development is an inalienable human right by virtue of which every human person and all peoples are entitled to participate in, contribute to and enjoy economic, social, cultural and political development, in which all human rights and fundamental freedoms can be fully realized.

2. The human right to development also implies the full realization of the right of peoples to self-determination, which includes, subject to the relevant provisions of both International Covenants on Human Rights, the exercise of their inalienable right to full sovereignty over all their natural wealth and resources.

Article 2

1. The human person is the central subject of development and should be the active participant and beneficiary of the right to development.

2. All human beings have a responsibility for development, individually and collectively, taking in to account the need for full respect for their human rights and fundamental freedoms as well as their duties to the community, which alone can ensure the free and complete fulfilment of the human being and they should therefore promote and protect an appropriate political, social and economic order for development.

3. States have the right and the duty to formulate appropriate national development policies that aim at constant improvement of the well-being of the entire population and of all individuals, on the basis of their active, free and meaningful participation in development and in the fair distribution of the benefits resulting there from.

Article 3

1. States have the primary responsibility for the creation of national and international conditions favourable to the realization of the rights to development.

2. The realization of the rights to development requires full respect for the principles of international law concerning friendly relations and cooperation among States in accordance with the Charter of the United Nations.

3. States have the duty to cooperate with each other in ensuring development and eliminating obstacles to development. State should realize their rights and fulfil their duties in such a manner as to promote a new international economic order based on sovereign equality, interdependence, mutual interest and cooperation among all States, as to encourage the observance and realization of human rights.

Article 4

1. States have the duty to take steps, individually and collectively, to formulate international development policies with a view to facilitating the full realization of the rights to development.

2. Sustained action is required to promote more rapid development of developing countries. As a complement to the efforts of developing countries, effective international cooperation is essential in providing these countries with appropriate means and facilities to foster their comprehensive development.

Article 5

State shall take resolute steps to eliminate the massive and fragrant violations of the human rights of peoples and human beings affected by situations such as those resulting from apartheid, all forms of racism and racial discrimination, colonialism, foreign domination and occupation, aggression, foreign interference and threats against national sovereignty, national unity and territorial integrity, threats of war and refusal to recognize the fundamental right of peoples to self-determination.

Article 6

1. All States should cooperate with a view to promoting, encouraging and strengthening universal respect for an observance of all human rights and fundamental freedoms for all without any distinction as to race, sex, language or religion.

2. All human rights and fundamental freedoms are indivisible and interdependent; equal attention and urgent condition should be given to the implementation, promotion and protection of civil, political, economic, social and cultural rights.

3. State should take steps to eliminate obstacles to development resulting from failure to observe civil and political rights, as well as economic, social and cultural rights.

Article 7

All State should promote the establishment, maintenance and strengthening of international peace and security and, to that end, should do their utmost to achieve general and complete disarmament under effective international control, as well as to ensure that the resources released by effective disarmament measures are used for comprehensive development, in particular that of the developing countries.

Article 8

1. States should undertake, at the national level, all necessary measures for the realization of the right to development and shall ensure, inter-alias, equality of

opportunity for all in their access to basic resources, education, health services, food, housing, employment and the fair distribution of income. Effective measure should be undertaken to ensure that women have an active role in the development process. Appropriate economic and social reforms should be carried out with a view to eradicating all social injustices.

2. States should encourage popular participation in all spheres as an important factor in development and in the full realization of all human rights.

Article 9

1. All the aspects of the right to development set forth in the present Declaration are indivisible and interdependent and each of them should be considered in the context of the whole.

2. Nothing in the present Declaration shall be construed as being contrary to the purposes and principles of the United Nations, or as implying that any State, group or person has a right to engaged in any activity or to perform any act aimed at the violation of the rights set forth in the Universal Declaration of Human Rights and in the International Covenants on Human Rights.

Article 10

Steps should be taken to ensure the full exercise and progressive enhancement of the right to development, including formulation, adoption and implementation of policy, legislative and other measures at the national and international levels.

A BRIEF ANALYSIS ON DECLARATION ON THE RIGHT TO DEVELOPMENT

The right to self Determination : The Right to self-determination is one of the most basic collective rights. By virtue of the right of self-determination people have right not only to freely determine their political status but also to freely pursue their economic, social and cultural development. Thus, right of self-determination includes right to development.

The right to Development : The right to development encompasses within its ambit all human rights and fundamental freedoms including right of self-determination: Article 1 of the Declaration on the right to Development runs as follows :

"The right to development is an inalienable human right by virtue of which every human person and all people are entitled to participate in, contribute to and enjoy economic, social, cultural and political development, in which all human rights and fundamental freedoms can be fully realised." Further, "The human rights to development also implies the full realisation of the right of people to self determination, which includes, subject to the relevant provisions of both international convents on human rights, the exercise of their inalienable right to full sovereignty over all their natural wealth and resources."

Thus, right to development is of multidimensional character incorporating all civil, political, economic, social and cultural rights necessary for the full development of individual and the protection of his dignity"[13] Louis B. Sohn has said that the right to development "requires careful balancing of the interests of the community and of the individuals. A healty regard for the rights of the individual is indispensable for a state's success in pursuing its right to development."

The general framework of human rights which were affirmed in International Declaration and Covenants was mainly concerned with rights of individuals. Various new issues and concerns have led to the emergence of new human rights and their international recognition. A landmark development in the formulation and recognition of new human rights is the Declaration on the Rights to Development which was adopted by the General Assembly of the United Nations on 4 December 1986. This Declaration is particularly significant for its importance to the developing countries even though the necessary means for enforcing it are lacking.

ELEVEN

International Human Rights Law and Organizations

International law now contains many functioning human rights treaties. A number of them have been ratified by more than three-quarters of the world's countries. This section sketches the development of international measures to promote and protect human rights. The efforts to protect human rights through international treaties began in 1919 in the League of Nations and expanded after World War II in international organizations such as the United Nations, the Council of Europe, the Organization of American States, and the African Union. The international promotion and protection of human rights complements the legal protection of human rights at the national level.

HISTORICAL OVERVIEW

When a government violates the human rights of its residents they may be able to appeal to the country's laws or bill of rights and get a court to order that the violations stop and that the government provide remedies. If suitable national laws and bills of rights are unavailable, however, victims of human rights violations may seek help from international law and organizations. Traditionally, international law did not confer rights and protections on individual persons; its concern was exclusively the rights and duties of countries or states. Victims of human rights violations could appeal to heaven, and invoke standards of natural justice, but there were no international organizations working to formulate and enforce legal rights of individuals. After World War I the League of Nations had some success in using minority rights treaties to protect national minorities in Europe, but the effort ended with the rise of Nazi Germany and the beginning of World War II.

Countries fighting Hitler's Germany decided that after their victory a new international organization would be needed to promote international peace and security, and that securing human rights in all countries would help lessen the dangers of falling back into large wars. Indeed, prior to the official formation of the United Nations, the Allies imposed human rights obligations on Italy and Central European powers in peace treaties. Similar obligations were imposed on Germany and Japan during the Allied occupation. The United Nations was created in 1945. Its *Charter* established goals of protecting future generations from the "scourge of war" and promoting "fundamental human rights" and the "dignity and worth of the human person."

Not long after its founding the UN established a committee with the charge of writing an international bill of rights. This document was to be similar to historic bills of rights such as the French Declaration of the Rights of Man and of the Citizen (1789) and the United States Bill of Rights (1791), but was to apply to every person in every country. This international bill of rights emerged in December 1948 as the *Universal Declaration of Human Rights*. Although some diplomats had hoped for a binding human rights treaty that countries joining the UN would have to adopt, the Universal Declaration was a set of recommended standards rather than a binding treaty. By now, however, almost all of the norms in the Universal Declaration have been incorporated in widely-ratified UN human rights treaties.

The Universal Declaration has been astoundingly successful in setting the pattern for subsequent human rights treaties and in getting countries to include its list of rights in national constitutions and bills of rights (Morsink 1999). The Universal Declaration, and the treaties that followed it, largely define what people today mean when they speak of human rights. The Universal Declaration proposed six families of rights including security rights, due process rights, liberty rights, rights of political participation, equality rights, and social rights. The inclusion of social rights to goods such as education and an adequate standard of living took the Declaration beyond its 18th century antecedents.

The Universal Declaration was born at a time that made its success difficult. The Declaration's approval by the General Assembly coincided with the beginning of the Cold War — an ideological and geopolitical conflict between capitalist and communist countries that continued almost until 1990. Ideological differences and hostilities might have stalled the human rights movement but not human rights advances in Europe. In the early 1950s Western European countries formed the Council of Europe and created *the European Convention for the Protection of Human Rights and Fundamental Freedoms*. This international treaty entered into force on September 3, 1953, and was binding upon countries that ratified it. The European Convention established basic rights similar to those in the Universal Declaration, but included provisions for enforcement and adjudication. The European Convention gave birth to the European Court of Human Rights, whose job is to receive, evaluate, and investigate complaints, mediate disputes, issue judgements, and interpret the Convention. The human rights set forth in the Convention are legally enforceable rights to which member states are bound. In creating the European Convention and Court, the countries of Western Europe gradually proved that effective protection of human rights could be provided at the international level.

Inspired by the success of the European Convention, the United Nations followed a similar path, creating numerous treaties aimed at the enforcement and adjudication of the rights set forth in the Universal Declaration. These documents establish legal obligations among the ratifying countries to implement international rights within their national legal and political systems. By 2000 the main human rights treaties had been ratified by a large majority of the world's countries. As Ann Bayefsky writes, "Every UN member state is a party to one or more of the six major human rights treaties. 80% of states have ratified four or more".

Regional arrangements, similar to those in Europe, exist in the Americas and Africa Efforts to protect human rights through international law have obviously not been totally successful — lots of human rights violations still occur today in all parts of the world. International human rights law is a work in progress, and has developed much farther than one could have expected in 1950 or even in 1975.

UNITED NATIONS HUMAN RIGHTS TREATIES

International human rights treaties transform lists of human rights into legally binding state obligations. The first such United Nations treaty was the *Genocide Convention,* approved in 1948 —just one day before the Universal Declaration. The Convention defines genocide and makes it a crime under international law. The Convention requires states to enact national legislation prohibiting genocide, to try to punish persons or officials who commit genocide, and to allow persons accused of genocide to be transported to countries capable of trying the charge. It also calls for action by UN bodies to prevent and suppress acts of genocide (Genocide Convention, articles 5, 7, 9). Currently the Genocide Convention has more than 130 parties (1948). The *International Criminal Court*, created by the Rome Treaty of 1998, is authorized to prosecute genocide at the international level, along with crimes against humanity and war crimes.

After the creation of the Universal Declaration, the Human Rights Commission proceeded to try to create treaties that would make the rights in the Universal Declaration into norms of international law. Because of the Cold War, the effort went ahead at a glacial pace. To accommodate the ideological division between those who believed in the importance of social rights and those who did not, or who thought that social rights could not be enforced in the same way as civil and political rights, the Commission ultimately decided to create two separate treaties. Drafts of the two International Covenants were submitted to the General Assembly for approval in 1953, but approval was much delayed. Almost twenty years after the Universal Declaration, the United Nations General Assembly finally approved the International Covenant on Civil and Political Rights and the International Covenant on Economic, Social, and Cultural Rights (both 1966). The Civil and Political Covenant contains most of the civil and political rights found in the Universal Declaration. The Social Covenant contains the economic and social rights found in the second half of the Universal Declaration. These treaties embodying Universal Declaration rights received enough ratifications to become operative in 1976 and have now become the most important UN human rights treaties. To date, these treaties have been ratified by about 75 percent of the world's countries (See Status of Ratifications of the Principal Human Rights Treaties).

A country ratifying a UN human rights treaty agrees to respect and implement within domestic law the rights the treaty covers. It also agrees to accept and respond to international scrutiny and criticism of its compliance. It does not necessarily agree to make the human rights norm directly enforceable in domestic courts. That usually requires implementing legislation.

A common method of treaty implementation within the UN is the creation of a standing committee (or treaty body) to monitor states' performance, and to which member states are required to submit periodic reports on compliance. The Civil and Political Covenant, which has been ratified by more than 150 countries illustrates this approach. Rather than creating a human rights court, the Covenant created the Human Rights Committee (HRC), to promote compliance with its norms. The eighteen members of the HRC serve as independent experts rather than as state representatives. This potentially gives them some independence from the positions of their governments. The HRC frequently expresses its views as to whether a particular practice is a human rights violation, but it is not authorized to issue legally binding decisions.

The HRC is responsible for publishing "general comments" regarding the interpretation of the Civil and Political Covenant, reviewing periodic state reports on implementation of the Covenant, and receiving and investigating complaints of human rights violations made by states and individuals. The Committee holds public sessions in which it hears from non-governmental organizations such as Amnesty International and meets with representatives of the state making the report. The HRC then publishes "Concluding Observations" that evaluate human rights compliance by the reporting country. This process requires countries to hold discussions with the Human Rights Committee and have their human rights problems exposed to world public opinion. The reporting procedure is useful in encouraging countries to identify their major human rights problems and to devise methods of dealing with them over time. Unfortunately, the reporting system has few teeth when dealing with countries that stonewall or fail to report, and the Human Rights Committee's conclusions often receive little attention.

In addition to the required reporting procedure, the HRC has the authority to consider state complaints alleging human rights violations by another member state. The Civil and Political Covenant also has an optional provision requiring separate ratification that authorizes the HRC to receive, investigate, and mediate complaints from individuals alleging that their rights under the Covenant have been violated by a participating state. By 2006, 105 of the 155 states adhering to the Covenant had ratified this optional provision.

Many other UN human rights treaties are implemented in roughly the same way as the Civil and Political Covenant. These include the International Convention on the Elimination of All Forms of Racial Discrimination (1966), the *Convention on the Elimination of All Forms of Discrimination Against Women* (1979), the Convention on the Rights of the Child (1989), the Convention against Torture and Other Cruel, Inhuman or Degrading Treatment or Punishment (1984), and the Migrant Workers Convention (1990). These human rights treaties create their own treaty bodies to monitor compliance and implementation. The proliferation of treaty bodies and reporting requirements has led to considerable overlap and inefficiency within the UN human rights system (Bayefsky 2001).

The standard UN system for implementing human rights is not very powerful. It is stronger on the promotion of human rights than on their protection through adjudication. Unlike the regional systems in Europe and the Americas, it does not have an international human rights court with powers to order states to change their practices or compensate a victim. Its tools are largely limited to consciousness-raising, persuasion, mediation, and exposure of violations to public scrutiny.

Other United Nations Human Rights Agencies

Human Rights treaties are only one part of the UN's human rights program. In fact, the UN has several agencies and courts, independent of its human rights treaties, to address continuing human rights abuses. Three notable agencies are the *High Commissioner for Human Rights* (OHCHR) which serves as a full-time advocate for human rights within the UN; *Human Rights Council,* which took over the main functions of the now defunct Human Rights Commission in addressing gross human rights violations; and the *Security Council,* which has the authority to impose diplomatic and economic sanctions, sponsor peacekeeping missions, and authorize military interventions in cases of human rights emergencies.

THE HIGH COMMISSIONER FOR HUMAN RIGHTS

In 1993, following recommendations included in the World Conference on Human Rights in Vienna, the United Nations General Assembly established the office of the High Commissioner for Human Rights as part of the UN Secretariat. The OHCHR coordinates the many human rights activities within the UN, working closely with treaty bodies, such as the Human Rights Committee, and other UN agencies such as the Human Rights Council. The High-Commissioner assists in the development of new treaties and procedures, sets the agenda for human rights agencies within the UN and provides advisory services to governments. Most importantly, the High Commissioner serves as a full-time advocate for human rights within the United Nations. The OHCHR also has field offices throughout the world, including offices in Central Asia, East and Southern Africa, the Pacific, Latin America, and the Middle East.

THE HUMAN RIGHTS COUNCIL

In 2006 the longstanding UN Human Rights Commission was replaced by a new Human Rights Council. The Human Rights Commission was a 56 member committee, authorized by the UN Charter, consisting of state representatives. The stated goals of the replacement were to eliminate "double standards and politicization." The new Council's responsibilities include "promoting universal respect for the protection of all human rights," addressing gross human rights violations, making recommendations to the General Assembly and "responding promptly to human rights emergencies." The Council's other responsibilities include providing direct assistance to UN member states to help them meet their human rights responsibilities through communication, technical assistance, and capacity building.

The Council consists of 47 members, elected directly and individually by the General Assembly with membership based on equitable geographic distribution. Council members serve terms of three years with a limitation of no more than two consecutive terms. Procedures for Council membership are aimed at keeping countries with very poor human rights records off the Commission. Members must be elected by an absolute majority of the General Assembly, requiring 96 votes in a secret ballot, rather than a simple majority of General Assembly members present. The General Assembly also acts as a check on the Council, with the ability to suspend Council members whose countries commit gross human rights violations. The Council will meet no fewer than three times per year for at least ten weeks, with the ability to hold special sessions when necessary. For now the Council will adopt the procedures and responsibilities of the Human Rights Commission, but has a year to review and change them.

THE SECURITY COUNCIL

The Security Council's mandate under Article 24 of the UN Charter is the maintenance of international peace and security. The fifteen-member body consists of 5 permanent and 10 elected members. Nine votes are needed to approve any measures. Any of the five permanent members (China, France, Russia, the United Kingdom, and the United States) can exercise their veto power to prevent a given action from succeeding. The permanent membership of five countries, with their veto power, is a clear concession to economic and military power within the Security Council. The Security Council can issue binding decisions regarding international security or peace, authorize military interventions and impose diplomatic and economic sanctions.

REGIONAL HUMAN RIGHTS SYSTEMS

Regional arrangements supplement the UN system by promoting and protecting human rights in particular parts of the world. Three regions — Europe, the Americas, and Africa — have formulated their own declarations and conventions for the protection and enforcement of human rights. Because of their locations, regional agencies and courts have better chances of effectively investigating alleged violations promptly and securing relief for victims. Regional agencies are also likely to be more attuned to the culture and identity of the region and may accordingly have a deeper understanding of problems, circumstances, and possible reforms.

The European System

The *European Convention for the Protection of Human Rights* (1950) demonstrated to the world the possibility of enforcing internationally human rights norms. Article 3 of the *Statute of the Council of Europe* requires member states to accept the principles of human rights and fundamental freedoms within their jurisdictions. The Council even defines its post-1989 role as that of a "human rights watchdog" for post-communist European countries.

The European Convention formulates human rights norms, legally binds member states to respect these norms, and creates a system of adjudication and enforcement. The European Convention's commitment clause requires all member states to secure these fundamental rights to every person within their jurisdictions. The first section of the European Convention then sets forth the fundamental rights covered in the convention, while the second section establishes the European Court of Human Rights.

The rights set forth in the European Convention are similar to the first twenty-one articles of the Universal Declaration, covering standard civil and political rights. Social rights were treated in a separate document, the *European Social Charter.* The European Convention defines its rights in greater detail than the Universal Declaration. A good example of this is seen in the right to life. While the Universal Declaration simply sets forth, "[everyone has the right to life...," the European Convention's formulation is far more specific, requiring a *mens rea* as a necessary condition for violation and defining specific exceptions to this right (see Article 2).

The European system originally had both a Commission and a Human Rights Court to ensure that member states fulfilled their human rights obligations. In 1998, the European Convention was amended to abolish the Commission, expand and reorganize the Court, and make the Court a full-time operation. Countries that ratify the European Convention agree to respect and implement a list of rights, but they also agree to the investigation, mediation, and adjudication of human rights complaints. The European Court of Human Rights, based in Strasbourg, France, is composed of one judge from each participating state in the Council of Europe. The judges, however, are appointed as independent jurists rather than as state representatives. Citizens from the participating countries with human rights complaints who have been unable to find a remedy in their national courts may petition the European Court of Human Rights. Complaints by governments about human rights violations in another participating country are also permitted, but are rarely made. If the Court agrees to hear a complaint, it investigates and adjudicates it. Before issuing a judgment, the Court attempts to mediate the dispute. If conciliation fails, the Court will issue a judgment with supporting judicial opinions and impose a remedy. Through this process a large body of international human rights jurisprudence has developed.

Participating governments almost always accept the Court's judgments. Compliance occurs because governments are committed to the European Convention and to the rule of law, and because their membership in good standing in the Council of Europe would be endangered were they to defy the Court.

The Inter-American System

The *Organization of American States* (OAS) is the oldest regional organization of states. In 1948, 21 states signed the *OAS Charter,* establishing the regional organization and affirming their commitment to democracy, liberty, and equality before the law. One OAS principle, set forth in Article 3 of the charter, is the "fundamental rights of the individual without distinction as to race, nationality, creed, or sex." The Inter-American system consists of two main documents, the *American Declaration of the Rights and*

Duties of Man and the *American Convention on Human Rights* and two main treaty bodies, the *Inter-American Commission on Human Rights* and the *Inter-American Court of Human Rights*. All 35 of the independent countries in the Americas currently comprise the Organization of American States.

Even before the UN adopted the Universal Declaration, the Organization of American States approved the American Declaration (1948). Like the Universal Declaration, the American Declaration encompasses the entire range of human rights. Additionally, the declaration includes an explicit list of duties, ranging from general duties toward society and one's children, to an individual's duty to vote, work, and pay taxes (Articles 29-38).

Despite its early beginnings, the Inter-American system of human rights progressed more slowly than its counterparts. Not until 1969 did the OAS adopt the American Convention on Human Rights, which entered into force in June of 1978. The Convention gave legal force to most of the rights established in the American Declaration with a commitment clause requiring states to adopt legislative or other measures necessary for full implementation of these rights. Similar to the European Convention on Human Rights, the American Convention protects civil and political rights as well as property rights and freedom from exile and collective expulsion for aliens. The Convention does not, however, cover social rights. Those are found in the *Protocol of San Salvador* (1988). The American Convention is unique in its inclusion of a right to seek asylum. To date, 25 of the 35 OAS member states have adopted the Convention.

The Inter-American Commission on Human Rights was established in 1959 and conducted its first investigation in 1961. The Commission is the first of two permanent bodies for promoting and protecting human rights in the Americas and consists of seven members elected by the OAS General Assembly who serve in their personal capacities.

The Commission's main functions include investigating individual complaints and preparing reports on countries with severe human rights problems. To this end the Commission is authorized to :

- Receive and investigate individual petitions regarding human rights violations
- Publish reports regarding human rights situations in member states
- Visit member states and investigate general human rights conditions or particular problem areas
- Publish studies on specific subject areas, such as indigenous rights and women's rights
- Make human rights recommendations to member states
- Submit cases to, or request advisory opinions from the Inter-American Court of human rights.

In 1979 the OAS adopted the Statute of the Inter-American Court of Human Rights, officially creating the Inter-American Court and defining its jurisdiction. The Court is authorized to interpret and enforce the Convention. The Court is composed of seven judges who serve a six year term in their individual capacity. Because judges serve in their individual capacity, the statute of the court explicitly prohibits them from holding positions that are incompatible with a judicial position, namely, positions in the executive branch of government, officials of international organizations. The Court's jurisdiction is limited to cases submitted by state parties and the Inter-American Commission involving the interpretation or application of the American Convention. The Court generally holds public hearings and delivers decisions in public sessions, ensuring its transparency. The Court issued its first decision in 1980, and to date has issued over 65 decisions.

Thus far, the Commission has been a far more important actor than the Court in the implementation of the American Convention. The Commission's jurisdiction is limited to individual cases alleging a human rights violation by OAS member states. Currently the Commission is processing more than 800 individual cases.

The African System

The newest regional human rights system covers the countries of the African continent. In 2000 the Organization of African Unity tranformed itself into the *African Union*. The *Constitutive Act* whereby this was accomplished reaffirmed Africa's determination "to promote and protect human and peoples' rights." The African Union's objectives include the promotion and protection of human rights in accordance with the *African Charter of Human and Peoples' Rights* and "other relevant human rights instruments." As of 2006 the African Union consists of 53 state parties.

The African Charter on Human and Peoples' Rights was created in 1981 and entered into force in 1986. This treaty obligates ratifying countries to recognize the rights and duties listed and to adopt legislation or measures to bring them into effect (Article 2). The African Charter is divided into two parts. The first part sets forth rights and duties and the second part establishes safeguards for them. Like the American Convention on Human Rights, the African Charter does not simply identify rights but also explicitly imposes duties upon individuals (Articles 27-29). These individual duties, included perhaps to counter claims that human rights promote excessive individualism, consist of duties to family, society, state, and the international community.

The African Charter explicitly posits group rights — the rights of peoples. Examples of such rights include the right of a group to freely dispose of its natural resources in the exclusive interest of its members (Article 21), and the right of a colonized or oppressed group to free themselves from domination (Article 20).

The Charter created an African Commission on Human and Peoples' Rights to promote and ensure the protection of human and peoples' rights in Africa, (Article 30). The Commission meets twice a year and consists of eleven members of the African community who serve six year terms in their personal capacities. The functions of the Commission are the promotion of human rights, the protection of these rights, interpretation of the African Charter, and the performance of "any other tasks" requested by the AU (Article 45). The Commission is also authorized to perform studies regarding problems in the area of human rights; formulate rules addressing human rights problems; investigate alleged human rights violations by any appropriate means; and prepare reports discussing human rights abuses; and make recommendations to the AU Assembly (Articles 45-54). Furthermore, states are required to submit regular reports to the Commission on their human rights problems and efforts to address them (Article 62).

An *African Court of Human and Peoples' Rights* is currently under construction.

The African system has enormous human rights problems to address, frequently faces non-cooperation by governments, and has inadequate resources to play a major role. But despite its limited legal and economic resources the African Union seems to be slowly constructing international mechanisms to promote and protect human rights in Africa.

Other Regions

Other regions of the world have yet to establish transnational human rights systems. No regional system exists in Asia, and the members of the *League of Arab States* have yet to ratify their *Arab Charter of Human Rights* despite its adoption more than a decade ago.

THE INTERNATIONAL CRIMINAL COURT

Once human rights norms are established internationally, the question arises about what should be done by way of punishment and accountability for political, military, and ethnic leaders who have organized and carried out severe human rights violations. The International Criminal Court (ICC) is designed to prevent impunity for human rights crimes, genocide, war crimes, and crimes against humanity. The ICC was based on the models and experience of the *Nuremberg Tribunal,* the *International Tribunal for the Former Yugoslavia,* and the *International Criminal Tribunal for Rwanda.*

The ICC was created in 1998 when 120 States adopted the *Rome Statute of the International Criminal Court* setting forth the jurisdiction and functions of the Court. By April 11, 2002 the Rome Statute obtained the requisite number of ratifications, and entered into force on July 1, 2002. Within fifteen months the state parties to the Rome Statute adopted the Rules of Procedure and Evidence, Elements of Crimes, and Agreement on Privileges and Immunities, and elected the Court's 18 judges.

The ICC is intended to be complementary to States' national systems for prosecuting war crimes and human rights violations and its jurisdiction is limited to "the most serious crimes of concern to the international community as a whole" (Rome Statute, Article 1). The Statute sets forth the following four crimes over which the ICC may exercise jurisdiction: (1) genocide; (2) crimes against humanity; (3) war crimes; and (4) the crime of aggression against another state. The ICC may not, however, exercise jurisdiction over crimes of aggression until members of the Court adopt a satisfactory definition of the crime and set out conditions for the Court's exercise of jurisdiction for this crime (Article 5.2). Until this is accomplished the ICC's jurisdiction is limited to 1-3.

The Rome Statute creates an independent Office of the Prosecutor who is responsible for receiving petitions, conducting investigations, and prosecuting the gravest international crimes (Articles 34, 42). The Prosecutor may accept referrals made by State Parties or by the United Nations Security Council, and may also accept information about crimes from individuals and nongovernmental organizations. Furthermore, the ICC may only exercise its authority when either "the State in which the crime was committed (the 'territorial State') or the State of which the accused is a national (the 'State of nationality') is a party to the Statute or has specifically accepted the jurisdiction of the Court".

The United States has refused to ratify the ICC, and it is unclear whether this will prevent the ICC from being fully effective. Both the Clinton and George W. Bush administrations had reservations about turning decisions to prosecute international crimes over to an independent prosecutor rather than keeping such decisions within the Security Council. The underlying worry, no doubt, was that U.S. officials and soldiers would be possible targets of politically motivated prosecutions.

PROMOTION OF HUMAN RIGHTS BY STATES

Perhaps the most important role that states play in international human rights law is in defining and establishing that law by creating and ratifying human rights treaties. Treaties are generally authored by committees of state representatives, and they are ratified by executive and legislative consent at the national level. Once a treaty is established, states help give it life by creating domestic legislation to implement it, conforming their conduct to its norms, and using it has a standard for domestic and international evaluation and criticism.

Article 56 of the United Nations Charter obligates member states to take "joint and separate action" for the achievement of United Nations purposes of observance of human rights and fundamental freedoms for all. Individual efforts take several forms, including the incorporation of international human rights documents into domestic law and state actions attempting to resolve human rights crises in other countries.

Within a country, means of promoting international human rights include incorporating international norms into a state's constitution and criminal law; creating limits on federalism, such as subordinating localities to the federal government; and, promoting human rights through propaganda and education. Perhaps the most basic method is enforcement through law at the national level. For example, to comply with the Genocide Convention a country must make genocide a crime within its own legal system. Much international law is obeyed because its norms have been incorporated into the legal systems of countries (Hathaway 2005). Since the end of the Cold War, numerous states have formulated new or revised constitutions that include human rights. A sampling of these states includes Romania (1991), Slovenia (1991), Congo (1992), Lithuania (1992), Albania (1993), Russian Federation (1993), Moldova (1994), Tunisia (1995), Cameroon (1996), and Poland (1997) (Alston 1999).

A recent example of the incorporation in domestic law of international norms is found in the United Kingdom Human Rights Act of 1998. The Act protects rights similar to the ones in the European Convention on Human Rights, including the right to life, liberty, security and a fair trial, and the prohibition of torture, slavery, forced labor. Here the state uses its own internal legal system to enforce human rights norms. A resident of the UK, instead of having to go to the European Court of Human Rights located in Strasbourg, France, can bring a human rights claim to local courts or tribunals. By imposing international and domestic obligations, self-enforcement measures ultimately serve as an in-house check on governments to ensure compliance with their human rights obligations.

Another mechanism for state promotion of human rights is the creation of national human rights commissions. Their functions include educating people on human rights, promoting human rights, and advising local governments about human rights. Representatives of state commissions may even participate in annual United Nations human rights sessions, enabling a state's human rights problems or successes to receive attention at the international level. Countries with national human rights commissions include Australia, Canada, Fiji, India, Ireland, Mexico, Nepal, the Philippines, and Uganda, to name a few.

States often take actions, unilaterally or together with other states, intended to promote and protect human rights in other countries. For example, in the late 1990s Australia led the military effort to restore peace and respect for human rights in East Timor. A new crisis erupted in 2006 and Australia, Portugal, New Zealand, and Malaysia again sent troops to suppress the violence. States use diplomacy, publishing reports and statements, conditioning access to trade or aid on human rights improvements, economic sanctions, and military intervention to promote human rights in other countries.

Humanitarian intervention is the use of force by one state to prevent or stop gross human rights violations and other humanitarian disasters in another state (Teson 2005). Obviously, military intervention conflicts with the idea of non-intervention, a cornerstone of international law. Non-intervention discourages the use of force against the political and territorial sovereignty of states, and in doing so promotes international peace and security. Perhaps humanitarian intervention, like self-defense, is an exception to the principle of non-intervention.

There is always the risk of a state pursuing its own foreign policy goals under the guise of "humanitarian intervention." This issue is currently being debated over the United States' intervention in Iraq (See *Human Rights Watch: The War in Iraq: Not a Humanitarian Intervention.* War can be rationalized by calling it "humanitarian intervention" and emphasizing high-minded motives.

Still, there are situations in which military intervention is the only possible means of ending a consistent pattern of gross human rights violations. Humanitarian intervention relies on the presumption that sovereign nations have an obligation to respect fundamental human rights. When state officials perpetrate human rights crimes and the government fails to bring them to justice, the responsibility of the international community is triggered. International organizations have been widely criticized for failing to intervene early and decisively during the genocide in Rwanda.

Efforts by states help to add real power to the international human rights system. The countries of Western Europe, Canada, Australia, and the United States, have been the historic pillars of the human rights establishment. They have lent their considerable support and clout to the system, keeping it going during hard times and helping it expand and flourish in better times. Although they have human rights problems of their own and have not always risen to the challenge of human rights emergencies, they have sometimes provided military and peacekeeping forces at considerable cost to themselves in money and lives. They have often worked closely with the Security Council in these efforts. They do not, however, have a standing legal commitment to do this, except their commitment under the UN Charter to support the actions of the Security Council.

Non-governmental Organizations

Nongovernmental organizations such as Human Rights Watch and Doctors Without Borders are extremely active at the international level in the areas of human rights, war crimes, and humanitarian aid. Nongovernmental organizations (NGOs) allow for collaborations between local and global efforts for human rights by "translating complex international issues into activities to be undertaken by concerned citizens in their own community". The functions of international NGOs include investigating complaints, advocacy with governments and international governmental organizations, and policy making. Local activities including fundraising, lobbying, and general education.

Although they do not have the authority to implement or enforce international law, NGOs have several advantages to state organizations in the human rights system. Much of their work includes information processing and fact finding, in which NGOs educate people about their human rights and gather information regarding human rights abuses in violating countries. In this process NGOs have the benefit of access to local people and organizations and are often able to get direct and indirect access to critical information about current human rights violations. Once they gather information, NGOs can design campaigns to educate the international community of these abuses.

A key function of NGOs is advocacy — urging support for human rights and attempting to influence governments or international groups with regard to specific actions. Advocacy involves education, persuasion, public exposure, criticism and provoking specific responses to human rights abuses. Representatives of NGOs are seen everywhere in the international human rights system. Many international human rights NGOs attend and often participate in the meetings of UN human rights bodies. They provide information about human rights situations through their reports and testimony. They shape the agendas, policies, and treaties of the UN through participation and lobbying (Korey 1998). Notable examples include NGO involvement in the development of the Universal Declaration of Human Rights and the UN Declaration on Torture and Other Cruel, Inhuman or Degrading Treatment.

NGOs with affiliates around the world include Amnesty International, Human Rights Watch, the International Commission of Jurists, the International Federation of Human Rights, Minority Group Rights, Doctors without Borders, and Oxfam. Besides these high profile NGOs there are thousands of local and national organizations working on human rights issues. For a comprehensive list of such organizations see *Non-governmental Organizations Research Guide.*

THE FUTURE OF HUMAN RIGHTS LAW

A person who has read the foregoing account of human rights law may wonder whether it has made any difference. If so much international human rights law exists, why is the world such a mess?

A simple answer with much truth in it is that the world's human rights problems are large and deeply entrenched, and that human rights law and organizations are, by comparison, not very strong — particularly within the United Nations. Countries with the worst human rights records often do not much participate in the UN system (for example, one forth of the world's countries have not ratified the Civil and Political Covenant), and many others participate in a formal and hypocritical way.

Regional systems, particularly in Europe and the Americas, do somewhat better. They have their own human rights courts, are more powerful, and enjoy more serious and sincere participation by many (but not all) of their members.

The first 50 years of the human rights movement were handicapped by the Cold War. With that handicap removed, the 1990s were a period of growth and improvement in human rights law and institutions. The period since 2001 has seen a preoccupation with terrorism that has taken much attention and energy away from other human rights problems.

Success in promoting human rights requires hard-to-achieve success in other areas including building more capable, responsive, efficient, and non-corrupt governments, dealing with failed states, increasing economic productivity (to pay for the protections and services that human rights require), improving the power and status of women, improving education, and managing international tensions and conflicts. Realizing human rights worldwide is a project for centuries, not decades.

Still, there are some grounds for optimism. Human rights are more widely accepted than they have ever been. They have become part of the currency of international relations, and most countries participate in the human rights system. Treaty arrangements help encourage and pressure countries to deal with their human rights problems. The human rights project continues and has not failed.

TWELVE

Human Rights in India

The Universal Declaration of Human Rights inspired Constitutions of those states which emerged after its adoption.Universal Declaration of Human Rights was adopted at the time when Indian Constitution was being drafted and hence almost all the rights enumerated in the declaration finds a place in the fundamental rights; justiciable or non-justiciable. However, in India the Human Rights or Civil liberties have their own history. It has its origin in the national movement. Granting of some basic rights to people was one of the objectives of national movement. The Swaraj Bill of India, 1895 spoke about freedom of speech, right to privacy and equality, right of franchise and punishment for specific offences only. The constitutions of India Bill 1895 contained provisions about the rights of citizens. It contains freedom of speech, equality before law, personal liberty, free education from the State etc.

There was a gradual broadening of the sphere of the rights of the citizens. They were no longer confined to political rights but comprise other civil rights too. They were not yet called fundamental rights. The Congress Resolution on Self determination contains as a first step in the practical application the principle of self determination in India, free speech and freedom from arbitrary arrest etc. The *Common Wealth of India Bill,* 1925 which was drafted and signed by prominent Indian political leaders was sent to the Labour Party of England introduced in Parliament contained rights of citizens. This document, for the first time gave the name 'Fundamental Rights' to the rights of citizens. It provided for personal liberty, freedom of conscience, freedom of speech and assembly, free elementary education, right to use roads, public places etc., equality before law and no discrimination on the ground of the sex. The Constitution recommended in the *Nehru Committee Report (1928)* contained a complete chapter on fundamental rights. It enlisted a number of rights like earlier documents and reiterated personal liberty, freedom of religion, freedom of speech and assembly, free elementary education, equality before law etc. It made a marked advance by incorporating social welfare provisions in the Fundamental Rights. It impose a duty on Parliament to make laws for the maintenance of health and fitness for work of all citizens securing of a living wage for every worker the protection of Motherhood, welfare of children and economic consequences of old age, infirmity and unemployment.

The national leaders continued their struggle for fundamental rights. Now, the content of fundamental rights came to include within its ambit the economic emancipation of the masses. The Resolution of Karachi Congress, 1931 is a very important document from this point of view. It formulates fundamental rights integrated with economic programme. It provided for a living wage for industrial workers, limited hours of labour, healthy conditions of work, protection against economic consequences of old age, sickness and unemployment, labour to be freed from Serfdom or Conditions bordering on Serfdom; protection of women workers and specially adequate provisions for leave during maternity period: prohibition against employment of children of school going age in factories etc. It included also a number of provisions regarding school welfare and upliftment. The declarations were reiterated in subsequent resolutions of the Congress.

With the passage of time, the content of Fundamental Rights came to include within its ambit the economic emancipation of the masses. The *Resolution of Karachi Congress, 1931* is a very important document from this point of view. It formulated fundamental rights integrated with economic programme. It contained provisions for a living wage for industrial workers, limited hours of labour, healthy conditions of work, protection against economic consequences of old age, sickness and unemployment, labour to be freed from Serfdom or Conditions bordering on Serfdom; protection of women workers and specially adequate provisions for leave during maternity period: prohibition against employment of children of school going age in factories etc. It also included a number of provisions regarding social welfare and upliftment. The declarations were reiterated in subsequent resolutions of the Congress.

However, the fundamental rights did not find place in the *Government of India Act,* 1935. But the demand for the fundamental rights continued to be made. The Act of 1935 was declared unacceptable by almost all the political parties. The demand for convening a constituent assembly for framing a Constitution for India grew and demand that fundamental rights should form a part of Constitution was emphasized. The Constitutional proposal of the Sapru Committee contained very forceful arguments in support of the incorporation of fundamental rights in Indian Constitution. Ultimately, power was transferred to a national government and a Constituent Assembly was formed for framing a constitution. The attainment of Socio economic justice also became an important objective to be acheived by the nation.

This Charter reflects India's Spirit to promote and guarantee human rights and fundamental Rights without distinction. Indian Constitution also provides for an effective machinery for the enforcement of fundamental rights. If a fundamental right is interfered by the executive or by a Federal or State Law, any person entitled to the right can move the Supreme Court to get the Executive act or Law declared unconstitutional Initially the attitude of judiciary in India towards the Directive Principles was not favourable and it had nullified many important legislations embodying socio-economic reforms. However, with the passage of time, there has been a shift in the attitude of the Indian judiciary towards socio-economic rights contained in part IV of the Indian constitution. The court felt the necessity of a change in its earlier outlook.

In India a number of welfare measures have been introduced, for instance, *Employees Provident Fund Act and Miscellaneous Provisions Act, 1952, Drugs and Cosmetics Act, Consumer Protection Act, 1986, The Criminal Procedure Code 1973* has been amended for giving fair trial to the criminals and limiting pre-trial of the confinement detention. Capital punishment though not abolished has been restricted to exceptional cases of inhuman murders.

India is the greatest champion of the Human Rights in the third world. However, the fact remains that there is a wide gap between theory and practice. It should not be forgotten that the emphasis in the Indian Constitution is on the individual citizen and not on the States. The guaranteed human rights have a definite purpose of saving executive arbitrariness and tyrannical conduct. The Supreme Court, the highest Court of the land, is the final interpreter and guardian of the Constitution and of the fundamental human rights of the people. In the course of its functioning for about half a century, the Supreme Court of India had many opportunities to elucidate the scope, amplitude and mode of operation of its power of judicial review, especially under Article 21 of the Constitution. It is to be pointed out that the Supreme Court's opinion have not displayed that consistency which one usually expects from the highest judicial organs in the country.

The framers of the Constitution of India adopted American pattern of incorporating the Bill of Rights in the Constitution itself. Prior to independence of India, *The Swaraj Bill of India, 1895* contained provisions about the freedom of Speech and expression, right of equality etc. It was felt by the political leaders that the human rights should be given priority so as to take cognizance of human dignity. Fundamental Rights drafted on the basis of the basic human rights were included by the framers of the Constitution in Part II so as to ensure that every individual, in general and every citizen, in particular should be conferred with some basic rights in accordance with the basic norms of democratic country which should not be withdrawn. On the basis of working experience of the Constitution of India till date, it could be safely commented that basic human rights incorporated in Part III dealing with Fundamental Rights have been considered to sacrosanct and inviolable by all the political parties who had been in power except during the brief period of emergency from 1975 to 1977, which witnessed suspension of Fundamental Rights and resulted in commission of wide spread attackes by government instrumentalities.

In order to achieve this and other objectives, the Constitution laid down various right in Parts III and IV which are known as Fundamental Rights and Directive Principles of State Policy respectively. While the former guarantees certain rights to the individuals, latter gives direction to the State to provide some other rights to its people in specified matters. Directive, though not enforceable before the Courts, are not to be regarded inferior to the fundamental rights. The Constitution under Article

37 lays down that the provisions contained in this part shall not be enforceable by any Court. But the principles laid down therein are nevertheless fundamental in governance of the country. It shall be the duty of the State to apply these principles in making laws. It may be stated that fundamental rights and directive principles together constitute the conscience of the Constitution. In Keshvanand Bharti V. State of Kerala, Chandrachud, J. observed that our constitution aims at bringing about a synthesis between fundamental rights and the Directive Principles of State Policy by giving to the former place of pride and to the latter a place of permanence.

FUNDAMENTAL RIGHTS IN INDIAN CONSTITUTION

When India obtained independence on 15 August 1947, the task of developing a constitution for the nation was undertaken by the *Constituent Assembly of India,* composing of elected representatives under the presidency of Rajendra Prasad. While members of Congress composed of a large majority, Congress leaders appointed persons from diverse political backgrounds to responsibilities of developing the constitution and national laws. Notably, *Bhimrao Ramji Ambedkar* became the chairperson of the drafting committee, while *Jawaharlal Nehru* and *Sardar Vallabhbhai Patel* became chairpersons of committees and sub-committees responsible for different subjects. A notable development during that period having significant effect on the Indian constitution took place on 10 December 1948 when the *United Nations General Assembly* adopted the *Universal Declaration of Human Rights* and called upon all member states to adopt these rights in their respective constitutions. The fundamental rights were included in the First Draft Constitution (February 1948), the Second Draft Constitution (17 October 1948) and final Third Draft

Constitution (26 November 1949) prepared by the *Drafting Committee.*

Preamble to the constitution, India's fundamental and supreme law is a brief introductory statement that set out the guiding principles of the constitution. The preamble is not an integral part of the Indian Constitution in the sense that it is enforceable in a court of law, however, Supreme Court of India has, in the Kesavananda case, recognised that preamble may be used to interpret ambiguous areas of the constitution where differing interpretation present themselves. However, the preamble is useful as an interpretive tool only if there is an ambiguity in the article itself and should not be treated as a right best owing part of the constitution.

As originally exacted the preamble described the state as a "sovereign democratic republic". In 1976 the Forty-second Amendment changed to read "sovereign socialist secular democratic republic".

Preamble of the Indian Constitution

WE, THE PEOPLE OF INDIA, having solemnly resolved India into a *Soverign Socialist Secular Democratic Republic* and to secure to all its citizen :

JUSTICE, social, economic and political;

LIBERTY OF THOUGHT, expression, belief, faith and worship.

EQUALITY, of status and of opportunity;

and to promote among them all.

FRATERNITY assuring the dignity of the individual and the unity and integrity of the Nation; IN OUR CONSTITUENT ASSEMBLY this twenty six day of November, 1949 do HEREBY ADOPT, ENACT AND GIVE TO OURSELVES THIS CONSTITUTION.

The Fundamental Rights and Directive Principles of State Policy are sections of the constitution that prescribe the fundamental obligations of the state to its citizens and the duties of the citizens to the state. These sections comprise a constitutional bill of Rights for government policy-making and behaviour and conduct of the citizens. These sections are considered vital elements of the constitution, which was developed between 1947 and 1949 by the constituent assembly and adopted on Twenty-sixth of January 1950.

Fundamental Rights in India Constitution

The Fundamental Rights are defined as basic human rights of all citizens. These rights, defined in Part III of the constitution, apply irrespective of race, place of birth, religion, caste creed or gender. They are enforceable by the courts subject to some restrictions.

Significance and characteristics of Fundamental Rights

The fundamental rights were included in the constitution because they were considered essential for the development of the personality of every individual and to preserve human dignity. The writers of the constitution regarded democracy of no avail if civil liberties, like freedom of speech and religion were not recognized and protected by the State. According to them, "democracy" is, in essence, a government by opinion and therefore, the means of formulating public opinion should be secured to the people of a democratic nation. For this purpose, the constitution guaranteed to all the citizens of India the freedom of speech and expression and various other freedoms in the form of the fundamental rights.

All people, irrespective of race, religion, caste or sex, have been given the right to move the *Supreme Court* and the *High Courts* for the enforcement of their fundamental rights. It is not necessary that the aggrieved party has to be the one to do so. Poverty stricken people may not have the means to do so and therefore, in the public interest, anyone can commence litigation in the court on their behalf. This is known as *"Public interest litigation"*. In some cases,

High Court judges have acted on their own on the basis of newspaper reports.

These fundamental rights help not only in protection but also the prevention of gross violations of human rights. They emphasize on the fundamental unity of India by guaranteeing to all citizens the access and use of the same facilities, irrespective of background. Some fundamental rights apply for persons of any nationality whereas others are available only to the citizens of India. The right to life and personal liberty is available to all people and so is the right to freedom of religion. On the other hand, *freedoms of speech* and *expression* and freedom to reside and settle in any part of the country are reserved to citizens alone, including *non-resident Indian citizens*. The right to equality in matters of public employment cannot be conferred to *overseas citizens of India*.

Fundamental rights primarily protect individuals from any arbitrary state actions, but some rights are enforceable against individuals. For instance, the Constitution abolishes *untouchability* and also prohibits begar (forced labour). These provisions act as a check both on state action as well as the action of private individuals. However, these rights are not absolute or uncontrolled and are subject to reasonable restrictions as necessary for the protection of general welfare. They can also be selectively curtailed. The Supreme Court has ruled that all provisions of the Constitution, including fundamental rights can be amended. However, the *Parliament* cannot alter the basic structure of the constitution. Features such as *secularism* and *democracy* fall under this category. Since the fundamental rights can only be altered by a *constitutional amendment*, their inclusion is a check not only on the *executive branch* but also on the *Parliament* and state legislatures.

A *state of national emergency* has an adverse effect on these rights. Under such a state, the rights conferred by Article 19 (freedoms of speech, assembly and movement, etc.) remain suspended. Hence, in such a situation, the legislature may make laws which go against the rights given in Article 19. Also, the *President* may by order suspend the right to move court for the enforcement of other rights as well.

Right to Equality

Right to equality is an important right provided for in Articles 14, 15, 16, 17 and 18 of the constitution. It is the principal foundation of all other rights and liberties, and guarantees the following :

- ***Equality before law :*** Article 14 of the constitution guarantees that all citizens shall be equally protected by the laws of the country. It means that the State cannot discriminate against a citizen on the basis of caste, creed, colour, sex, religion or place of birth. According to the *Electricity Act* of 26 January 2003 the Parliament has the power to create special courts for the speedy trial of offences committed by persons holding high offices. Creation of special courts is not a violation of this right.

- ***Social equality and equal access to public areas :*** Article 15 of the constitution states that no person shall be discriminated on the basis of caste, colour, language etc. Every person shall have equal access to public places like public parks, museums, wells, bathing ghats and temples etc. However, the State may make any special provision for women and children. Special provisions may be made for the advancements of any socially or educationally backward class or *scheduled castes* or *scheduled tribes*.

- ***Equality in matters of public employment :*** Article 16 of the constitution lays down that the State cannot discriminate against anyone in the matters of employment. All citizens can apply for government jobs. There are some exceptions. The Parliament may enact a law stating that certain jobs can only be filled by applicants who are domiciled in the area. This may be meant for posts that require knowledge of the locality and language of the area.

The State may also reserve posts for members of backward classes, scheduled castes or scheduled tribes which are not adequately represented in the services under the State to bring up the weaker sections of the society. Also, there a law may be passed which requires that the holder of an office of any religious institution shall also be a person professing that particular religion. According to the *Citizenship (Amendment) Bill,* 2003, this right shall not be conferred to *Overseas citizens of India.*

- ***Abolition of untouchability :*** Article 17 of the constitution abolishes the practice of *untouchability.* Practice of untouchability is an offense and anyone doing so is punishable by law. The *Untouchability Offences Act* of 1955 (renamed to *Protection of Civil Rights Act* in 1976) provided penalties for preventing a person from entering a place of worship or from taking water from a tank or well.

- ***Abolition of Titles*** **:** Article 18 of the constitution prohibits the State from conferring any titles. Citizens of India cannot accept titles from a foreign State. The British government had created an aristocratic class known as *Rai Bahadurs* and *Khan Bahadurs* in India — these titles were also abolished. However, *Military* and *academic* distinctions can be conferred on the citizens of India. The awards of *Bharat Ratna* and *Padma Vibhushan* cannot be used by the recipient as a title and do not, accordingly, come within the constitutional prohibition". The Supreme Court, on 15 December 1995, upheld the validity of such awards.

Right to Freedom

The Constitution of India contains the right to freedom, given in articles 19, 20, 21 and 22, with the view of guaranteeing individual rights that were considered vital by the framers of the constitution. The right to freedom in Article 19 guarantees the following six freedoms :

- *Freedom of speech* and *expression,* which enable an individual to participate in public activities. The phrase, *"freedom of press"* has not been used in Article 19, but freedom of expression includes freedom of press. Reasonable restrictions can be imposed in the interest of public order, security of State, decency or morality.

- Freedom to assemble peacefully without arms, on which the State can impose reasonable restrictions in the interest of public order and the sovereignty and integrity of India.

- Freedom to form associations or unions on which the State can impose reasonable restrictions on this freedom in the interest of public order, morality and the sovereignty and integrity of India.

- Freedom to move freely throughout the territory of India though reasonable restrictions can be imposed on this right in the interest of the general public, for example, restrictions may be imposed on movement and travelling, so as to control *epidemics.*

- Freedom to reside and settle in any part of the territory of India which is also subject to reasonable restrictions by the State in the interest of the general public or for the protection of the *scheduled tribes* because certain safeguards as are envisaged here seem to be justified to protect indigenous and tribal peoples from exploitation and coercion. *Article 370* restricts citizens from other Indian states and Kashmiri women who marry men from other states from purchasing land or *property* in Jammu and Kashmir.

- Freedom to practice any profession or to carry on any occupation, trade or business on which the State may impose reasonable restrictions in the interest of the general public. Thus, there is no right to carry on a business which is dangerous or immoral. Also, professional or technical qualifications may be prescribed for practicing any profession or carrying on any trade.

The constitution also guarantees the right to life and personal liberty, which in turn cites specific provisions in which these rights are applied and enforced :

- Protection with respect to conviction for offences is guaranteed in the right to life and personal liberty. According to Article 20, no one can be awarded punishment which is more than what the law of the land prescribes at that time. This legal axiom is based on the principle that no criminal law can be made retrospective, that is, for an act to become an offence, the essential condition is that it should have been an offence legally at the time of committing it. Moreover, no person accused of any offence shall be compelled to be a witness against himself. "Compulsion" in this article refers to what in law is called *"Duress"* (injury, beating or unlawful imprisonment to make a person do something that he does not want to do). This article is known as a safeguard against self incrimination. The other principle enshrined in this article is known as the principle of *double jeopardy,* that is, no person can be convicted twice for the same offence, which has been derived from Anglo Saxon law. This principle was first established in the *Magna Carta.*

- Protection of life and personal liberty is also stated under right to life and personal liberty. Article 21 declares that no citizen can be denied his life and liberty except by law. This means that a person's life and personal liberty can only be disputed if that person has committed a crime. However, the *right to life* does not include the *right to die* and hence, *suicide* or an attempt thereof, is an offence. (Attempted suicide being interpreted as a crime has seen many debates. The Supreme Court of India gave a landmark ruling in the year 1994. The court repealed section 309 of the Indian penal code, under which people attempting suicide could face prosecution and prison terms of up to one year." In the year 1996 however another Supreme Court ruling nullified the earlier one. "Personal liberty" includes all the freedoms which are not included in

Article 19 (that is, the six freedoms). The right to travel abroad is also covered under "personal liberty" in Article *21.*

• In 2002, through the 86th Amendment Act, Article 21 (A) was incorporated. It made the right to primary education part of the right to freedom, stating that the State would provide free and compulsory education to children from six to fourteen years of age. Six years after an amendment was made in the Indian Constitution, the union cabinet cleared the Right to Education Bill in 2008. It was tabled in Parliament for approval now it is fundamental right of every child to get free and compulsory education upto the age of 14 yrs.

• Rights of a person arrested under ordinary circumstances is laid down in the right to life and personal liberty. No one can be arrested without being told the grounds for his arrest. If arrested, the person has the right to defend himself by a *lawyer* of his choice. Also an arrested citizen has to be brought before the nearest *magistrate* within 24 hours. The rights of a person arrested under ordinary circumstances are not available to an enemy alien. They are also not available to persons detained under the *Preventive Detention Act.* Under *preventive detention*, the government can imprison a person for a maximum of three months. It means that if the government feels that a person being at liberty can be a threat to the law and order or to the unity and integrity of the nation, it can detain or arrest that person to prevent him from doing this possible harm. After three months such a case is brought before an advisory board for review.

The constitution also imposes restrictions on these rights. The government restricts these freedoms in the interest of the independence, sovereignty and integrity of India. In the interest of morality and public order, the government can also impose restrictions. However, the right to life and personal liberty cannot be suspended. The six freedoms are also automatically suspended or have restrictions imposed on them during a state of emergency.

Right against Exploitation

Child labour and *Begar* is prohibited under Right against exploitation. The right against exploitation, given in Articles 23 and 24, provides for two provisions, namely the abolition of trafficking in human beings and Begar (forced labor), and abolition of employment of children below the age of 14 years in dangerous jobs like factories and mines. *Child_labour* is considered a gross violation of the spirit and provisions of the constitution. Begar, practised in the past by landlords, has been declared a crime and is punishable by law. Trafficking in humans for the purpose of slave *trade* or *prostitution* is also prohibited by law. An exception is made in employment without payment for compulsory services for public purposes. Compulsory military *conscription* is covered by this provision.

Right to Freedom of Religion

Right to freedom of religion, covered in Articles 25, 26, 27 and 28, provides *religious freedom* to all citizens of India. The objective of this right is to sustain the principle of *secularism* in India. According to the Constitution, all religions are equal before the State and no religion shall be given preference over the other. Citizens are free to preach, practice and propagate any religion of their choice.

Religious communities can set up charitable institutions of their own. However, activities in such institutions which are not religious are performed according to the laws laid down by the government. Establishing a charitable institution can also be restricted in the interest of public order, morality and health. No person shall be compelled to pay taxes for the promotion of a particular religion. A State run institution cannot impart education that is pro-religion. Also, nothing in this article shall affect the operation of any existing law or prevent the State from making any further law regulating or restricting any economic, financial, political or other secular activity which may be associated with religious practice, or providing for social welfare and reform.

Cultural and Educational Rights

As India is a country of many languages, religions, and *cultures,* the Constitution provides special measures, in Articles 29 and 30, to protect the rights of the minorities. Any community which has a language and a script of its own has the right to conserve and develop it. No citizen can be discriminated against for admission in State or State aided institutions.

All minorities, religious or linguistic, can set up their own educational institutions in order to preserve and develop their own culture. In granting aid to institutions, the State cannot discriminate against any institution on the basis of the fact that it is administered by a minority institution. But the right to administer does not mean that the State can not interfere in case of maladministration. In a precedent-setting judgment in 1980, the Supreme Court held that the State can certainly take regulatory measures to promote the efficiency and excellence of educational standards. It can also issue guidelines for ensuring the security of the services of the teachers or other employees of the institution. In another landmark judgement delivered on 31 October 2002, the Supreme Court ruled that in case of aided minority institutions offering professional courses, admission could only be through a common entrance test conducted by State or a university. Even an unaided minority institution ought not to ignore the merit of the students for admission.

Right to Constitutional Remedies

Right to constitutional remedies empowers the citizens to move a *court* of law in case of any denial of the fundamental rights. For instance, in case of imprisonment, the citizen can ask the court to see if it is according to the provisions of the law of the country. If the court finds that it is not, the person will have to be freed. This procedure of asking the courts to preserve or safeguard the citizens' fundamental rights can be done in various ways. The courts can issue various kinds of *writs.* These writs are *habeas corpus, mandamus, prohibition, quo warranto* and *certiorari*. When a national or state emergency is declared, this right is suspended by the central government.

AMENDMENTS

Changes to the fundamental rights require a *constitutional amendment* which has to be passed by a special majority of both houses of Parliament. This means that an amendment requires the approval of two-thirds of the members present and voting. However, the number of members voting should not be less than the *simple majority* of the house — whether the *Lok Sabha* or *Rajya Sabha*.

The right to education at elementary level has been made one of the fundamental rights under the *Eighty-Sixth Amendment* of 2002.

Right to Property

The Constitution originally provided for the *right to property* under Articles 19 and 31. Article 19 guaranteed to all citizens the right to acquire, hold and dispose off property. Article 31 provided that "no person shall be deprived of his property save by authority of law." It also provided that compensation would be paid to a person whose property has been taken for public purposes.

The provisions relating to the right to property were changed a number of times. The *Forty-Forth Amendment* of 1978 deleted the right to property from the list of fundamental rights. A new provision, Article 300-A, was added to the constitution which provided that "no person shall be deprived of his property save by authority of law". Thus if a legislature makes a law depriving a person of his property, there would be no obligation on the part of the State to pay anything as compensation. The aggrieved person shall have no right to move the court under Article 32. Thus, the right to property is no longer a fundamental right, though it is still a constitutional right. If the government appears to have acted unfairly, the action can be challenged in a court of law by citizens.

The liberalisation of the economy and the government's initiative to set up special economic zones has led to many protests by farmers and have led to calls for the reinstatement of the fundamental right to private property. The Supreme Court has sent a notice to the government questioning why the right should not be brought back. As in 2007 the Supreme Court unanimously said that the fundamental rights are a basic structure of the constitution and cannot be removed or diluted.

Right to Education

On 1 April 2010, India joined a group of few countries in the world, with a historic law making education a fundamental right of every child coming into force. Making elementary education an entitlement for children in the 6-14 age group, the Right of Children to Free and Compulsory Education Act, 2009 will directly benefit children who do not go to school at present.

Prime Minister Manmohan Singh announced the operationalisation of the Act. Children, who had either dropped out of schools or never been to any educational institution, will get elementary education as it will be binding on the part of the local and State governments to ensure that all children in the 6-14 age group get schooling. As per the Act, private educational institutions should reserve 25 per cent seats for children from the weaker sections of society. The Centre and the States have agreed to share the financial burden in the ratio of 55:45, while the Finance Commission has given Rs. 25,000 crore to the States for implementing the Act. The Centre has approved an outlay of Rs. 15,000 crore for 2010-2011.

Right to Constitutional Remedies

The Right to Constitutional Remedies empowers citizens to approach the *Supreme Court of India* to seek enforcement, or protection against infringement, of their Fundamental Rights. Article 32 provides a guaranteed remedy, in the form of a Fundamental Right itself, for enforcement of all the other Fundamental Rights, and the Supreme Court is designated as the protector of these rights by the Constitution. The Supreme Court has been empowered to issue writs, namely *habeas corpus, mandamus, prohibition, certiorari* and *quo warranto,* for the enforcement of the Fundamental Rights, while the High Courts have been empowered under Article 226 - which is not a Fundamental Right in itself – to issue these *prerogative writs* even in cases not involving the violation of Fundamental Rights. The Supreme Court has the jurisdiction to enforce the Fundamental Rights even against private bodies, and in case of any violation, award compensation as well to the affected individual. Exercise of jurisdiction by the Supreme Court can also be *suo motu* or on the basis of a *public interest litigation.* This right cannot be suspended, except under the provisions of Article 359 when a state of emergency is declared.

CRITICAL ANALYSIS OF FUNDAMENTAL RIGHTS

The fundamental rights have been criticised for many reasons. Political groups have demanded that the *right to work,* the right to economic assistance in case of *unemployment,* old age, and similar rights be enshrined as constitutional guarantees to address issues of poverty and economic insecurity, though these provisions have been enshrined in the Directive Principles of State Policy. The right to freedom and personal liberty has a number of limiting clauses, and thus have been criticized for failing to check the sanctioning of powers often deemed "excessive". There is also the provision of preventive detention and suspension of fundamental rights in times of *Emergency.* The provisions of acts like the *Maintenance of Internal*

Security Act (MISA) and the *National Security Act* (NSA) are a means of countering the fundamental rights, because they sanction excessive powers with the aim of fighting internal and cross-border *terrorism* and political violence, without safeguards for civil rights. The phrases "security of State", "public order" and "morality" are of wide implication. People of alternate sexuality is criminalized in India with prison term up to 10 years. The meaning of phrases like "reasonable restrictions" and "the interest of public order" have not been explicitly stated in the constitution, and this ambiguity leads to unnecessary litigation. The freedom to assemble peacably and without arms is exercised, but in some cases, these meetings are broken up by the police through the use of non-fatal methods. *"Freedom* of *press"* has not been included in the right to freedom, which is necessary for formulating *public opinion* and to make *freedom* of *expression* more legitimated. Employment of child labour in hazardous job environments has been reduced, but their employment even in non-hazardous jobs, including their prevalent employment as domestic help violates the spirit and ideals of the *constitution*. More than 16.5 million children are employed and working in India. India was ranked 88 out of 159 in 2005, according to the degree to which *corruption* is perceived to exist among public officials and politicians worldwide. The right to equality in matters regarding public employment shall not be conferred to *Overseas citizens of India,* according to the *Citizenship (Amendment) Bill,* 2003.

DIRECTIVE PRINCIPLES OF STATE POLICY

The Directive Principles of State Policy are guidelines to the central and state governments of India, to be kept in mind while framing laws and policies. These provisions, contained in Part IV of the Constitution of India, are not enforceable by any court, but the principles laid down therein are considered fundamental in the governance of the country, making it the duty of the state to apply these principles in making laws to establish a just society in the country. The principles are inspired by the Directive Principles given in the constitution of Ireland and also by the Gandhian principles; and relate to social justice, economic welfare, foreign policy and legal and administrative matters.

Directive principles are classified under the following categories; Gandhian, economic and socialistic, political and administrative, justice and legal, environmental and protection of monuments and peace and security.

The Directive Principles of State Policy, embodied in Part IV of the Constitution, are directions given to the State to guide the establishment of an economic and social democracy, as proposed by the *Preamble*. They set forth the *humanitarian* and *socialist* instructions that were the aim of social revolution envisaged in India by the Constituent Assembly. The State is expected to keep these principles in mind while framing laws and policies, even though they are *non-justiciable* in nature. The Directive Principles may be classified under the following categories: ideals that the State ought to strive towards achieving; directions for the exercise of legislative and executive power; and rights of the citizens which the State must aim towards securing.

Despite being non-justiciable, the Directive Principles act as a check on the State; theorised as a yardstick in the hands of the electorate and the opposition to measure the performance of a government at the time of an election.

Article 37, while stating that the Directive Principles are not enforceable in any court of law, declares them to be "fundamental to the governance of the country" and imposes an obligation on the State to apply them in matters of legislation. Thus, they serve to emphasise the *welfare state* model of the Constitution and emphasise the positive duty of the State to promote the welfare of the people by affirming social, economic and political justice, as well as to fight *income inequality* and ensure individual dignity, as mandated by Article 38.

Article 39 lays down certain principles of policy to be followed by the State, including (Providing an adequate means of livelihood for all citizens, *equal pay for equal work* for men and women, proper working conditions, reduction of the concentration of wealth and means of production from the hands of a few, and distribution of community resources to "subserve the common good". These clauses highlight the Constitutional objectives of building an *egalitarian* social order and establishing a welfare state, by bringing about a social revolution assisted by the State, and have been used to support the *nationalisation* of mineral resources as well as public utilities. Further, several legislations pertaining to *agrarian reform* and *land tenure* have been enacted by the federal and state governments, in order to ensure equitable distribution of land resources.

Articles 41 – 43 mandate the State to endeavour to secure to all citizens the *right to work,* a *living wage, social security, maternity relief,* and a decent *standard* of *living.* These provisions aim at establishing a socialist state as envisaged in the Preamble. Article 43 also places upon the State the responsibility of promoting *cottage industries,* and the federal government has, in furtherance of this, established several Boards for the promotion of *khadi. handlooms* etc., in coordination with the state governments.

Article 39A requires the State to provide free *legal aid* to ensure that opportunities for securing justice are available to all citizens irrespective of economic or other disabilities.

Article 43A mandates the State to work towards securing the participation in the management of industries. The State, under Article 46, is also mandated to promote the interests of and work for the economic uplift of the *scheduled castes and scheduled tribes* and protect them from discrimination and exploitation. Several enactments, including two Constitutional amendments, have been passed to give effect to this provision.

Article 44 encourages the State to secure a *uniform civil code* for all citizens, by eliminating discrepancies between various *personal laws* currently in force in the country. However, this has remained a "dead letter" despite numerous reminders from the Supreme Court to implement the provision.

Article 45 originally mandated the State to provide free and compulsory education to children between the ages of six and fourteen years, but after the 86th Amendment in 2002, this has been converted into a Fundamental Right and replaced by an obligation upon the State to secure childhood care to all children below the age of six.

Article 47 commits the State to raise the standard of living and improve public health, and prohibit the consumption of *intoxicating* drinks and drugs injurious to health. As a consequence, partial or total *prohibition* has been introduced in several states, but financial constraints have prevented its full-fledged application.

The State is also mandated by Article 48 to organise agriculture and *animal husbandry* on modern and scientific lines by improving breeds and *prohibiting slaughter of cattle*. Article 48A mandates the State to *protect the environment* and safeguard the forests and wildlife of the country, while Article 49 places an obligation upon the State to ensure the preservation of monuments and objects of national importance.

Article 50 requires the State to ensure the separation of judiciary from executive in public services, in order to ensure *judicial independence* and federal legislation has been enacted to achieve this objective.

The State, according to Article 51, must also strive for the promotion of international peace and security, and Parliament has been empowered under Article 253 to make laws giving effect to *international treaties*.

CRITICAL ANALYSIS OF DIRECTIVE PRINCIPLES OF STATE POLICY

Many critics have called Directive Principles of State Policy as not better than 'New Year Greetings'. Even the rational of inserting such high sounding promises has been questioned. It has been asserted that Directive are in the form of half wishes having no legal sanction behind them. Government is not bound to implement them. Critics point out :

1. Fewer children are now employed in hazardous environments, but their employment in non-hazardous jobs, prevalently as domestic help, violates the spirit of the constitution in the eyes of many critics and human rights advocates. More than 16.5 million children are in employment.

2. India was ranked 88 out of 159 countries in 2005, according to the degree to which corruption is perceived to exist among public officials and politicians.

3. Corruption has now spread like wild fire, every where. Now corruption is eating the very vital nerve of the Nation.

4. The recent financial corruption in organising Common Wealth Games, is talk of the day and may give blow to National reputation.

5. The implementation of a *uniform civil code* for all citizens has not been achieved owing to widespread opposition from various religious groups and *political parties*. The *Shah Bano case* (1985-86) provoked a political firestorm in India when the Supreme Court ruled that *Shah Bano*, a Muslim woman who had been divorced by her husband in 1978 was entitled to receive *alimony* from her former husband under Indian law applicable for all Indian

women. This decision evoked outrage in the Muslim community, which sought the application of the *Muslim personal law* and in response the Parliament passed the Muslim Women (Protection of Rights on Divorce) Act, 1986 overturning the Supreme Court's verdict. This act provoked further outrage, as jurists, critics and politicians alleged that the fundamental right of equality for all citizens irrespective of religion or gender was being jettisoned to preserve the interests of distinct religious communities. The verdict and the legislation remain a source of heated debate, with many citing the issue as a prime example of the poor implementation of Fundamental Rights.

Despite all this, it can not be said that these principles are absolutely useless. They have their own ability and significance. The Directive Principles are just like a polestar that provide direction. Their basic aim is to persuade the government to provide social and economic justice in all spheres of life, keeping in view its limited material resources at the earliest possible. Many of them have been implemented very successfully. Actually no government can afford to ignore these instructions as they are the mirror of public opinion and also reflect the basic spirit of the Preamble of our Constitution. Some of the steps taken in this direction are being listed below:

1. Land reforms have been introduced and Jagirdari and Zamindari systems have been abolished.

2. There has been rapid industrialisation and tremendous increase in the agricultural production through Green Revolution.

3. National Commission for the Welfare of Women has been established.

4. Ceiling has been placed on land and property to fix the limit of person's holdings.

5. The privy purses of ex-princes have been abolished.

6. Life Insurance, General Insurance and most of the banks have been nationalised.

7. In order to reduce economic disparity, Right to Property has been deleted from the chapter on Fundamental Rights.

8. Subsidized public distribution schemes have been launched to help the poor people.

9. The rules require that both men and women are paid equal wages for equal work.

10. Untouchability has been abolished. Sincere efforts have been made for the upliftment of the SCs, STs and of other Backward Classes.

11. Through 73rd and 74th Amendments to the constitution (1991 & 1992 respectively), Panchayati Raj has been given the constitutional status with more powers.

12. One-third of the total number of seats have been reserved for women in Panchayats at every level; and in the case of *Bihar*, half the seats have been reserved for women.

13. Small scale and village industries and Khadi Gram Udyog have been encouraged to bring prosperity to the rural areas.

14. The year 1990-1991 was declared as the "Year of Social Justice" in the memory of B.R. Ambedkar. The government provides free textbooks to students belonging to scheduled castes and tribes pursuing medicine and engineering courses. During 2002-2003, a sum of Rs. 4.77 crore (47.7 million) was released for this purpose.

15. The *Equal Remuneration Act* of 1976 provides for equal pay for equal work for both men and women.

16. The *Sampoorna Grameen Rozgar Yojana* (Universal Rural Employment Programme) was launched in 2001 to attain the objective of providing gainful employment for the rural poor. The programme was implemented through the *Panchayati Raj institutions.*

17. The judiciary has been separated from the executive "in all the states territories except *Jammu and Kashmir* and *Nagaland.*"

18. India's foreign policy has been influenced by the Directive Principles. India supported the *United Nations* in peace-keeping activities, with the *Indian Army* having participated in 37 UN peace-keeping operations.

The above steps on the part of central and state governments indicate that many Directive Priciples of State Policy have been implemented to lay down the formations of a secular, socialistic welfare state. However, still there is long way to go to achieve all of them in full.

There are many hinderances in the non-implementation of Directive Principles of State Policy. The main reasons are – lack of political will among political parties, lack of awareness and organized action on the part of the people and limited material resources.

RELATIONSHIP BETWEEN THE FUNDAMENTAL RIGHTS, DIRECTIVE PRINCIPLES AND FUNDAMENTAL DUTIES

The Directive Principles have been used to uphold the Constitutional validity of legislation in case of a conflict with the fundamental rights Articles 31C, added by the 25th Amendment in 1971, provided that any law made to give effect to the Directive Principles in Article 39(b) – (c) would not be invalid on the grounds that they derogated from the Fundamental Rights conferred by Articles 14, 19 and 31.

The application of this article was sought to be extended to all the Directive Principles by the 42nd Amendment in 1976, but the Supreme Court struck down the extension as void on the ground that it violated the basic structure of the Constitution. The Fundamental Rights and Directive Principles have also been used together in forming the basis of legislation for *social welfare*. The Supreme Court, after the judgment in the *Kesavananda Bharati* case, has adopted the view of the Fundamental Rights and Directive Principles being complementary to each other, each supplementing the other's role in aiming at the same goal of establishing a welfare state by menas of social revolution. Similarly, the Supreme Court has used the Fundamental Duties to uphold the Constitutional validity of statutes which seeks to promote the objects laid out in the Fundamental Duties. These Duties have also been held to be obligatory for all citizens, subject to the State enforcing the same by means of a valid law. The Supreme Court has also issued directions to the State in this regard, with a view towards making the provisions effective and enabling a citizens to properly perform their duties.

Here we have defined the six fundamental rights as per the constitution of India:

1. *Right to Equality*
2. *Right to Particular Freedom*
3. *Cultural and Educational Rights*
4. *Right to Freedom of Religion*
5. *Right Against Exploitation and*
6. *Right to Constitutional Remedies*

Chronology of Human Rights in India

- 1829 - The practice of sati was formally abolished by *Governor General William Bentick* after years of campaigning *by Hindu reform movements* such as the

Brahmo Samaj of Ram Mohan Roy against this orthodox Hindu funeral custom of self-immolation of widows after the death of their husbands.

• 1929 - *Child Marriage Restraint Act,* prohibiting marriage of minors is passed.

• 1947 - India achieves *political independence* from the *British Raj.*

• 1950 - The *Constitution of India* establishes a sovereign *democratic republic* with universal adult franchise. Part 3 of the Constitution contains a *Bill of Fundamental Rights* enforceable by the Supreme Court and the High Courts. It also provides for reservations for previously disadvantaged sections in education, employment and political representation.

• 1952 - *Criminal Tribes Act* 1871 repealed by government, former "criminal tribes" categorized as *"denotified"* and *Habitual Offenders Act* (1952) enacted.

• 1955 - Reform of family law concerning Hindus gives more rights to Hindu women.

• 1958 -*Armed Forces (Special Powers) Act*, 1958

• 1973 - *Supreme Court of India* rules in *Kesavananda Bharati* that the basic structure of the Constitution (including many fundamental rights) is unalterable by a constitutional amendment.

• 1975-77 - *State of Emergency in India* - extensive rights violations took place.

• 1978 - SC rules in *Menaka Gandhi v. Union of India* that the right to life under Article 21 of the Constitution cannot be suspended even in an emergency.

• 1978-Jammu and Kashmir Public Safety Act, 1978.

• 1984 - *Operation Blue Star* and the subsequent 1984 *Anti-Sikh riots.*

• 1985-6 - The *Shah Bano* case, where the Supreme Court recognised the Muslim woman's right to maintenance upon divorce, sparks protests from Muslim clergy. To nullify the decision of the Supreme Court, the *Rajiv Gandhi* government enacted *The Muslim Women* (*Protection of Rights on Divorce*) *Act* 1986.

• 1989 - *Scheduled Caste and Scheduled Tribe (Prevention of Atrocities) Act, 1989* is passed.

• 1989-present - *Kashmiri insurgency* sees *ethnic cleansing* of *Kashmiri Pandits*, desecrating Hindu temples, killing of Hindus and Sikhs, and abductions of foreign tourists and government functionaries.

• 1992 - A constitutional amendment establishes *Local Self-Government (Panchayati Raj)* as a third tier of governance at the village level, with one-third of the seats reserved for women. Reservations were provided for scheduled castes and tribes as well.

• 1992 - *Babri Masjid* demolished by Hindu mobs, resulting in riots across the country.

• 1993 - *National Human Rights Commission* is established under the *Protection of Human Rights Act.*

• 2001 - Supreme Court passes extensive orders to implement the right to food.

• 2002 - Violence in Gujarat, targeting its Muslim minority, claims more than 2000 innocent lives.

• 2005 - A powerful *Right to Information Act* is passed to give citizen's access to information held by public authorities.

• 2005 - *National Rural Employment Guarantee Act (NREGA)* guarantees universal right to employment.

• 2006 - Supreme Court orders police reforms in response to the poor human rights record of Indian police.

• 2009 - *Delhi High Court* delcarės that *Section 377 of the Indian Penal Code,* which outlaws a range of unspecified "unnatural" sex acts, is unconstitutional when applied to homosexual acts between private consenting individuals, effectively decriminalising homosexual relationships in India.

THIRTEENTH

Universal Declaration of Human Rights and Constitution of India

It is to be noted that many of rights incorporated in the Universal Declaration of Human Rights find place in the Preamble of Indian Constitution. The resolve made in the preamble regarding rights of individuals finds elaborate expression in Part III i.e., the 'Fundamental Rights and in part IV i.e., Directive Principles of State Policy of Indian Constitution. India has not only incorporated an elaborate Bill of Right in her Constitution but efforts have been made to translate these into reality. We find that India has incorporated the elaborate provision of the Declaration of Human Rights, 1948 in the Constitution. The chart given hereinafter reflects that the spirit of providing for human rights pervaded the minds of the founding fathers of the Indian Constitution as much as it did the minds of the makers of Universal Declaration of Human rights 1948. It would be expedient to present a brief account of the "Fundamental Rights" and 'Directive Principles of State Policy' which go to guarantee, protect and secure human rights.

HUMAN RIGHTS VIS-A-VIS FUNDAMENTAL RIGHTS

This Charter reflects India's spirit to promote and guarantee human rights and fundamental rights without distinction. Indian Constitution also provides for an effective machinery for the enforcement of fundamental rights. If a fundamental right is interfered by the executive or by a Federal or State Law, any person entitled to the right can move the Supreme Court to get the Executive act or Law declared unconstitutional. Initially the attitude of judiciary in India towards the Directive Principles was not favourable and it had nullified many important legislations embodying socio-economic reforms. However, with the passage of time there has been a shift in the attitude of the Indian judiciary towards socio-economic rights contained in part IV of the Indian constitution. The court felt the necessity of a change in its earlier outlook.

In India a number of welfare measures have been introduced, for instance, *Employees Provident Fund Act and Miscellaneous Provisions Act, 1952, Drugs and Cosmetics Act, Consumer Protection Act, 1986, The Criminal Procedure Code 1973* has been amended for giving fair trial to the criminals and limiting pre-trial of the confinement detention. Capital punishment though not abolished has been restricted to exceptional cases of inhuman murders.

India is the greatest champion of the Human Rights in the third world. However, the fact remains that there is a wide gap between theory and practice. It should not be forgotten that the emphasis in the Indian Constitution is on the individual citizen and not on the States. The guaranteed human rights have a definite purpose of saving executive arbitrariness and tyrannical conduct. The Supreme Court, the highest Court of the land, is the final interpreter and guardian of the Constitution and of the fundamental human rights of the people. In the course of its functioning for about half a century, the Supreme Court of India had many opportunities to elucidate the scope, amplitude and mode of operation of its power of judicial review, especially under Article 21 of the Constitution. It is to be pointed out that the Supreme Court's opinion have not displayed that consistency which one usually expects from the highest judicial organs in the country.

The framers of the Constitution of India adopted American pattern of incorporating the Bill of Rights in the Constitution itself. Prior to Independence of India, *The Swaraj Bill of India, 1895* contained provisions about the freedom of Speech and expression, right of equality etc. It was felt by the political leaders that the human rights should be given priority so as to take cognizance of human dignity. Fundamental rights drafted on the basis of the basic human rights were included by the framers of the Constitution in Part II so as to ensure that every individual, in general and every citizen, in particular should be conferred with some basic rights in accordance with the basic norms of democratic country which should not be withdrawn. On the basis of working experience of the Constitution of India till date, it could be safely commented that basic human rights incorporated in Part III dealing with Fundamental Rights have been considered to be sacrosanct and inviolable by all the political parties who had been in power except during the brief period of emergency from 1975 to 1977, which witnessed suspension of Fundamental Rights and resulted in commission of wide spread attackes by government instrumentalities.

In order to achieve this and other objectives, the Constitution laid down various right in Parts III and IV which are known as Fundamental Rights and Directive Principles of State Policy respectively. While the former guarantees certain rights to the individuals, latter gives direction to the State to provide some other rights to its people in specified matters. Directive, though not enforceable before the Courts, are not to be regarded inferior to the fundamental rights. The Constitution under Article 37 lays down that the provisions contained in this part shall not be enforceable by any Court. But the principles laid down therein are nevertheless fundamental in governance of the country. It shall be the duty of the State to apply these principles in making laws. It may be stated that fundamental rights and directive principles together constitute the conscience of the Constitution. In *Keshvanand Bharti* V. *State of Kerala*, Chandrachud, J. observed that our constitution aims at bringing about a synthesis between fundamental rights and the Directive Principles of State Policy by giving to the former place of pride and to the latter a place of permanence.

India has ratified the International Covenant on Civil and Political Rights and International Covenant on Economic, Social and Cultural Rights. By ratification, it has been established on the international plane its consent to be bound by them. It has been obligation to provide to the individuals the rights contained in two covenants. A question arises as to how far the rights enshrined in the Covenants are consistent with the rights stipulated in the Constitution. The provisions of the two covenants are discussed separately with reference to the constitution of India.

Universal Declaration of Human Rights	*Provision of the Indian Constitution*
Art 1 : All men are born free and are equal in dignity and in their rights.	Art 14 : The State shall not deny to any person equality before the law or the equal protection of the laws within the territory of India.
Art 2 : No Discrimination on the ground of race, colour, sex, language, religion, birth.	Art 15 : The State shall not discriminate against any citizen on grounds only of religion, race,

Universal Declaration of Human Rights	*Provision of the Indian Constitution*
	caste, sex, place of birth or any of them.
Art 3 : Right to life.	Art 21 : No person shall be deprived of his life or personal liberty except according to procedure established by law.
Art 4 : No slavery.	Art 23 : Traffic in human beings and begar and other forms of forced labour are prohibited and any contravention of this provision shall be an offence punishable in accordance with law.
Art 5 : No torture, cruelty, inhuman or Degrading treatment.	Art 21 : *State of Maharashtra* vs. *Ravikant S. Patil*. (1991) 2 SCC 373. Handcuffing and parading of under trial prisoner was held violative of rights under Article 21. 3 SCC 161 and (1991) 4 SCC 177. Right to live with human dignity held to be enshrined in Article 21. *Maneka Gandhi* vs. *Union of India* (1978) 1 SCC 248. The expression "personal liberty" under Art. 21 is a phrase of wide amplitude and covers a variety of rights which go to constitute personal liberty of man including right to safety of his person.
Art 6 : Right to recognition everywhere as a person before the law.	Art 14 and 21

Universal Declaration of Human Rights	*Provision of the Indian Constitution*
Art 7 : Equality before law.	Art 14 :
Art 8 : Right to effective remedy.	Art 32 : 1. The rights to move the Supreme Court by appropriate proceedings for the enforcement of the rights conferred by part III of the Constitution is guaranteed. 2. Supreme Court shall issue directions or orders or writs, including writs in the nature of habeas corpus, mandamus, prohibition, quo warranto and certorari whichever may be appropriate, for the enforcement of any of the rights conferred by this part. Art 226 : Nowithstanding anything in Art 32, every High Court shall have power, throughout the territories in relation to which it exercises jurisdiction, to issue to any person or authority, including in appropriate cases, any Government, within those terrtories directions, orders or writs, including writs in the nature of habeas corpus, mandamus, prohibition, quowarranto and certiorari, or any of them, for the enforcement of any of the rights conferred by Part III and for any other purpose.
Art 9 : Arbitrary arrest and detention.	Art 22 : 1. No person who is arrested shall be detained in custody without being informed, as soon as may be, of the grounds

Universal Declaration of Human Rights	*Provision of the Indian Constitution*
	for such arrest nor shall he be denied the right to consult, and to be defended by, a legal practitioner of his choice. 2. Every person who is arrested and detained in custody shall be produced before the nearest magistrate within a period of twenty-four hours of such arrest excluding the time necessary for the journey from the place of arrest to the court of the magistrate and no such person shall be detained in custody beyond the said period without the authority of a magistrate.
Art 10 : Public hearing and fair trial.	Art 39 (A) : The State shall secure that the operation of the legal system promotes justice, on a basis of equal opportunity, and shall, in particular, provide free legal aid, by suitable legislation or schemes or any other way, to ensure that opportunities for securing justice are not denied to any citizen by reason of economic or other disabilities.
Art 11 : Presumption of innocence and Criminal Law until prove guilty in public trial. No retrospective declaration of offence nor retrospective objective of higher sentence by retrospective amendments.	Art 304 (CCP) : Where in a trial before the Court, the accused is not represented by a pleader, and where it appears to the Court that the accused has not sufficient means to engage a pleader, the Court shall assign a pleader for his defence at the expense of the State. Art 303 (CCP) : Any person accused of an offence before a

Universal Declaration of Human Rights	*Provision of the Indian Constitution*
	Criminal Court, or against whom proceedings are instituted under this Code, may of right be defened by a pleader of his choice. Art 327 (CCP) : The place in which any Criminal Court is held for the purpose of inquiring into or trying any offence shall be deemed to be an open Court, to which the public generally may have access, so far as the same can conveniently contain them. The principle of common Law, the Doctrine of Rule of Law, Presumption of innocence till guilt is established.
Art 12 : Privacy, family, home correspondence, reputation, protection of law against interference of force.	Art 20 : 1. No person shall be convicted of any offence except for violation of the law in force at the time of the commission of the act charged as an offence, nor be subjected to a penalty greater than that which might have been inflicted under the law in force at the time of the commission of the offence. Each one is conversed by the law enacted by Parliament and is protected.
Art 13 : (i) Freedom of Movement and Residence. (ii) Right live and return to country.	Art 19 : (d) To move freely throughout the territory of India. (e) To reside and settle in any part of the territory of India. Provisions of the Passport Act.
Art 14 : Rights to Religion.	Art 25 : All persons are equally entitled to freedom of con-science

Universal Declaration of Human Rights	*Provision of the Indian Constitution*
	and free profession, practice and propagation of religion.
Art 15 : (i) Right to Nationality. (ii) Change of nationality.	Art 5 : At the commencement of this Constitution, every person who has his domicile in the territory of India and (a) who was born in the territory of India; or (b) either of whose parents was born in the territory of India; or (c) who has been ordinarily resident in the territory of India for not less than five years immediately preceding such commencement, shall be a citizen of India.
Art 16 : Marriage and Family.	Art 9 : No person shall be a citizen of India by virtue of Article 5 or be deemed to be a citizen of India is virtue of Article 6 or Article 8, if he has voluntarily acquired the citizenship of any foreign state. Art 10 : Every person who is deemed to be a citizen of India under any of the forgoing provision of this Part shall, subject to the provisions of any law that may be made by Parliament, continue to be such citizen. Covered by suitable legisiation applicable to people of different religions.
Art 17 : Property.	Art 300 (A) : Person not be deprived of property save by authority of law.

Universal Declaration of Human Rights	*Provision of the Indian Constitution*
Art 18 : Freedom of thought and conscience.	Art 25 (A) : All person are equally entitled to freedom of con-science and the right freely to profess, practise and propagate religion.
Art 19 : Freedom of information and expression.	Art 19 (A) : All citizens shall have the right to speech and expression.
Art 20 : Peaceful assembly and association.	Art 19 (B) : All citizens shall have the right to assemble peaceably and without arms. Art 19 (C) : To form associations or unions.
Art 21 : (i) Democracy.	Art 325 : There shall be one general electoral role for every territorial constituency for election to either House of Parliament or to the House or either House of the Legislature of a State and no person shall be ineligible for inclusion in any such roll or claim to be included in any electoral roll for any such constituency on grounds only of religion, race, caste, sex or any of them.
Art 22 : Right to Social Security. Art 23 : Right to work. Right to equal pay. Remuneration keeping human dignity.	Art 41 : The state shall, within the limits of its economic capacity and development, make effective provision for securing the right to work, to education and to public assistance in case of unemployment, old age, sickness and disablement and in other cases of undeserved want.

Universal Declaration of Human Rights	*Provision of the Indian Constitution*
Right to form and join unions.	Art 39 (A) : The State shall, in particular, direct its policy towards securing-that the citizens-men and women, have the right to an adequate means of livelihood. Art 43 : The State shall endeavour to secure, by suitable legislation or economic organization or in any other way, to all workers, agriculture, industrial or otherwise, work, a living wage, conditions of work ensuring a decent standard of life and full employment of leisure and social and cultural opportunities and, in particular, the State shall endeavour to promote cottage industries on an individual or cooperative basis in rural areas. Art 19 (1) : Art 43 :
Art 24 : Rights to rest, reasonable working hours. Art 25 : (i) Standard of living adequate for health and well-being. Motherhood and children.	Art 47 : The State shall regarded the raising of the level of nutrition and the standard of living of its people and the improvement of public health as among its primary duties and, in particular, the State shall endeavour to bring about prohibition of the consumption except for medicinal purpose of intoxicating drinks and of drugs which are injurious to health. Art 39 (f) : The state shall in particular, direct its policy towards securing-that children are given opportunities and

Universal Declaration of Human Rights	*Provision of the Indian Constitution*
	facilities to develop in a healthy manner and in conditions of freedom and dignity and that childhood and youth are protected against exploitation and against moral and material abandonment. Art 42 : The state shall make provision for securing just and human conditions of work and for maternity relief.
Art 26 : Right to Education.	Art 45 : The state shall endeavour to provide within a period of ten years from the commencement of this constitution, for free compulsory education for all children until they complete the age of fourteen years.
Art 27 : (i) Free participation in cultural life. (ii) Protection of moral material interest.	Art 51 A(f) : To value and preserve the rich heritage of our composite culture.
Art 28 : Social and international order.	Art 38 : Art 51 : That State shall endeavour to (a) promote international peace and security; (b) maintain just and honourable relations between nations; (c) foster respect for international law and treaty obligations in the dealings of organised people with one another; and (d) encourage settlement of international disputes by arbitration.

Universal Declaration of Human Rights	*Provision of the Indian Constitution*
Art 29 : Duties.	Art 51 (A) : It shall be duty of every citizen of India-(a) to abide by the Constitution and respect its ideals and institutions, the National Flag and the National Anthem: (b) to cherish and follow noble ideas which inspired our national struggle for freedom; (c) to uphold and protect the sovereignty, unity and integrity of India; (d) to defend the country and render national service when called open to do so; (e) to promote harmony and the spirit of common brotherhood amongst all the people of India transcending religious, linguistic and regional or sectional diversities; to renounce practices derogatory to the dignity of women; (f) to value and preserve the rich heritage of our composite culture: (g) to protect and improve the natural environment including forests, lakes, rivers and wild life, and to have compassion for living creatures; (h) develop the scientific temper, humanism and the spirit of inquiry and roform; (i) to safeguard public property and to adjure violence; and (j) to strive towards excellence in all spheres of individual and collective activity so that the nation constantly rises to higher levels of endeavour and achievement.

FOURTEENTH

International Covenant on Civil and Political Rights and Constitution of India

India has ratified the International Covenant on Civil and Political Rights and International Covenant on Economic, Social and Cultural Rights. By ratification, it has been established on the international plane its consent to be bound by them. It has been obligation to provide to the individuals the rights contained in two covenants. A question arises as to how far the rights enshrined in the Covenants are consistent with the rights stipulated in the Constitution. Provisions of the two Covenants have been discussed separately with reference to the Indian Constitution.

The Constitution provides a number of rights to individuals in Part III i.e., called Fundamental Rights or justiciable rights. The expression fundamental denotes that these rights are inherent in all the human being and are essential for the individuals for blossoming of the human personality and soul. These rights represent the basic values of a civilized society. The Constitution makers declared that they shall be given a place of pride in the Constitution. Therefore, they elevated them to the status of fundamental rights. These rights are calculated to protect the dignity of the individuals and create conditions in which every human being can develop his personality to the fullest extent.

Fundamental rights differ from ordinary rights in a sense that the former are inviolable. No law, ordinance, custom, usage or administrative order can abridge or take them away. Any law which is violative of any of the fundamental rights is void. These are binding on the legislature as well as on the executive. In *A.D.M., Jabalpur* v. *S. Shukla*. It was observed that the object of making certain general aspects of rights fundamental is to guarantee them against illegal invasion of these rights by executive, legislative or judicial organ of the State. The founding fathers of the Constitution thought it necessary to incorporate them for the welfare of the people. They were perhaps moved by the atrocities committed on people during the World War II, and were also influenced largely by the liberties granted in the Atlantic Charter, the U.N. Charter and the Universal Declaration of Human Rights.

The Supreme Court of India has recognized these rights as 'natural rights' or human rights. The Chief Justice Patanjli Shastri has referred to fundamental rights as 'those great and basic rights which are recognized and guaranteed as the natural rights inherent in the status of a citizen of a free Country. Similarly, the Chief Justice Subba Rao in *L.C. Golak Nath* V. *State of Punjab*, has very rightly observed that fundamental rights are the modern name for what have been traditionally known as natural rights. They are moral rights which every human being everywhere at all times ought to have simply because of the fact that in contradiction with other beings, he is rational or moral. The rights enshrined in Part III are the rights.

International Covenant on Civil and Political Rights	*Constitution of India*
Article 1. All human being are born free and equal in dignity and rights. They are endowed with reason and conscience and should act toward one another in a spirit of brotherhood.	Preamble the People of India having solemnly resolved to constitute India into a Sovereign, Socialist, Secular Democratic Republic and to secure to all Citizen : *Justice*_social, economic and political; *Liberty* of thought, expression, belief, faith and worship; *Equality* of status, and opportunity and to promote among them all : *Fraternity* assuring the dignity of the individual and the unit and integrity of the National; In our Constituent Assembly This Twenty Sixth Day of November, 1949 do Hereby Adopt: Enact: and Give to Ourselves this Constitution.
Article 14(1). All are equal before the law are entitled without any discrimination to equal protection of the law. All are entitled to equal protection against any discrimination in violation and against any incitement in such discrimination.	Article 14. Equality Before Law and Equal Protection of the Laws : The State shall not deny to any person equality before the law and equal protection of the laws within the terriority of India.
Article 26. Everyone is entitled to all rights and freedom, without distinction of any kind, such as race, colour, sex, language, religion, political or other opinion, national or social origin, property, birth or other Status.	Article 15. Prohibition of Discrimination on Grounds of Religion, Race, Caste, Sex or Place of Birth-(1) The State shall not discriminate against any citizen on ground only of religion, race, caste, sex, place of birth or any of them.

International Covenant on Civil and Political Rights	*Constitution of India*
	(2) No citizen shall, on grounds only of religion, race, caste, sex, place of birth or any of them, subject to any disability, liability, restriction, or condition with regard to- (a) Access to shops, public restaurants, hotels and places of public entertainment. (b) The use of wells, tanks, bathing ghats, roads, and places of public resort maintain wholly or partly out of state funds or dedicated to the use of the general public.
Article 25 (1). Every one has the rights of equal access to public service in his country.	Article 17. Equality Of Opportunity In Matters Of Public Employement - (1) There shall be equality of opportunity for the citizen in matter relating to employment to any office under the State. (2) No citizen shall, on grounds only of religion, race, caste, sex, descent, place of birth, residence or any of them, be ineligible for, or discriminated against in respect of any employment of office under the State.
Article 19(1)&(2). Every has the right to freedom of opinion and expression, this rights includes freedom to hold opinion without interference and to seek, receive and impart and ideas through any media and regardless of frontier.	Article 19. Protection of Certain Rights Regarding of Speech, etc. (1) citizen shall have the rights (a) to freedom of speech and expression;

International Covenant on Civil and Political Rights	*Constitution of India*
Article 22. Everyone has the rights to freedom of movement and residence within the borders of each State.	Article 19 (1) (e). All citizens shall have the rights to reside and settle in any part of the territory of India.
Article 17 (1) Every one has the rights to own property alone as well as in association with others.	Article 19 (1) (f) Omitted by 44m Amendment to the Constitution. Article 300-A Person Not To Be Deprived Of Property Save Of Property Save By Authority Of Law - No person shall be deprived of his property save by authority of law.
Article 6(1) & 9(1). Everyone has the rights to life, liberty and security of person.	(2) Article 21. Protection of Life And Personal Liberty-No person shall be deprived of his life or personal liberty except according to produce established by law.
Article 9(2)(3)&(4). No one shall be subject to arbitrary arrest detention or exile.	Article 22 (1) Arrest person has II rights 1. Rights to be informed the grounds of arrest. 2. Rights to consult a lawyer of his own choice. 3. Rights to be produced before a Magistrate within 24 hours of arrest. 4. The freedom from detention beyond the said period except by the order of Magistrate.
Article 14(3)(g). No one shall be subject to torture, or to cruel or in human or regarding treatment or punishment.	Article 20 (3) Prohibition Of Traffic In Human Being And Forced Labour-(1) Traffic in human being and others similar forms of forced labour are prohibited and any contravention of this provision shall be an offence

International Covenant on Civil and Political Rights	*Constitution of India*
	punishable in according with law. (2) Nothing on this Article shall prevent the State from imposing compulsory service, and in imposing such service the state shall not make any discrimination on ground only of religion, race, caste, or class, or any of them.
Article 15 (1) No one shall be held guilty of any penal offence on account of any act or omission which did not constitute a penal offence, under national or international law at the time when it was committed. Nor shall a heavier penalty be applicable at the time the penal offence was committed.	Article 20. Protection In Respect Of Conviction For Offence- (1) No person shall be convicted of any offence except for the violation of one in force at the time of the commission of the Act charged as an offence nor be subjected to penalty greater than that which might have been inflicted under the law in force at the time of the commission of the offence.
Article 18(1). Everyone has the rights to freedom of thought, conscience and religion, this rights include freedom to change his religion or belief and freedom, either alone or in community with others and in public or private, to manifest his religion or belief in teaching practice, worship and observance.	(5) Article 25. Freedom Of Conscience And Free Profession: Practice And Propagation of Religion - (1) Subject to public order, morality and health, and to the other provision of this Part (Part III) all person are equally entitled to freedom of conscience and the right freely to profess, practice and propagate religion. (2) Nothing in this Article shall affect the operation of any existing law or prevent the state from making any law:

International Covenant on Civil and Political Rights	*Constitution of India*
	(a) regulating or restricting the economic.., financial, political or other secular activity which religious practice; (b) providing for social welfare and reform or the throwing upon of Hindu religious institution of a public character to all classes and section of Hindu.
Article 17 (2). No one shall be arbitrary deprived of his property.	Article 31. Person Not To Be Deprived of Property Save By Authority of Law: No person shall be deprived of his property save authority of law.
Article 8. Everyone has the right to an effective remedy by the competent national tribunals for acts violating the fundamental rights granted to him by the constitution or by law.	Article 32. Remedies For Enforcement Of Rights Conferred By This Part (i.e., Part III)-(1) The Rights to move the Supreme Court by enforcement proceedings for the enforcement of the rights guaranteed.

Thus, there is no basic difference. The constitution of India and Universal Declaration of Human Rights were drafted almost simultaneously. Framers of Indian Constitution were influenced by the Concept of human rights in the UN Charter and also by the deliberations for the Universal Declaration. The Constitution incorporated most of the human rights which were later embodied in the International Covenant.

FIFTEEN

Covenant on Economic, Social and Cultural Rights and The Indian Constitution

These rights which are not provided in the Constitution but are stipulated in the covenant as justiciable to be included in the Directive Principles. Similar rights were included in Part IV as Directive Principles State Policy non justiciable rights. The Directive Principles of the State Policy covered under part IV of the Constitution of India could be safely said to be fundamental in respect of regulation and governance of the country. Basically, these Directive Principles are intended to promote social welfare in consonance with basic object of the human rights which claim global recognition and needs to be enforced at national level.

Directive Principles of the State Policy play a significant role by imposing obligation upon the state to implement them so as to protect the interest of common masses including the working class. Directive Principles of State Policy are mainly intended to promote welfare of the people and strive for securing social and economic justice to the workers. The following table shows the different Articles of the Covenant and Constitution wherein identical rights are stipulated.

Rights	*Covenant on Economics, Social and Cultural Rights*	*Indian Constitution*
1. Equal pay for Equal work for both men and women	Art 7 (a) (1)	Art 39 (d)
2. Opportunities & facilities for children to develop in a healthy manner.	Art 10 (3)	Art 39 (f)
3. Right to work, to education and to public assistance in certain cases.	Art 6(10)	Art 41
4. Provisions for just and humane conditions of work and maternity relief.	Art 7(b)	Art 42
5. Provisions for securing just and humane conditions of work and for maternity relief.	Art 10(2)	Art 42
6. Living wage etc., for workers.	Art 7 (a) (ii)	Art 43
7. Reasonable limitation of working hours and periodic holidays with pa.	Art 7 (d)	Art 43

Rights	*Covenant on Economics, Social and Cultural Rights*	*Indian Constitution*
8. Provision for free and compulsory education for children.	Art13(2)(a)	Art 45
9. Duty of the State to raise the level of nutrition and the standard of living and to improve public health.	Art 11	Art 47

The above table shows that various directives for providing living wages to workers, ensuring just humane conditions of work, motivating the workers to participate in the management of a company, providing equal opportunity to all workers irrespective of their sex in terms of employment and promotion opportunities, prohibiting employment of children in hazards occupational employment etc, have been explicitly included in part IV from Article 36 to 51 of the constitution of India.

Thus, the right to equal pay for equal work both men and women, the right to protect the childhood and youth from exploitation, the right to secure just and human conditions of work and for maternity relief, the right to work, the right to a decent standard of life and full enjoyment of leisure and social and cultural opportunities and the right to raise the level of standard of living and right to free and compulsory education have been recognized in the Constitution as well as in the Covenants.

For accomplishing these objectives relevant legalization have been enacted and enforced which mainly include *The Factories Act, 1948; The Minimum Wages Act, 1948; Employees State Insurance Act, 1948; The Mines Act, 1952; Employees Provident Funds and Miscellaneous Provisions Act, 1952; Payment of Bonus Act, 1965;* the *Payment of Gratuity Act, 1972;* etc. Undoubtedly these legislative measures have come to rescue of the workers, particularly, the industrial workers and those engaged in organized sector of employment. It would not be out of place to bring forth at this juncture significant observations of Dr. Nagendra Singh that the universal adult franchise and democratic form of government envisaged by the Constitution provides guarantee against violation of human rights. Ultimately democracy, public opinion and awareness of one's own rights would be the best guarantees protection of human values and basic freedoms. There could not be an iota of doubt that these basic human rights which have been duly recognized in the form of Constitutional guarantees have been duly taken care of, particularly in a democratic set up of society and have proved to be of much relevance for protecting the interest of a common man and more specifically that of the worker. With regard to the working class engaged in the organized sector of employment, these Constitutional mandates have certainly played a significant role so as to ensure them social and economic stability. But at the same time the outcome is very much disappointing so far as the workers engaged in unorganized sector are concerned, who are subjected to exploitation and victimization by their employers mainly, due to absence of strong trade unions over there as well as on account of ineffective implementation process due to corruption and political interference. Due to those reasons unorganized workers are presently compelled to lead a miserable life in contravention of basic human rights.

All the provisions of the covenant on economic, social and cultural rights are binding on India except those in respect of which reservation has been made in the instrument of accession. The Government should take steps with a view to provide these liberties to the individuals. The great importance of these right are also due to their close relationship with the Civil and Political Rights. These two sets of rights of the human beings are indivisible and cannot be segregated from one another. The full realization of the civil and political rights is impossible without the enjoyment of economic, social and cultural rights.

SIXTEEN

Philosophical Analysis of the Concept of Human Rights

Human rights are rights that attach to human beings and function as moral guarantees in support of our claims towards the enjoyment of a minimally good life. In conceptual terms, human rights are themselves derivative of the concept of a right. This section focuses upon the philosophical analysis of the concept of a 'right' in order to clearly demonstrate the various constituent parts of the concept from which human rights emerge. In order to gain a full understanding of both the philosophical foundations of the doctrine of human rights and the different ways in which separate human rights function, a detailed analysis is required.

MORAL VS. LEGAL RIGHTS

The distinction drawn between moral rights and legal rights as two separate categories of rights is of fundamental importance to understand the basis and potential application of human rights. Legal rights refer to all those rights found within existing legal codes. A legal right is a right that enjoys the recognition and protection of the law. Questions as to its existence can be resolved by simply locating the relevant legal instrument or piece of legislation. A legal right cannot be said to exist prior to its passing into law and the limits of its validity are set by the jurisdiction of the body which passed the relevant legislation. An example of a legal right would be my daughter's legal right to receive an adequate education, as enshrined within the United Kingdom's Education Act (1944). Suffice it to say, that the exercise of this right is limited to the United Kingdom. No child has no legal right to receive an adequate education from a school board in Southern California. Legal positivists argue that the only rights that can be said to legitimately exist are legal rights, rights that originate within a legal system. On this view, moral rights are not rights in the strict sense, but are better thought of as moral claims, which may or may not eventually be assimilated within national or international law. For a legal positivist, such as the 19th century legal philosopher Jeremy Bentham, there can be no such thing as human rights existing prior to, or independently from legal codification. For a positivist determining the existence of rights is no more complicated than locating the relevant legal statute or precedent. In stark contrast, moral rights are rights that, it is claimed, exist prior to and independently from their legal counterparts. The existence and validity of a moral right is not deemed to be dependent upon the actions of jurists and legislators. Many people argued, for example, that the black majority in apartheid South Africa possessed a moral right to full political participation in that country's political system, even though there existed no such legal right. What is interesting is that many people framed their opposition to apartheid in rights terms. What many found so morally repugnant about apartheid South Africa was precisely its denial of numerous fundamental moral rights, including the rights not to be discriminated against on grounds of colour and rights to political participation to the majority of that country's inhabitants. This particular line of opposition and protest could only be pursued because of a belief in the existence and validity of moral rights. A belief that fundamental rights which may or may not have received legal recognition elsewhere, remained utterly valid and morally compelling even, and perhaps especially, in those countries whose legal systems had not recognized these rights. A rights-based opposition to apartheid South Africa could not have been initiated and maintained by appeal to legal rights, for obvious reasons. No one could legitimately argue that the legal political rights of non-white South Africans were being violated under apartheid, since no such legal rights existed. The systematic denial of such rights did, however, constitute a gross violation of those peoples' fundamental moral rights.

From the above example it should be clear that human rights cannot be reduced to, or exclusively identified with legal rights. The legal positivist's account of justified law excludes the possibility of condemning such systems as apartheid from a rights perspective. It might, therefore, appear tempting to draw the conclusion that human rights are best identified as moral rights. After all, the existence of the UDHR and various International Covenants, to which South Africa was not a signatory in most cases, provided opponents of apartheid with a powerful moral argument. Apartheid was founded upon the denial of fundamental human rights. Human rights certainly share an essential quality of moral rights, namely, that their valid existence is not deemed to be conditional upon their being legally recognized. Human rights are meant to apply to all human beings everywhere, regardless of whether they have received legal recognition by all countries everywhere. Clearly, there remain numerous countries that wholly or partially exclude formal legal recognition to fundamental human rights. Supporters of human rights in these countries insist that the rights remain valid regardless, as fundamental moral rights. The universality of human rights positively entails such claims. The universality of human rights as moral rights clearly lends greater moral force to human rights. However, for their part, legal rights are not subject to disputes as to their existence and validity in quite the way moral rights are. It would be a mistake to exclusively identify human rights with moral rights. Human rights are better thought of as both moral rights and legal rights. Human rights originate as moral rights and their legitimacy is necessarily dependent upon the legitimacy of the concept of moral rights. A principal aim of advocates of human rights is for these rights to receive universal legal recognition. This was, after all, a fundamental goal of the opponents of apartheid. Human rights are best thought of, therefore, as being both moral and legal rights. The legitimacy claims of human rights are tied to their status as moral rights. The practical efficacy of human rights is, however, largely dependent upon their developing into legal rights. In those cases where specific human rights do not enjoy legal recognition, such as in the example of apartheid above, moral rights must be prioritised with the intention that defending the moral claims of such rights as a necessary prerequisite for the eventual legal recognition of the rights in question.

CLAIM RIGHTS AND LIBERTY RIGHTS

To gain an understanding of the functional properties of human rights it is necessary to consider the more specific distinction drawn between claim rights and liberty rights. It should be noted that it is something of a convention to begin such discussions by reference to W.N. Hohfeld's (1919) more extended classification of rights. Hohfeld identified four categories of rights: liberty rights, claim rights, power rights, and immunity rights. However, numerous scholars have subsequently tended to collapse the last two within the first two and hence to restrict attention to liberty rights and claim rights. The political philosopher Peter Jones (1994) provides one such example.

Jones restricts his focus to the distinction between claim rights and liberty rights. He conforms to a well-established trend in rights' analysis in viewing the former as being of primary importance. Jones defines a claim right as consisting of being owed a duty. A claim right is a right one holds against another person or persons who owe a corresponding duty to the right holder. To return to the example of my daughter. Her right to receive an adequate education is a claim right held against the local education authority, which has a corresponding duty to provide her with the object of the right. Jones identifies further necessary distinctions within the concept of a claim right when he distinguishes between a positive claim right and a negative claim right. The former are rights one holds to some specific good or service, which some other has a duty to provide. My daughter's claim right to education is therefore a positive claim right. Negative claim rights, in contrast, are rights one holds against others' interfering in or trespassing upon one's life or property in some way. My daughter could be said to possess a negative claim right against others attempting to steal her mobile phone, for example. Indeed, such examples lead on to the final distinction Jones identifies within the concept of claim rights: rights held 'in personam' and rights held 'in rem'. Rights held in personam are rights one holds against some specifically identified duty holder, such as the education authority. In contrast, rights held in rem are rights held against no one in particular, but apply to everyone. Thus, my daughter's right to an education would be practically useless were it is not held against some identifiable, relevant, and competent body. Equally, her right against her mobile phone being stolen from her would be highly limited if it did not apply to all those capable of potentially performing such an act. Claim rights, then, can be of either a positive or a negative character and they can be held either in personam or in rem.

Jones defines liberty rights as rights which exist in the absence of any duties not to perform some desired activity and thus consist of those actions one is not prohibited from performing. In contrast to claim rights, liberty rights are primarily negative in character. For example, I may be said to possess a liberty right to spend my vacation lying on a particular beautiful beach in Greece. Unfortunately, no one has a duty to positively provide for this particular exercise of my liberty right. There is no authority or body, equivalent to an education authority, for example, who has a responsibility to realize my dream for me. A liberty right can be said, then, to be a right to do as one pleases precisely because one is not under an obligation, grounded in others' claim rights, to refrain from so acting. Liberty rights provide for the capacity to be free, without actually providing the specific means by which one may pursue the objects of one's will. For example, a multi-millionaire and a penniless vagrant both possess an equal liberty right to holiday in the Caribbean each year.

SUBSTANTIVE CATEGORIES OF HUMAN RIGHTS

The above section was concerned to analyse what might be termed as the 'formal properties' of rights. This section, in contrast, proceeds to consider the different categories of substantive human rights. If one delves into all of the various documents that together form the codified body of human rights, one can identify and distinguish between five different categories of substantive human rights. These are as follows: rights to life; rights to freedom; rights to political participation; rights to the protection of the rule of law; rights to fundamental social, economic, and cultural goods. These rights span the so-called three generations of rights and involve a complex combination of both liberty and claim rights. Some rights, such as the right to life, consists of both liberty and claim rights in roughly equal measure. Thus, the adequate protection of the right to life requires the existence of liberty rights against others trespassing against one's person and the existence of claim rights to have access to basic prerequisites to sustaining one's life, such as an adequate diet and health-care. Other rights, such as social, economic, and cultural rights, for example, are weighed more heavily towards the existence of various claim rights, which require the positive provision of the objects of such rights. The making of substantive distinctions between human rights can have controversial, but important consequences. Human rights are typically understood to be of equal value, each right is conceived of as equally important as every other. On this view, there can exist no potential for conflict between fundamental human rights. One is simply meant to attach equal moral weight to each and every human right. This prohibits arranging human rights in order of importance. However, conflict between rights can and does occur. Treating all human rights as of equal importance prohibits any attempt to address or resolve such conflict when it arises. Take the example of a hypothetical developing world country with severely limited financial and material resources. This country is incapable of providing the resources for realising all of the human rights for all of its citizens, though it is committed to doing so. In the meantime, government officials wish to know which human rights are more absolute than others, which fundamental human rights should it immediately prioritise and seek to provide for? This question, of course, cannot be answered if one sticks to the position that all rights are of equal importance. It can only be addressed if one allows for the possibility that some human rights are more fundamental than others and that the morally correct action for the government to take would be to prioritise these rights. A refusal to do so, no matter how consistent it may be philosophically, would be tantamount to dogmatically sticking one's head in the metaphorical sands. Attempting to make such distinctions is, of course, a philosophically fraught exercise. It clearly requires the existence of some more ultimate criteria against which one can 'measure' the relative importance of separate human rights. This is a highly controversial issue within the philosophy of human rights and one which I shall return to when I consider how philosophers attempt to justify the doctrine of human rights. What remains to be addressed in our analysis of the concept of a human right are the questions of what adequately implementing human rights generally requires, and upon whom does this task fall; who has responsibility for protecting and promoting human rights and what is required of them to do so?

SCOPE OF HUMAN RIGHTS AND DUTIES

Human rights are said to be possessed equally, by everyone. A conventional corollary of this claim is that everyone has a duty to protect and promote the human rights of everyone else. However, in practice, the onus for securing human rights typically falls upon national governments and international, inter-governmental bodies. Philosophers such as Thomas Pogge (1995) argue that the moral burden for securing human rights should fall disproportionately upon such institutions precisely because they are best placed and most able to effectively perform the task. On this reading, non-governmental organizations and private citizens have an important role to play in supporting the global protection of human rights, but the onus must fall upon the relevant national and international institutions, such as the governments of nation-states and such bodies as the United Nations and the World Bank. One might wish to argue that, for example, human rights can be adequately secured by the existence of reciprocal duties held between individuals across the globe. However, 'privatizing' human rights in this fashion would ignore two particular salient factors: individuals have a tendency to prioritise the moral demands of those closest to them, particularly members of their own family or immediate community; individuals' ability to exercise their duties is, to a large extent, determined by their own personal financial circumstances. Thus, global inequalities in the distribution of wealth fundamentally undermine the ability of those in the poorer countries to reciprocate assistance provided them by those living in wealthier countries. Reasons such as these underlie Pogge's insistence that the onus of responsibility lies at the level of national and international institutions. Adequately protecting and promoting human rights require both nation-states ensuring the adequate provision of services and institutions for their own citizens and the co-operation of nation-states within international institutions acting to secure the requisite global conditions for the protection and promotion of everyone's human rights.

What must such bodies actively do to adequately secure individuals' human rights? Does my daughter's human right to receive an adequate education require the education authority to do everything possible to assist and enhance my child's education? Does it require the provision of a world-class library, frequent study trips abroad, and employing the most able and best-qualified teachers? The answer is, of course, no. Given the relative scarcity of resources and the demands placed upon those resources, we are inclined to say that adequately securing individuals' human rights extends to the establishment of decent social and governmental practice so as to ensure that all individuals have the opportunity of leading a minimally good life. In the first instance, national governments are typically held to be primarily responsible for the adequate provision of their own citizens' human rights. Philosophers such as Brian Orend endorses this aspiration when he writes that the object of human rights is to secure 'minimal levels of decent and respectful treatment.' It is important to note, however, that the duty ensure the provision of even minimal levels of decent and respectful treatment cannot be strictly limited by national boundaries. The adequate protection and promotion of everyone's human rights does require, for example, the more affluent and powerful nation-states providing sufficient assistance to those countries currently incapable of adequately ensuring the protection of their own citizens' basic human rights. While some may consider Orend's aspirations for human rights to be unduly cautious, even the briefest survey of the extent of human suffering and deprivation in many parts of the world today is sufficient to demonstrate just how far we are from realizing even this fairly minimal standard.

National and international institutions bear the primary responsibility of securing human rights and the test for successfully fulfilling this responsibility is the creation of opportunities for all individuals to lead a minimally good life. The realization of human rights requires establishing the conditions for all human beings to lead minimally good lives and thus should not be confused as an attempt to create a morally perfect society. The impression, that many have of human rights as being unduly Utopian, testifies less to the inherent demands of human rights and more to the extent to which even fairly modest aspirations are so far from being realized in the world today. The actual aspirations of human rights are, on the face of it, quite modest. However, this should not distract from a full appreciation of the possible force of human rights. Human rights call for the creation of politically democratic societies in which all citizens have the means of leading a minimally good life. While the object of individual human rights may be modest, the force of that right is intended to be near absolute. That is to say, the demands of rights are meant to take precedence over other possible social goals. Ronald Dworkin has coined the term 'rights as trumps' to describe this property. He writes that, 'rights are best understood as trumps over some background justification for political decisions that states a goal for the community as a whole.' In general, Dworkin argues, considerations of rights claims must take priority over alternative considerations when formulating public policy and distributing public benefits. Thus, for example, a minority's possession of rights against discriminatory treatment should trump any and all considerations of the possible benefits that the majority would derive from discriminating against the minority group. Similarly, an individual's right to an adequate diet should trump other individuals' desires to eat lavish meals, despite the aggregate gain in pleasure these individuals would derive. For Dworkin, rights as trumps expresses the fundamental ideal of equality upon which the contemporary doctrine of human rights rests. Treating rights as trumps is a means for ensuring that all individuals are treated in an equal and like fashion in respect of the provision of fundamental human rights. Fully realizing the aspirations of human rights may not require the provision of 'state of the art' resources, but this should not detract from the force of human rights as taking priority over alternative social and political considerations.

PHILOSOPHICAL JUSTIFICATION OF HUMAN RIGHTS

We have established that human rights originate as moral rights but that the successful passage of many human rights into international and national law enables one to think of human rights as, in many cases, both moral rights and legal rights. Furthermore, human rights may be either claim rights or liberty rights, and have a negative or a positive complexion in respect of the obligations imposed by others in securing the right. Human rights may be divided into five different categories and the principal object of securing human rights is the creation of the conditions for all individuals to have the opportunity to lead a minimally good life. Finally, human rights are widely considered to trump other social and political considerations in the allocation of public resources. Broadly speaking, philosophers generally agree on such issues as the formal properties of human rights, the object of human rights, and the force of human rights. However, there is much less agreement upon the fundamental question on how human rights may be philosophically justified. It would be fair to say that philosophers have provided many different, at times even conflicting, answers to this question. Philosophers have sought to justify human rights by appeal to single ideals such as equality, autonomy, human dignity, fundamental human interests, the capacity for rational agency, and even democracy. For the purposes of clarity and relative simplicity I will focus upon the two, presently most prominent, philosophical attempts to justify human rights: interests theory and will theory. Before I do that, it is necessary to address the prior question.

Do Human Rights Require Philosophical justification?

Many people tend to take the validity of human rights for granted. Certainly, for many non-philosophers human rights may all too obviously appear to rest upon self-evidently true and universally valid moral principles. In this respect, human rights may be perceived as empirical facts about the contemporary world. Human rights do exist and many people do act in accordance with the correlative duties and obligations respecting human rights entails. No supporter of human rights could possibly complain about such perceptions. If nothing else, the prevalence of such views is pragmatically valuable for the cause of human rights. However, moral philosophers do not enjoy such licence for epistemological complacency. Moral philosophers remain concerned by the question of the philosophical foundations of human rights. There is a good reason why we should all be concerned with such a question. What might be termed the 'philosophically naive' view of human rights effectively construes human rights as legal rights. The validity of human rights is closely tied to, and dependent upon, the legal codification of human rights. However, as was argued earlier, such an approach is not sufficient to justify human rights. Arguments in support of the validity of any moral doctrine can never be settled by simply pointing to the empirical existence of particular moral beliefs or concepts. Morality is fundamentally concerned with what ought to be the case, and this cannot be settled by appeals to what is the case, or is perceived to be the case. From such a basis, it would have been very difficult to argue that apartheid South Africa, to take an earlier example, was a morally unjust regime. One must not confuse the law with morality, per se. Nor consider the two to be simply co-extensional. Human rights originate as moral rights. Human rights claim validity everywhere and for everyone, irrespective of whether they have received comprehensive legal recognition, and even irrespective of whether everyone is in agreement with the claims and principles of human rights. Thus, one cannot settle the question of the philosophical validity of human rights by appealing to purely empirical observations upon the world. As a moral doctrine, human rights have to be demonstrated to be valid as norms and not facts. In order to achieve this, one has to turn to moral philosophy. Presently, two particular approaches to the question of the validity of human rights predominate: what might be loosely termed as the 'interests theory approach' and the 'will theory approach'.

The interests theory approach

Advocates of the interests theory approach argue that the principal function of human rights is to protect and promote certain essential human interests. Securing human beings' essential interests is the principal ground upon which human rights may be morally justified. The interests approach is thus primarily concerned to identify the social and biological prerequisites for human beings leading a minimally good life. The universality of human rights is grounded in what are considered to be some basic, indispensable, attributes for human well-being, which all of us are deemed necessarily to share. Take, for example, an interest each of us has in respect of our own personal security. This interest serves to ground our claim to the right. It may require the derivation of other rights as prerequisites to security, such as the satisfaction of basic nutritional needs and the need to be free from arbitrary detention or arrest, for example. The philosopher John Finnis provides a good representative of the interests theory approach. Finnis argues that human rights are justifiable on the ground of their instrumental value for securing the necessary conditions of human well-being. He identifies seven fundamental interests, or what he terms 'basic forms of human good', as providing the basis for human rights. These are: life and its capacity for development; the acquisition of knowledge, as an end in itself; play, as the capacity for recreation; aesthetic expression; sociability and friendship; practical reasonableness, the capacity for intelligent and reasonable thought processes; and finally, religion, or the capacity for spiritual experience. According to Finnis, these are the essential prerequisites for human well-being and, as such, serve to justify our claims to the corresponding rights, whether they are of the claim right or liberty right variety.

Other philosophers who have defended human rights from an interests-based approach have addressed the question of how an appeal to interests can provide a justification for respecting and, when necessary, even positively acting to promote the interests of others. Such questions have a long heritage in western moral and political philosophy and extend at least as far back as the 17th Century philosopher Thomas Hobbes. Typically, this approach attempts to provide what James Nickel has termed 'prudential reasons' in support of human rights. Taking as the starting point the claim that all human beings possess basic and fundamental interests, advocates of this approach argue that each individual owes a basic and general duty to respect the rights of every other individual. The basis for this duty is not mere benevolence or altruism, but individual self-interest. As Nickel writes, 'a prudential argument from fundamental interests attempts to show that it would be reasonable to accept and comply with human rights, in circumstances where most others are likely to do so, because these norms are part of the best means for protecting one's fundamental interests against actions and omissions that endanger them.' (ibid). Protecting one's own fundamental interests requires others' willingness to recognize and respect these interests, which, in turn, requires reciprocal recognition and respect of the fundamental interests of others. The adequate protection of each individual's fundamental interests necessitates the establishment of a co-operative system, the fundamental aim of which is not to promote the common good, but the protection and promotion of individuals' self-interest.

For many philosophers the interests approach provides a philosophically powerful defence of the doctrine of human rights. It has the apparent advantage of appealing to human commonality, to those attributes we all share, and, in so doing, offers a relatively broad-based defence of the plethora of human rights considered by many to be fundamental and inalienable. The interests approach also provides for the possibility of resolving some of the potential disputes which can arise over the need to prioritise some human rights over others. One may do this, for example, by hierarchically ordering the corresponding interests identified as the specific object, or content, of each right.

However, the interests approach is subject to some significant criticisms. Foremost amongst these is the necessary appeal interests' theorists make to some account of human nature. The interests-approach is clearly operating with, at the very least, an implicit account of human nature. Appeals to human nature have, of course, proven to be highly controversial and typically resist achieving the degree of consensus required for establishing the legitimacy of any moral doctrine founded upon an account of human nature. For example, combining the appeal to fundamental interests with the aspiration of securing the conditions for each individual leading a minimally good life would be complicated by social and cultural diversity. Clearly, as the economic philosopher Amartya Sen (1999) has argued, the minimal conditions for a decent life are socially and culturally relative. Providing the conditions for leading a minimally good life for the residents of Greenwich Village would be significantly different from securing the same conditions for the residents of a shanty town in Southern Africa or South America. While the interests themselves may be ultimately identical, adequately protecting these interests will have to go beyond the mere specification of some purportedly general prerequisites for satisfying individuals' fundamental interests. Other criticism of the interests approach have focused upon the appeal to self-interest as providing a coherent basis for fully respecting the rights of all human beings. This approach is based upon the assumption that individuals occupy a condition of relatively equal vulnerability to one another. However, this is simply not the case. The model cannot adequately defend the claim that a self-interested agent must respect the interests of, for example, much less powerful or geographically distant individuals, if she wishes to secure her own interests. On these terms, why should a purely self-interested and overweight individual in, say Los Angeles or London, care for the interests of a starving individual in some distant and impoverished continent? In this instance, the starving person is not in a position to affect their overweight counterpart's fundamental interests. The appeal to pure self-interest ultimately cannot provide a basis for securing the universal moral community at the heart of the doctrine of human rights. It cannot justify the claims of universal human rights. An even more philosophically oriented vein of criticism focuses upon the interests' based approach alleged neglect of constructive human agency as a fundamental component of morality generally. Put simply, the interests-based approach tends to construe our fundamental interests as pre-determinants of human moral agency. This can have the effect of subordinating the importance of the exercise of freedom as a principal moral ideal. One might seek to include freedom as a basic human interest, but freedom is not constitutive of our interests on this account. This particular concern lies at the heart of the so-called 'will approach' to human rights.

The will theory approach

In contrast to the interests approach, the will theory attempts to establish the philosophical validity of human rights upon a single human attribute: the capacity for freedom. Will theorists argue that what is distinctive about human agency is the capacity for freedom and that this ought to constitute the core of any account of rights. Ultimately, then, will theorists view human rights as originating in, or reducible to, a single, constitutive right, or alternatively, a highly limited set of purportedly fundamental attributes. H.L.A. Hart, for example, inferentially argues that all rights are reducible to a single, fundamental right. He refers to this as 'equal right of all men to be free.' Hart insists that rights to such things as political participation or to an adequate diet, for example, are ultimately reducible to, and derivative of, individuals' equal right to liberty. Henry Shue (1996) develops upon Hart's inferential argument and argues that liberty alone is not ultimately sufficient for grounding all of the rights posited by Hart. Shue argues that many of these rights imply more than mere individual liberty and extend to include security from violence and the necessary material conditions for personal survival. Thus, he grounds rights upon liberty, security and subsistence. The moral philosopher Alan Gewirth has further developed upon such themes. Gewirth argues that the justification of our claims to the possession of basic human rights is grounded in what he presents as the distinguishing characteristic of human beings generally: the capacity for rationally purposive agency. Gewirth states that the recognition of the validity of human rights is a logical corollary of recognizing oneself as a rationally purposive agent since the possession of rights are the necessary means for rationally purposive action. Gewirth grounds his argument in the claim that all human action is rationally purposive. Every human action is done for some reason, irrespective of whether it be a good or a bad reason. He argues that in rationally endorsing some end, say the desire to write a book, one must logically endorse the means to that end; as a bare minimum one's own literacy. He then asks what is required to be a rationally purposive agent in the first place? He answers that freedom and well-being are the two necessary conditions for rationally purposive action. Freedom and well-being are the necessary means to acting in a rationally purposive fashion. They are essential prerequisites for being human, where to be human is to possess the capacity for rationally purposive action. As essential prerequisites, each individual is entitled to have access to them. However, Gewirth argues that each individual cannot simply will their own enjoyment of these prerequisites for rational agency without due concern for others. He bases the necessary concern for others' human rights upon what he terms the 'principle of generic consistency' (PGC). Gewirth argues that each individual's claim to the basic means for rationally purposive action is based upon an appeal to a general, rather than, specific attribute of all relevant agents. I cannot logically will my own claims to basic human rights without simultaneously accepting the equal claims of all rationally purposive agents to the same basic attributes. Gewirth has argued that there exists an absolute right to life possessed separately and equally by all of us. In so claiming, Gewirth echoes Dworkin's concept of rights as trumps, but ultimately goes further than Dworkin is prepared to do by arguing that the right to life is absolute and cannot, therefore, be overridden under any circumstances. He states that a 'right is absolute when it cannot be overridden in any circumstances, so that it can never be justifiably infringed and it must be fulfilled without any exceptions.' Will theorists then attempt to establish the validity of human rights upon the ideal of personal autonomy: rights are a manifestation of the exercise of personal autonomy. In doing so, the validity of human rights is necessarily tied to the validity of personal autonomy. On the face of it, this would appear to be a very powerful, philosophical position. After all, as someone like Gewirth might argue, critics of this position would themselves necessarily be acting autonomously and they cannot do this without simultaneously requiring the existence of the very means for such action, even in criticizing human rights one is logically pre-supposing the existence of such rights.

Despite the apparent logical force of the will approach, it has been subjected to various forms of criticism. A particularly important form of criticism focuses upon the implications of will theory for the so-called 'marginal cases'; human beings who are temporarily or permanently incapable of acting in a rationally autonomous fashion. This would include individuals who have diagnosed from suffering from dementia, schizophrenia, clinical depression, and also, individuals who remain in a comatose condition, from which they may never recover. If the constitutive condition for the possession of human rights is said to be the capacity for acting in a rationally purposive manner, for example, then it seems to logically follow, that individuals incapable of satisfying this criteria have no legitimate claim to human rights. Many would find this conclusion morally disturbing. However, a strict adherence to the will approach is entailed by it. Some human beings are temporarily or permanently lacking the criteria, Gewirth, for instance, cites as the basis for our claims to human rights. It is difficult to see how they could be assimilated within the community of the bearers of human rights on the terms of Gewirth's argument. Despite this, the general tendency is towards extending human rights considerations towards many of the so-called 'marginal cases'. To do otherwise would appear to many to be intuitively wrong, if not ultimately defensible by appeal to practical reason. This may reveal the extent to which many peoples' support of human rights includes an ineluctable element of sympathy, taking the form of a general emotional concern for others. Thus, strictly applying the will theorists' criteria for membership of the community of human rights bearers would appear to result in the exclusion of some categories of human beings who are presently recognized as legitimate bearers of human rights.

The interests theory approach and the will theory approach contain strengths and weaknesses. When consistently and separately applied to the doctrine of human rights, each approach appears to yield conclusions that may limit or undermine the full force of those rights. It may be that philosophical supporters of human rights need to begin to consider the potential philosophical benefits attainable through combining various themes and elements found within these (and other) philosophical approaches to justifying human rights. Thus, further attempts at justifying the basis and content of human rights may benefit from pursuing a more thematically pluralist approach than has typically been the case to date.

PHILOSOPHICAL CRITICISM OF HUMAN RIGHTS

The doctrine of human rights has been subjected to various forms of fundamental, philosophical criticism. These challenges to the philosophical validity of human rights as a moral doctrine differ from critical appraisals of the various philosophical theories supportive of the doctrine for the simple reason that they aim to demonstrate what they perceive to the philosophical fallacies upon which human rights are founded. Two such forms of critical analysis bear particular attention: one, which challenges the universalist claims of human rights, and another, which challenges the presumed objective character of human rights principles.

Moral relativism

Philosophical supporters of human rights are necessarily committed to a form of moral universalism. As moral principles and as a moral doctrine, human rights are considered to be universally valid. However, moral universalism has long been subject to criticism by so-called moral relativists. Moral relativists argue that universally valid moral truths do not exist. For moral relativists, there is simply no such thing as a universally valid moral doctrine. Relativists view morality as a social and historical phenomenon. Moral beliefs and principles are therefore thought of as socially and historically contingent, valid only for those cultures and societies in which they originate and within which they are widely approved. Relativists point to the vast array of diverse moral beliefs and practices apparent in the world today as empirical support for their position. Even within a single, contemporary society, such as the United States or Great Britain, one can find a wide diversity of fundamental moral beliefs, principles and practices. Contemporary complex societies are thus increasingly considered to be pluralist and multicultural in character. For many philosophers the multicultural character of such societies serves to restrict fundamentally the substance and scope of the regulative political principles governing those societies. In respect of human rights, relativists have tended to focus upon such issues as the presumed individualist character of the doctrine of human rights. It has been argued by numerous relativists that human rights are unduly biased towards morally individualist societies and cultures at the necessary expense of the communal moral complexion of many Asian and African societies. At best, some human rights' articles may be considered to be redundant within such societies, at worse they may appear to be positively harmful if fully implemented, replacing the fundamental values of one civilization with those of another and thereby perpetuating a form of cultural and moral imperialism.

The philosophical debate between universalists and relativists is far too complex to adequately summarise here. However, certain immediate responses to the relativist critique of human rights are immediately available. First, merely pointing to moral diversity and the presumed integrity of individual cultures and societies does not, by itself, provide a philosophical justification for relativism, nor a sufficient critique of universalism. After all, there have existed and continue to exist many cultures and societies whose treatment of their own people leaves much to be desired. Is the relativist genuinely asking us to recognize and respect the integrity of Nazi Germany, or any other similarly repressive regime? There can be little doubt that, as it stands, relativism is incompatible with human rights. On the face of it, this would appear to lend argumentative weight to the universalist support of human rights. After all, one may speculate as to the willingness of any relativist to actually forego their possession of human rights if and when the social surroundings demanded it. Similarly, relativist arguments are typically presented by members of the political elites within those countries whose systematic oppression of their people has attracted the attention of advocates of the human rights. The exponential growth of grass-root human rights organizations across many countries in the world whose cultures are alleged to be incompatible with the implementation of human rights, raises serious questions as to the validity and integrity of such 'indigenous' relativists. At its worst, the doctrine of moral relativism may be being deployed in an attempt to illegitimately justify oppressive political systems. The concern over the presumed incompatibility between human rights and communal moral systems appears to be a more valid issue. Human rights have undeniably conceived of the principal bearer of human rights as the individual person. This is due, in large part, to the Western origins of human rights. However, it would be equally fair to say that the so-called 'third generation' of human rights is far more attuned to the communal and collective basis of many individuals' lives. In keeping with the work of political philosophers such as Will Kymlicka, there is increasing awareness of the need to tailor human rights principles to such things as the collective rights of minorities and, for example, these minorities' claims to such things as communal land rights. While human rights remain philosophically grounded within an individualist moral doctrine, there can be no doubt that attempts are being made to adequately apply and human rights to more communally oriented societies. Human rights can no longer be accused of being 'culture-blind'.

Epistemological criticism of human rights

The second most important contemporary philosophical form of human rights' criticism challenges the presumed objective basis of human rights as moral rights. This form of criticism may be thought of as a river into which run many philosophical tributaries. The essence of these attempts to refute human rights consists in the claim that moral principles and concepts are inherently subjective in character. On this view moral beliefs do not emanate from a correct determination of a rationally purposive will, or even gaining insight into the will of some divine being. Rather, moral beliefs are fundamentally expressions of individuals' partial preferences. This position therefore rejects the principal ground upon which the concept of moral rights rests: that there exist rational and a priori moral principles upon which a correct and legitimate moral doctrine is to be founded. In modern, as opposed to ancient, philosophy this argument is most closely associated with the 18th Century Scottish philosopher David Hume. More recently versions of it have been defended by the likes of C.L. Stevenson, Ludwig Wittgenstein, J.L. Mackie, and Richard Rorty. Indeed, Rorty has argued that human rights are based not upon the exercise of reason, but a sentimental vision of humanity. He insists that human rights are not rationally defensible. He argues that one cannot justify the basis of human rights by appeal to moral theory and the canons of reason since, he insists, moral beliefs and practices are not ultimately motivated by an appeal to reason or moral theory, but emanate from a sympathetic identification with others; morality originates in the heart, and not in the head. Interestingly, though unambiguously sceptical about the philosophical basis of human rights, Rorty views the existence of human rights as a 'good and desirable thing', something whose existence we all benefit from. His critique of human rights is thus not motivated by an underlying hostility to the doctrine. For Rorty, human rights are better served by emotional appeals to identify with the unnecessary suffering of others, than by arguments over the correct determination of reason.

Rorty's emphasis upon the importance of an emotional identification with others is a legitimate concern. It may, for example, provide additional support for the philosophical arguments presented by the likes of Gewirth. However, as Michael Freeman has recently pointed out, 'Rorty's argument... confuses *motivation and justification.* Sympathy is an emotion. Whether the action we take on the basis of our emotions is justified depends on the reasons for the action. Rorty wishes to eliminate unprovable metaphysical theories from philosophy, but in his critique of human-rights theory he goes too far, and eliminates reasoning. Rorty's own account of the basis and scope of moral knowledge ultimately prohibits him from claiming that human rights is a morally desirable phenomenon, since he explicitly rules out the validity of appealing to the independently verifiable criteria required to uphold any such judgement. What we require from Rorty is an independent reason for accepting his conclusion. It is precisely this that he denies, may be legitimately provided by moral philosophy.

Rorty aside, the general critique of moral objectivity has a long and very well-established heritage in modern moral philosophy. It would be false to claim that either the objectivists or the subjectivists have scored any ultimate 'knock-down' over their philosophical opponents. Human rights are founded upon the claim to moral objectivity, whether by appeal to interests or the will. Any critique of moral objectivism is bound, therefore, to have repercussions for the philosophical defence of human rights. As I noted above, philosophers such as Alan Gewirth and John Finnis, in their separate and different ways, have attempted to establish the rational and objective force of human rights. The reader, interested in pursuing this particular theme further, is therefore recommended to pursue a close philosophical analysis of either, or both, of these two philosophers.

CONCLUSION

Human rights have a long historical heritage. The principal philosophical foundation of human rights is a belief in the existence of a form of justice valid for all peoples, everywhere. In this form, the contemporary doctrine of human rights has come to occupy centre stage in geo-political affairs. The language of human rights is understood and utilized by many people in very diverse circumstances. Human rights have become indispensable to the contemporary understanding of how human beings should be treated, by one another and by national and international political bodies. Human rights are best thought of as potential moral guarantees for each human being to lead a minimally good life. The extent to which this aspiration has not been realized represents a gross failure by the contemporary world to institute a morally compelling order based upon human rights. The philosophical basis of human rights has been subjected to consistent criticism. While some aspects of the ensuing debate between philosophical supporters and opponents of human rights remain unresolved and, perhaps, irresolvable, the general case for human rights remains a morally powerful one. Arguably, the most compelling motivation for the existence of humanity may rest upon the exercise of imagination. Try imagining a world without human rights!

SEVENTEEN

Epilogue

The Idea of human rights pre-dates the United Nations. Yet it was only with the setting up of this body that it finally achieved formal, universal recognition.

The history of human rights is a fascinating one. It has roots in all the great events of the world, and it has sustained the struggle for freedom and equality everywhere.

The international community has grown and changed enormously in the course of the twentieth century and it was one particularly agonizing convulsion—the Second World War—that prompted the victors to try to assemble a forum, firstly to deal with some of the War's consequences, but foremost to help provide a way to prevent such appalling events in the future. This was the United Nations.

The magnitude of the task was, and still is, clearly recognized. The attempt to define various universal declarations of human rights remains essential to the whole enterprise. Writing twenty years after the War, for example, in a review of The United Nations and Human Rights, the then Secretary-General, U Thant, declared that: "The establishment of human rights provides the foundation upon which rests the political structure of human freedom; the achievement of human freedom generates the will as well as the capacity for economic and social progress; the attainment of economic and social progress provides the basis for true peace". He saw in the promotion and protection of human rights-in the "ascending spiral", as he called it, "of human freedom and progress; prosperity and peace-the livery essence" and the "deepest meaning and motivation" of the United Nations Organization.

Fifteen years later Secretary-General Javier Perez de Cuellar, in summarizing Untied Nations Action, in the Field of Human Rights, endorsed the "place of honour" the Universal Declaration had won as the "basic international code of conduct by which performance in promoting and protecting human rights is to be measured", While regretting the continuance of flagrant violations, he acknowledged a deep and common-concern for human rights and the need to stimulate and reinforce them through effective programmes of teaching education and information

Very few people appreciate how extensive the attempt since 1945 has been to arrive at general agreement of this kind, and how much has been achieved. The reference point remains the Universal Declaration of Human Rights referred to above, and first proclaimed in 1948, it sets out a list of basic rights-a "common standard of achievement" in the words of the Declaration itself-for everyone in the world, whatever their race, colour, sex, language, religion, political or other opinion, national or social origin, property, birth or other status.

After extensive discussion and debate, two more international instruments were concluded, providing legal obligations to State parties—they were the international Covenant on Economic, Social and Cultural Rights, and the International Covenant on Civil and Political Rights. These both were adopted in 1966, and they entered into force ten years later. An Optional Protocol to the latter Covenant also provided machinery for the handling of complaints from individuals under specified circumstances.

These three documents together constitute the International Bill of Human Rights. They have directly inspired, or they parallel, in whole or in part, a very wide range of complementary instruments—on self-determination and the granting of independence to colonial countries and peoples; on the prevention of discrimination, whether by race, sex, employment, occupation, religion, belief, or in education (with a special convention on the crime of apartheid); on war crimes and crimes against humanity (including genocide); on slavery, servitude, forced labour and similar institutions and practices; on the protection of persons subjected to detention or imprisonment (with minimum rules for the treatment of prisoners, the condemnation of torture and the like); on nationality, statelessness, asylum and refugees; on freedom of information (the international right to correct misleading news dispatches); on freedom of association (trade union rights); on employment policy; on the political rights of women; on marriage, the family, childhood and youth; on social welfare, progress and development (the eradication of hunger and malnutrition, the use of scientific and technological progress in the interests of peace and for the benefit of all, and the rights of people with physical and mental disabilities); on international cultural development and co-operation; and on the media and the contribution it might make to strengthening peace and 'international understanding, to countering racism, apartheid and incitement to war, and to the promotion of human rights.

HUMAN RIGHTS MYTH

No doubt, the Universal Declaration of Human Rights is a great achievement of Human Civilization; it is also an achievement that a chapter on Human Rights has now a place in the constitutions of most of the countries of the world. But paradoxically this is an age when Human Rights are crushed mercilessly everywhere in the world and Human Rights have become a big fraud.

Certain human rights have been incorporated in the written Constitution of many countries, but sometimes, the political leaders usurp all the powers of the government and become dictators. The holy scripts of the Constitution guaranteeing the fundamental rights are nullified. In the Asian countries of Pakistan, Bangla Desh and Sri Lanka, military Generals have snatched all the powers and have put the popular leaders behind bars. The democracy comes to an end in these countries and the human rights are suspended. The activities are restricted and life becomes insecure. Any other country's government is not allowed to help, because it is considered as an interference in the internal matter.

It is ironical as well as amusing that these are the very countries which profess to be the guardians and torch bearers of Human Rights. And leading the battle-cry has been the USA. Ever since Woodrow Wilson spoke of making the world safe for democracy, successive American Presidents and important governmental functionaries have reiterated their faith in human rights as the bedrock, not only of American Policy but to entire political system.

In 1978, Fidel Castro made a point at a mass rally. He asked, "What moral right does a government have to defend human rights in a country where millionaires and the poverty stricken exist side by side, where Indians are exterminated and blacks discriminated against, where women are prostituted, and where Latin Americans are ruthlessly exploited. How can there be any talk of human rights by the leaders of an empire dominated by the-mafia, gambling casinos and child prostitution are life, where the CIA is devising and implementing subversive programmes, organizing worldwide spying, and where the Pentagon is creating neutron bombs that are designed to destroy every living thing, leaving intact only material objects. This empire supports counter-revolution in the world, protects and encourages multinational's exploitation of wealth and human resources on every continent, pursues a policy of inequality and protectionism, and thoughtlessly condemns the world to hunger while squandering natural resources."

"How can anyone speak about human rights while instructing and supplying with arms the most reactionary, blood thirsty and venal governments in the world?"

"How can anyone speak about human rights while maintaining close ties with the South African racists who oppress, discriminate against and exploit 20 million Africans? How can anyone speak about human rights while supplying an enormous amount of sophisticated weapons to the Zionist aggressors who have annexed the lands of Arab people of Palestine and who refuse to return the Arab territories they have seized by force? How can government leaders speak about human rights when their intelligence agencies have organized assassinations of other countries' leaders, when they have bombed Vietnam with more than one hundred times the amount of explosives found in the atomic bombs dropped on Hiroshima and Nagasaki, when their troops have exterminated hundreds of Vietnamese. And this government never got around to apologizing for its actions, never compensated the other for its losses. How can the leaders of a country talk about human rights when they traditionally interfere in the affairs of Latin America and exploit the people there?"

"Finally, how can an imperialist state which forcibly maintains a military basis on other territories and subjects their people to a criminal economic blockade speak about human rights?"

"Each leader of the United States claims to be the champion of human rights, yet nothing has changed in their policy either in the Western hemisphere or in the world. Everything remains the same, and as always, gunboat and dollar diplomacy and the law of the strong prevails. The only thing that remains constant in US policy is falsehood."

It is, thus, obvious that the very concept of human rights has become, what can be called an 'ideological neutron bomb', which is being increasingly used by American to establish its Economic & Ideological Imperialism in the world.

More Examples of Human Rights Myth

The following facts clearly show that Human Rights is a myth and Human Rights Education is a big fraud.

More than one thousand million people in the world suffer from acute hunger today. Every year/more than fifteen million people die of hunger.

Twenty four people die of starvation and hunger every minute; every twenty four hours 35,000 people die of hunger.

Out of 24 people who die of hunger every minute, 18 are children below the age of 5 years.-

More people have died of starvation and hunger in the last two years than those who had died in two World Wars together.

More people died of starvation every two days than died in the bombing of Hiroshima.

In 1976 a terrible earthquake in China took a toll of two lakh lives. More people die of starvation in the world every seven days.

These startling facts have been reported by Hunger Project, an international institution set up in 1977. It is spread over 152 nations, with a membership of about 3 million. Its objective is to spread awareness about the grave situation of starvation and hunger on a global scale, particularly in the context of mankind having developed enough productive power to produce ample food to feed the entire population of the world, if only a proper system of distribution could be worked out. It has recently published a report which presents some disturbing facts carefully hidden by the rulers of advanced capitalist countries as well as the Third World countries pursuing the capitalist path. Here are some more startling excerpts from the report :

"Out of the 1,000 million persons living in starvation, the overwhelming majority belonged to Third World countries pursuing the capitalist path of development in Latin America, Africa and Asia. Of this starving population, 50 per cent of nearly 500 million people live in the five countries of India, Bangladesh, Nigeria, Pakistan and Indonesia. It is estimated that if starvation were eliminated from India alone, the extent of starvation in the world would be reduced by one-third. It is significant that the crusader for a computers-led entry of India into a twenty-first century of prosperity, by relying on the profit-chasing classes as the agents of growth, is shrewdly silent about how these millions of Indian people, constituting one-third of the worlds hungry, are to be free from starvation."

The Report further says: "The rulers of countries and the mass media which sensationalize famines and seek to evoke pity for the famine stricken do not point out that the deaths and the misery caused by regular, everyday starvation, are of far greater proportions than deaths due to famines. Famines are heart-rending and do call for relief, but those who provide charity and relief during highly publicized famine situations should awaken to the fact that the deaths and agony caused by permanent, if non-spectacular starvation, are far more extensive and destructive than those caused by occasionally erupting famines. In the last 100 years Africa experienced famines in one country or the other 25 times, Latin America six times, Europe three times, West Asia four times and Asia 12 times. However, the destruction of life due to continuous starvation is many times greater and even the after effects of continuous starvation are more damaging and far-reaching than those of famines. While not denying horrors of famines and other disasters, it should be realized that without creating conditions in which starvation can be eliminated the disastrous consequences of famines cannot be checked or eliminated.

Apart from the millions who die as a result of permanent starvation, many more millions are condemned to life-long disabilities. For instance, due to inadequate intake of certain vitamins more than a quarter children become blind every year. Almost an equal number becomes deaf and dumb.

Taking the Indian situation, by the government's own admission, 3000 children become blind in the country due to Vitamin-A deficiency every year. These figures are of blindness as reported by hospitals, which we know cover only 15 per cent of the population. We also know how hospital records are inadequate and carelessly compiled. According to studies conducted by the National Institute of Nutrition in Hyderabad, 63 per cent of children below three years of age and 45 per cent of children in the 3-5 years age group suffer from severe anaemic conditions due to iron deficiency. The starvation and hunger are far more widespread than recorded by official bodies."

No matter how startling the facts, they are mere numbers. And numbers in thesmevels, are lifeless. The abject poverty and hunger of people, the animal like existence of millions & millions has become a common sight. We have 'adjusted' ourselves to it. We are no longer moved. And so like the proverbial ostrich we bury our heads further in the sand, and keep on burrowing furiously to attain our narrow, private ends.

The cause of the extensive worldwide starvation is not non-availability of food. 1,000 million people are starving today inspite of the fact that more food is produced than is needed for feeding the entire population of the world.

The solution to the problem of starvation of millions, it follows, does not lie in just more and more production, but is tied up with the system of distribution of what is produced.

In other words, the report is quite clear that the problem of hunger and starvation is tied up with how society is structured and organized. The conclusion is inescapable: that the rulers of the world capitalist system, including their imitators in the Third World countries, are responsible for the condition of 1,000 million starving people. This should be viewed with the same concern as that created by the countries preparing to plunge mankind into the holocaust of an atomic war.

Thus, it is ironical as well as amusing that these are the very countries which profess to be the guardians and torch-bearers of Human Rights. And leading the battle cry has been the USA. Ever since Woodrow Wilson spoke of making the world safe for democracy, successive American presidents and important governmental functionaries have reiterated their faith in human rights as the bedrock not only of American policy but of the entire political system.

MODERN AGE OF PARADOXES

The modern age is an age of paradoxes. Two world wars have been fought 'to end wars', but the shadow of the third is haunting us. The sky all over the world is coloured with hypocricy, suspicion, hatred, misunderstanding and cut-throat competition for material gains. This is the age of cold war. Cold war may, at any moment, change into hot war and a single atom may atomize the whole universe.

The First World War was fought by the Allied Countries in the name of Democracy and Human Rights and was won. But after this war the world witnessed the emergence of totalitarian forms of government with their various symbols—red, black and brown—but each designed to establish a despotism over the bodies and minds of men and each founded on the principle that man is created for the state. They replaced the democratic slogan of liberty, equality-and fraternity by their own slogan of duty, discipline, sacrifice, man for the state and regimentation.

The Second World War was fought to end these totalitarian regimes which were a challenge to individual Freedom and Dignity of Man. No doubt, the war brought destruction of the black and brown forms of totalitarianism (Fascism and Nazism), but paradoxically it strengthened the red regime (U.S.S.R.) which emerged to challenge the democracies that had fought to preserve the ideals of freedom, with its own slogan of class-struggle, violent revolutions, proletariat dictatorship, withering away of the state and ultimately classless and stateless society—free from exploitation and oppression.

Communism is trying to establish a classless and stateless society to save the individual from exploitation and oppression. According to the communists, a classless and stateless society is the raison deter of peace, progress and prosperity and proletarian dictatorship is a stepping stone towards this goal. Once the transfer of the means of production into the hands of the community has been achieved, the state-that is to say, the instrument of coercion will no longer be necessary. It will wither away. Theoretically, the dictatorship of the proletariat, no doubt, was to create conditions for 'withering away' of the state. But, paradoxically the state has become all powerful and all pervasive. It has its iron hand not only on the political and economic life but also on the moral, cultural and intellectual life, nay its words are to be final in the domain of art and literature, philosophy and science. Under such a dictatorship of the communist party (rather the leader of the communist party) the individual is degraded, oppressed, tortured and controlled by fear. It seems that the state will never 'wither away' and the goal of classless and stateless society will remain only a dream. This sorry state of affairs is not confined to the U.S.S.R. alone, it also finds its full expression in the Russian satellites and Red China—the greatest challenge to the world. The hall-mark of this system is that the Individual seems to be deprived of liberty and freedom for which the human soul cries so loudly.

America is aware of the fact that communism is enemy number one of individual Freedom and Dignity of Man, but she does not realize the increasing likeness of methods and developments, towards which the struggle with the communist bloc is driving her. The Individual Freedom guaranteed by the constitution and protected by the Supreme Court still permeates American life and ideology. But the powers of the Committee for the Un-American Activities of the Federal Investigation Bureau, under the so-called Loyalty Order of 1947 and the pressure of publicity campaigns of newspapers and other organs of public opinion, subject statesmen, public servants, scientific workers and teachers to growing restrictions and intimidations under the label of communist sympathies or associations. The 'Voice of America' rivals with that of Moscow and Beijing in abuse. Today, the ideological gap between American and Communist is still very wide, but so far as methods in practice are concerned, both are coming close to each other. Behind all the tension and fury of the modern age, there has always been a measure of common values between the two camps. There is the same faith in boundless possibilities of technological perfection, a pride in the sheer bigness of scientific and industrial development, a naive optimism about man's ability to produce heaven on earth, by mastering nature and circumstances. Thus, not only totalitarian communism but big-scale capitalism is also leading to a very similar system of control, and the very existence of the individual is likely to be jeopardized.

Trade Unionism was started as a measure of collective self-defence of the under-privileged working class against the exploitation of the capitalism, but even in the most developed industrial countries it has now reached the stage in which the individual worker is left with less and less freedom. In practice, if not in theory, he must join the union or he will lose his livelihood. Under trade-unionism the innocent workers are exploited by the so-called labour leaders who are more dangerous than the capitalists, who are bigger parasites on society and who are a challenge to the society with their slogan of strike and violence.

Universal Education is being provided to liberate the masses, so that they may think or act independently, following their own judgement and conscience, but paradoxically they are losing their independent thinking, because they are more exposed than ever to the press, the radio, the television, the wireless, the film and the organized political mass meeting.

This is the age of Democracy — "Government of the people, for the people and by the people", but paradoxically even in the modern democratic states the average citizen usually speaks of "they", not "we", when referring to government action of taxation, defence or other matters. It is significant that in the last few decades leading political and social thinkers of different countries have studied the growth of the new "elite", a new oligarchy of rulers dominating the masses. The sociological studies of Frenchman Georges Sorel, the Italian Vilfredo Pareto, the Spainish Ortega Y Gasset, German Oswald Spengler find their counter part in Aldous Huxley's Picture of a completely mechanized and standardized 'Brave New World', together with the superficial trends towards democracy and the greater participation of the people in the political affairs, the technical means by which the small groups of people can guide and rule the masses, have grown immensely, in quantity and quality. Thus the modern democracy is democracy only in name.

THE MODERN AGE OF STATISM

We talk of democracy, socialism, communism and democratic socialism, but in fact, it is an age of statism; in the sense that the state, whether capitalistic or socialistic or communistic is gaining more and more say in our lives. "It was said in the beginning of this century that the modern state was Jenghiz Khan, with telegraph lines. Today it is more than that. It is Jenghiz Khan distant controls exercised by a hundred methods. It speaks with a million voices on the radio; overhears our conversation on the telephone. It pries into our secret thoughts by censoring letters. It controls the water we drink, the food we eat, the light we use, our modes of transportation and infact, practically everything in our lives". One may be proud of human rights enshrined in the constitutions of almost all the countries of the world. But, what chance has the individual inst such an institution, that is, highly centralized modern state — impersonal, all pervasive, unmoved by sentiments, armed both by the power of law and by every possible instrument of authority coercion?

THE INDIVIDUAL AT STAKE

In this modern age of paradoxes the Individual, degraded, oppressed and controlled by fear has become the victim of hatred, jealousy, violence and suspicion. He tends to be neurotic. The old ideals, i.e. philosophies of life which have brought him so far are unable to push him any further. He is trying to find out something and makes experiments with whatever crosses his mind. All that is nothing but search in the darkness and instead of solving problems, he is only making them more and more complicated. The individual is losing all hope and is feeling in secure. Slowly and slowly all the inner finer qualities of man are leaving him, making him increasingly gross and self-centred. As a consequem in all spheres of activities — moral, social, intellectual, economic, political, educational and cultural-he finds nothing, but confusion. In such a state of confusion the very existence of the Individual is at stake. He does not know what to do.

THE PROBLEMS OF THE MODERN AGE

Some of the problems which the individual is facing today are:

(a) How can the Individual regain the sense of his wholeness, so that he ceases to be neurotic?

(b) How can he regain awareness of his essential oneness with his fellows?

(c) How can a non-violent sanction for a society be developed that may take the place of external sanctions by which society is at present regulated?

The crisis in the modern civilization is the direct result of loss of faith. We have today a generation of men who are smart, superficial, trim, alert, ready to question and doubt, unwilling to believe in anything, and have no moral earnestness or love of truth. Our knowledge is diffused, directionless and we are all distraught in mind and tired in body and listless in out manners. We have a civilization built upon untruth and lovelessness. We have given ourselves to the cult of violence. We just shift and drift and cleverly erect defences to hide out real nature. The best lack all convictions and the worst are full of passionate interests. When the best lack all convictions and the worst are full of passionate interests, when the exponents of different isms, propagandists of contradictory socio-politico-economic values and enthusiasts of diametrically opposed parties do not hesitate to slaughter their opponents, humanity can be saved only by practicing Truth and Non-violence in life in such a way as was advocated by Gandhiji.

Equality, brotherhood and world-peace have been so ubiquitous, and yet never has humanity or human values stood nearer to the brink of total destruction than they do today. The world has been passing now through the after-effects of the two great world wars which have revealed the brute in man and shaken all confidence in his inner goodness. The world is being caught up again in a long and grim cold war for which even the most pacifist nations are engaged in coolly devising the most powerful instruments for the destruction of fellow beings. Today even democratic governments are being unconsciously led to adopt autocratic methods for saving democracy. The same is being done to get rid of terrorism. Thus the modern world faces a paradox.

The explanation for the paradox lies in the contradiction between the ends and the means that characterize the present age. When we use brute force to settle a problem, it sets into motion an opposite force of a like character. This in its turn necessitates the use of greater force, and so the chain of retaliation and counter-retaliation lengthens and strengthens.

Is there a way of breaking this vicious circle. Is there a force different and better suited for resolving tensions than brute force? Gandhiji showed us one. 'Satyagraha' i.e. the power of Truth was the name he gave it. He also called it 'soul force' because it pits against the material force of the opponent, the power of the spirit.

RECOVERY OF SPIRITUAL VALUES

The paradoxes of the modern world are because the material aspect of the world is almost completely divorced from its spiritual aspect. The material which knows no moral law, has become a law unto itself. While being influenced by materialistic philosophy, so much human energy, time, and money are devoted to the discovery of the truths of outer material nature, so little is being done to reveal and utilize the deeper truths of human nature. Even the most advanced people blindly assume the truth of the brute in man, plan human relations on this crude basis, and then apply all scientific talents to the perfection of destructive implements that can take care of brute, by threat and violence. In this process of killing the brute in the enemy by violence, man turns both himself and his enemy into greater brutes.

Human progress can be assured only if the life of the individual, society, country, and the world as a whole be more and more based on the fundamental moral principles of Truthfulness, Non-violence, Non-stealing. Self-control and Non-possession. The regeneration of moral life requires, as Gandhiji tried to show, the progressive planning of social, economic, and political life on these moral principles. Thus, if the physical world is to be established and saved from self-destruction, it must become part of a unified world order. It must, that is to say, be brought under the control of moral and spiritual law. It is to the recovery of spiritual values that we must look for the solution of our major, national and world-problems.

Human Rights cannot be protected by putting beautiful chapters in the International Charters and Constitution of different countries of the world, but can be protected and enjoyed only when we govern our life by spiritual and not material values. When every body is governed by spiritual values and perform his or her duties, automatically, no body's rights will be violated and every body's rights will be protected.

Thus, it is only when the foundation of society is based upon spiritual values, that Human Rights will become Reality.

APPENDICES

ONE

Land Marks of Human Rights Development

26 June 1945

Signing of the Charter of the United Nations and statute of the International Court of Justice, in San Francisco.

21 June 1946

Establishment of the commission on Human Rights under Economic and Social Council resolution 9 (11). At its first session, in 1947, the Commission establishes the Sub commission on prevention of Discrimination and Protection of Minorities on the basis of that resolution.

21 June 1946

Establishment of the Commission on the Status of Women under resolution 11 (II) of the Economic and Social Council.

9 December 1948

Adoption by the General Assembly of the Covenant on the Prevention and Punishment of the Crime of Genocide.

10 December 1948

Adoption by the General Assembly of the Universal Declaration of Human Rights.

2 December 1949

Adoption by the General Assembly of the Convention for the Suppression of the traffic in Persons and of the Exploitation of the Prostitution of Others.

4 November 1950

Adoption by the members of the Council of Europe of the Convention for the Protection of Human Rights and Fundamental Freedoms (European Convention on Human Rights).

1 December 1950

Creation of the Committee on Crime Prevention and Control under General Assembly resolution 415 (v). The Committee is responsible for preparing the United, Nations Congresses on the Prevention of Crime and the Treatment of Offenders, it is institutionalised in the form of the Commission on Crime Prevention and Criminal Justice by the Economic and Social Council on 6 February 1992.

28 July 1951

Adoption by a United Nations Conference of Plenipotentiaries of the Convention relating to the Status of Refugees.

20 December 1952

Adoption by the General Assembly of the Convention on the Political Rights of Women.

23 October 1953

Adoption by the General Assembly of the Protocol amending the Slavery Convention Signed at Geneva on 25 September 1926.

28 September 1954

Adoption by a Conference of Plenipotentiaries; of the Convention relating to the Status of Stateless Persons.

30 August 1955

Adoption by the First United Nations Congress on the Prevention of Crime and the Treatment of Offenders of the Standard Minimum Rules for the Treatment of Prisoners.

7 September 1956

Adoption by a Conference of Plenipotentiaries; of the Supplementary Convention on the Abolition of Slavery, the Slave trade, and Institutions and Practices Similar to Slavery.

29 January 1957

Adoption by the General Assembly of the Convention on the Nationality of Married Women.

25 June 1957

Adoption by the General Conference of the International Organization of the Convention on the Abolition of Forced Labour.

30 July 1959

Adoption by the Economic and Social Council of resolution 728 F (XXVIII), given the Commission on Human Rights certain responsibilities with regard to the treatment of communications dealing with human rights.

20 November 1959

Adoption by the General Assembly of the Declaration of the Rights of the Child.

14 December 1960

Adoption by the General Assembly of the Declaration on the Granting of Independence to Colonial Countries and Peoples.

30 August 1961

Adoption by a Conference of Plenipotentiaries of the Convention on the Reductipn of Statelessness.

7 November 1962

Adoption by the General Assembly of the Convention on Consent to Marriage, Minimum Age and Registration of Marriages.

14 December 1962

Adoption by the General Assembly of resolution 1803 (XVII) on permanent sovereignty over natural resources.

20 November 1963

Adoption by the General Assembly of the United-Nations Declaration on the Elimination of All forms of Racial Discrimination.

21 December 1965

Adoption by the General Assembly of the International convention on the Elimination of All forms of Racial Discrimination. This convention provides for the establishment of the committee on the Elimination of Racial Discrimination.

16 December 1966

Adoption by the General Assembly of the International covenant on Economic, social and cultural Rights. Adoption of the International covenant on civil and political Rights and of the corresponding-optional protocol. This covenant provides for the establishment of the Human Rights committee.

6 June 1967

Adoption by the Economic and Social Council of resolution 1235 (XLII), authorizing the Commission on Human Rights and the Sub commission on Prevention of Discrimination and Protection of Minorities to examine information relevant to gross violations of human rights and fundamental freedoms.

7 November 1967

Adoption by the General I Assembly of the Declaration on the Elimination of Discrimination against Women.

13 May 1968

Proclamation by the International Conference on Human Rights of the Protection of Teheran.

26 November 1968

Adoption by the General Assembly of the Convention on the Non-Applicability of Statutory Limitation to War Crimes and Crimes against Humanity.

22 November 1969

Adoption of the American convention on Human Right!

11 December 1969

Adoption by the General Assembly of the Declaration on Social, Progress and Development.

27 May 1970

Adoption by the Economic and Social council of resolution 1503 (XLVIII), establishing procedures allowing the Commission on Human Rights and the Sub commission on Prevention of Discrimination and Protection of Minorities to hold private meetings to consider communications relating to violations of Human rights and fundamental freedoms.

13 August 1971

Adoption by the Sub commission on Prevention of Discrimination and Protection of Minorities of resolution 1 (XXIV), concerning procedures for the implementation of Economic and Social Council resolution 1503(XLVIII).

30 November 1973

Adoption by the General Assembly of the International Convention on the Suppression and Punishment of the Crime of Apartheid. The Convention provides for the establishment of the Group of Three, which is to monitor its implementation.

9 December 1975

Adoption by the General Assembly of the Declaration on the Protection of All Persons from Being Subjected to Torture and Other Cruel, Inhuman or Degrading Treatment or Punishment.

8 June 1977

Adoption by the Diplomatic Conference on the Reaffirmation and Development of International Humanitarian Law applicable in Armed Conflict of the Protocol Additional to the Geneva Conventions of 12 August 1949, and relating to the Protection of Victims of Non-international Armed Conflicts (Protocol 11).

27 November 1978

Adoption by the General Conference of UNESCO of the Declaration on Race and Racial Prejudice.

17 December 1979

Adoption by the General Assembly of the Code of Conduct for Law Enforcement Officials.

18 December 1979

Adoption by the General Assembly of the Convention on the Elimination of All Forms of Discrimination against Women. The Covenant Provides for the establishment of the Committee on the. Elimination of Discrimination against Women.

June 1981

Adoption of the African Charter on Human and Peoples' Rights, by the Eighteenth Conference of Heads of State and Government of the Organization of African Unity.

25 November 1981

Adoption by the General Assembly of the Declaration on the Elimination of All Form of Intolerance and Discrimination Base on Religion-or Belief.

25 May 1984

Approval by the Economic and Social Council of the Safeguards Guaranteeing protection of the rights of those facing the death penalty.

12 November 1984

Adoption by the General Assembly of the Declaration on the Right of Peoples to Peace.

10 December 1984

Adoption by the General Assembly of the Convention against Torture and Other Cruel, Inhuman or Degrading Treatment or Punishment. The Convention provides for the establishment of the Committee against Torture.

28 May 1985

Adoption by the Economic and Social Council of resolution 1985/ 17 establishing the Committee on Economic, Social and Cultural Rights, responsible for - monitoring the implementation of the International Covenant on Economic, Social and Cultural Rights.

29 November 1985

Adoption by the General Assembly of the United Nations Standard Minimum Rules for the Administration of Juvenile Justice (The Beijing Rules).

29 November 1985

Adoption by the General Assembly of the Declaration of Basic Principles of Justice for Victims of Crime and Abuse of Power.

29 November 1985

Adoption by the Seventh United Nations Congress on the Prevention of Crime and the Treatment of Officers of the Basic Principles on the Independence of the Judiciary.

10 December 1985

Adoption by the General Assembly of the International Convention against Apartheid in Sports. The Convention provides for the establishment of the Commission against Apartheid in Sports.

13 December 1985

Adoption by the General Assembly of a resolution on the implementation of the Nairobi Forward-looking Strategies for the Advancement of Women.

4 December 1986

Adoption by the General Assembly of the Declaration on the Right to Development.

9 December 1988

Adoption by the General Assembly of the Body of Principles for the Protection of All Persons under Any Form of Detention or Imprisonment.

24 May 1989

Adoption by the Economic and Social Council of the Principles on the Effective Prevention and Investigation of Extra-legal, Arbitrary and Summary Executions.

20 November 1989

Adoption by the General Assembly of the Convention on the Rights of the child. The Convention provides for the establishment of the Committee on the Rights of the Child.

15 December 1989

Adoption by the General Assembly of the Second Optional Protocol to the fnternational Covenant on Civil and Political Rights, aiming at the Adoption of the Death Penalty. The Human Rights Committee is the monitoring body for the Protocol.

7 September 1990

Adoption by the Eighth United Nations Congress on the 'Prevention of Crime and the Treatment of Offenders of the Basic Principles on the Use of Force and Firearms by Law Enforcement Officials.

7 September 1990

Adoption by the English United Nations Congress on the Prevention of crime and the Treatment of Offenders of the Principles on the Role qf Lawyers.

7 September 1990

Adoption by the English United Nations Congress on the Prevention of Crime and the Treatment of Offenders of the Guidelines on the Role of Prosecutors.

30 September 1990

Adoption by the World Summit for Children of the World Declaration on the Survival, Protection and Development of Children and of the Plan of Action for Implementing the World Declaration.

14 December 1990

Adoption by the General Assembly of the United Nations Standard Minimum Rules for Non-custodial Measures (The Tokyo Rules); Basic Principles for the treatment of prisoners; the United Nations Guidelines for the Prevention of Juvenile Delinquency (The Riyadh Guidelines) and the United Nations Rules of the Protection of Juveniles Deprived of their Liberty.

18 December 1990

Adoption by the General Assembly of a resolution deciding to convene a World Conference on Human Rights in 1993.

18 December 1990

Adoption is the General Assembly of the International Convention On the Protection of the Rights of All Migrant Workers and Members of Their Families. The Convention provides for the establishment of the Committee on the Protection of the Rights of all Migrant Workers and Members of Their Families.

20 May 1991

Adoption by the Security Council of a Resolution establishing the United Nations Observer Mission in EL Salvador (ONUSAL).

7 April 992

Adoption by the Security Council of a resolution deciding to deploy the United Nations Protection Force (UNPROFOR) in the former Yugoslavia.

30 May 1992

Adoption by the Security Council of a resolution demanding that the parties to the conflict in Bosnia and Herzegovina allow the unimpeded delivery of humanitarian supplies.

14 September 1992

Adoption by the Security Council of a resolution authorizing the enlargement of the mandate of UNPROFOR.

16 November 1992

Adoption by the Security Council of a resolution condemning "ethnic cleansing" in Bosnia and Herzegovina.

18 December 1992

Adoption by the Security Council of a resolution demanding that the detention camps in-Bosnia and Herzegovina should be closed.

18 December 1992

Adoption by the General Assembly of the Declaration on the Protection of All Persons from Enforced Disappearance.

18 December 1992

Adoption by the General Assembly of the Declaration on the Rights of Persons Belonging to National or Ethnic, Religious and Linguistic Minorities.

22 February 1993

Adoption by the Security Council of a resolution establishing an International Tribunal for the Prosecution of persons responsible for serious violations of international humanitarian law committed in the territory of the former Yugoslavia since 1991.

20 April 1993

Adoption by the General Assembly of a resolution authorizing the participation of the United Nations jointly with the Organization of American States in an International Civilian Mission to Haiti (MICIVIH).

25 May 1993

Adoption by the Security Council of a resolution adopting the statute of the International Tribunal for the Prosecution of Persons Responsible for Serious Violations of International Humanitarian Law Committed in the Territory of the Former Yugoslavia since 1991.

14 June 1993

The Secretary-General, at the opening of the World Conference on Human Rights in Vienna, describes human rights as "the quintessential values through which we affirm together that we are a single human community".

25 June 1993

Adoption of the Vienna Declaration and Programme of Action at the closing of the World Conference on Human Rights.

20 December 1993

Adoption by the General Assembly of resolution 48/91, proclaiming the Third Decade to Combat Racism and Racial Discrimination.

20 December 1993

Adoption by the General Assembly of resolution 48/163, proclaiming the International Decade of the World's Indigenous People.

20 December 1993

Adoption by the General Assembly of resolution 48/141, establishing the post of United Nations High Commissioner for Human Rights.

23 February 1994

Adoption by the Security Council of a resolution establishing the civil police component of the United Nations Operation in Mozambique (ONUMOZ).

1 July 1994

Adoption by the Security Council of a resolution establishing a Commission of Experts to investigate violations of human rights in Rwanda.

19 September 1994

Adoption by the General Assembly of a resolution establishing the United Nations Mission for the Verification of Human Rights and of Compliance with the Commitments of the Comprehensive Agreement on Human Rights in Guatemala (MINUIGUA).

23 September 1994

Adoption by the 'Security Council of a resolution re-emphasising that "ethnic cleansing" constitutes a clear violation of international humanitarian law.

8 November 1994

Adoption by the Security Council of resolution 955 (1994), establishing an International Tribunal for Rwanda.

23 December 1994

Adoption by the General Assembly of resolution 49/184, Proclaiming the United Nations Decade for Human Rights Education (1995-2004).

3 March 1995

Adoption by the Commission on Human Rights-of a resolution establishing a working group to elaborate a draft declaration on the rights of indigenous people (resolution 1995/32), i.e (1994-2004).

1995

Bejining Declaration & platform for Action, Fourth World Conference on Women: Action for Equality, Development and peace.

1997

Guiding principles on International Diplacement, 1997.

1998

Declaration on the Right & Responsibility of Individuals, Groups and Organs of Society to Promote and Protect Universally Recognized Human Rights and Fundamental Freedom, 1998.

2000

U.N. millennium Declaration, 2000.

2000

Declaration of Articles on Nationality of Natural persons in relation to the succession of states, 2000.

2000

General Assembly Declaration of commitment on HIV/ AIDS, 2000.

2003

Norms on the Responsibilities of Trasnational Corporation and other Business Entyerprises with regard Human Rights, 2003.

2005

Basic principles of Guidelines on the Right to a Remedy and Reparation for victims of gross violations of International Human Rights Law and serious violations of International Humantarian Law, 2005.

Human Rights and Human Genome

1. Universal Declaration on the Human Genome and Human Rights 1997.

2. European convention for the protection of Human Rights and Dignity of the Human Being with Regard to the Application of Biology and Medicine (Convention on Human Rights and Biomedicine), 1997.
3. Additional Protocol to the European convention on Human Rights and Biomedicine, on the prohibition of cloning Human Beings, 1998.
4. Additional Protocol to the European Convention on Human Rights and Biomedicine, concerning Transplantation of Organs and Tissues of Human origin, 2002.
5. Additional Protocol to the European convention on Human Right and Biomedicine, concerning Biomedical Research, 2005.
6. UNESCO International Declaration on Human Genetic Data, 2003.
7. United Nations Declaration on Human Clonning 2005.
8. Universal Declaration on Bioethics and Human Rights, 2005.

TWO

The Right to Information Act, 2005

The following Act of Parliament received the assent of the President on the 15th June 2005, and is hereby published for general information:

An Act to provide for setting out the practical regime of rights to information for citizens to secure access to information under the control of public authorities, in order to promote transparency and accountability in the working of every public authority, the constitution of a Central Information Commission and State Information Commission and for matters connected therewith or incidental thereto.

WHEREAS the Commission of India has established democratic Republic;

AND WHEREAS democracy requires an informed citizenry and transparency of information which are vital to its functioning and also to contain corruption and to hold Governments and their instrumentalities accountable to the governed;

AND WHEREAS revelation of information in actual practice is likely to conflict with other public interests including efficient operations of the Governments, optimum use of limited fiscal resources and the preservation of confidentiality of sensitive information;

AND WHEREAS it is necessary to harmonise these conflicting interests while preserving the paramount of the democratic ideal;

NOW THEREFORE, it is expedient to provide for furnishing certain information to citizens who desire to have it.

BE it enacted by Parliament in the Fifty-sixth year of the Republic of India as follows:

CHAPTER-1

Preliminary

1. Short title, extent and commencement-

(1) This Act may be called the Right to Information Act, 2005.

2) It extends to the whole of India except the State of Jammu and Kashmir.

(1) The provisions of Sub-section 4, Sub-sections (1) and (2) of section 5, Sections 12, 13, 15, 16, 24, 27 and 28 shall come into force at once, and the remaining provisions of this Act shall come into force on the one hundred and twentieth day of its enactment.

2. Definitions-in this Act, unless the context otherwise requires,

(a) "Appropriate Government" means in relation to a public authority which is established, constituted, owned, controlled or substantially financed by funds provided directly or indirectly -

(I) by the Central Government or the Union Territory administration, the central Government;

(II) by the State Government, the State Government;

(b) "Central Information Commission" means the Central « Information Commission constituted under Sub-section (1) of Section 12;

(c) "Central Public Information Commission" means the Central Public Information Officer designated under Sub-section (1) and includes a Central Assistant Public Information Officer designated as such under Sub-section (2) of Section 5;

(d) "Chief Information Commissioner" and "information Commissioner" mean the Chief Information Commissioner and Information Commissioner appointed under Sub-section (3) of section 12;

(e) "competent authority" means -

(I) the Speaker in the case of the House of the People or the Legislative Assembly of a State or a Union Territory having such Assembly and the Chairman in the case of the Council of State of a Legislative Council of States;

(II) the Chief Justice of India in the case of the Supreme Court;

(III) the Chief Justice of the High Court in the Case of a High Court;

(IV) the President or the Governor, as the case may be, in the case of other authorities established or constituted by or under the Constitution;

(V) the administrator appointed under Article 239 of the Constitution;

(f) "information" means any material in any from, including records, documents, memos, e-mails, opinions, advices, press releases, circulars, orders, logbooks, contracts, reports, paper releases, circulars, orders logbooks, contracts, reports, papers, samples, models, data material held in any electronic from and information relating to any private body which cal be accessed by a public authority under any other law for the time being in force;

(g) "prescribed" means prescribed by rules made under this Act by the appropriate Government or the Competent authority, as the case may be;

(h) "public authority" means any authority or body or institution of self-government established or constituted-

(a) by or under the Constitution;

(b) by any other law made by Parliament;

(c) by any other law made by State Legislature;

(d) by notification issued or order made by the appropriate - Government, and includes any-

(I) body owned, controlled or substantially financed;

(II) non-Government organisation substantially financed;

directly or indirectly by funds provided by the appropriate Government;

(i) "**Record**" includes-

(a) any document, manuscript and file;

(b) any microfilm, microfiche and facsimile copy of a document;

(c) any reproduction of image or images embodied in such microfilm (whether enlarged or not); and

(d) any other material produced by a computer or any other device;

(j) "Right to Information" means the right to information accessible under that Ace which is held by or under the control of any public authority and includes the right to-

(I) inspection of work, documents, records;

(II) taking notes, extracts or certified copies of documents or records;

(III) taking certified samples of material;

(IV) obtaining information in the form of diskettes, floppies, tapes, video cassettes or in any other electronic mode or through printouts where such information is stored in a computer or in any other device;

(k) "State Information Commission" means the State Information Commission constituted under Sub-section (1) of Section 15;

(I) "State Chief Information Commission" and "State Information Commissioner" mean the State Chief Information Commissioner and the State information Commissioner appointed under Sub-section (3) of Section 15;

(m) "State Public Information Officer" means the State Public Information Officer designated under Sub-section (1) and includes a State Assistant Public Information Officer designated as such under Sub-section (2) of Section 5;

(n) "Third party" means a person other than the citizen making a request for information and includes a public authority.

CHAPTER-II

Right to information and obligations of public authorities

3. Right to information - Subject to the provisions of this Act, all citizens shall have the right to information.

4. Obligation of public authorities - (1) Every public authority shall -

(a) Maintain all its records duly catalogued and indexed in a manner and the from which facilitates the right to information under this Act and ensure that all records that are appropriate to be computerised are within a reasonable time and subject to availability of resources, computerised and connected through a network all over the country on different systems so that access to such records is facilitated;

(b) publish within one hundred and twenty days from the enactment of this Act,-

(I) the particulars of its organisation, function and duties;

(II) the powers and duties of its officers and employees;

(III) the procedure followed in the decision making process, including channels of supervision and accountability;

(IV) the norms set by it for the discharge of its functions;

(V) the rules, regulations, instructions and records, held by it or under its control or used by its employees for discharging its functions;

(VI) a statement of the categories of documents that are held by it or under its control;

(VII) the particulars of any arrangement that exists for consultation with, or representation by, the members of the public in relation to the formulation of its policy or implementation thereof;

(VIII) a statement of the boards, councils, committees and other bodies consisting of two or more persons constituted as its part or for the purpose of its advice, and as to whether meetings of those boards, councils, committees and other bodies are open to the public, or the minutes of such meetings are accessible for public;

(IX) a directory of its officers and 'employees;

(X) the monthly remuneration received each of its officers and employees, including'the system of compensation as provided in its regulations;

(XI) the budget allocated to each of its agency, indicating the particulars of all plans, proposed expenditures and reports on disbursements made;

(XII) the manner of execution of subsidy programmes, including the amounts allowed and the details of beneficiaries of such programmes;

(XIII) particulars of recipients of concessions, permits or authorisations granted by it;

(XIV) details in respect of the information, available to or held by it, reduced in an electronic form;

(XV) the particulars of facilities available to citizens for obtaining information, including the working hours of a library or reading room, if maintained for public use;

(XVI) the names, designations and other particulars of the Public Information Officers;

(XVII) such other information as may be prescribed, and thereafter update these publications every year;

(c) publish all relevant facts while formulating important policies or announcing the decisions which affect public;

provide reasons for its administrative or quasi-judicial decisions to affected persons.

(2) It shall be a constant endeavour of every public authority to take steps in accordance with the requirements of Clause (b) of Sub-section (1) to provide as much information *suo mofu* to the public at regular intervals through various means of communications, including internet, so that the public have minimum resort to the use of this Act to obtain information.

(1) For the purposes of Sub-section (1), every information shall be disseminated widely and in such from and manner which is easily accessible to the public.

All materials shall be disseminated taking into consideration the cost effectiveness, local language and the most effective method of communication in that local area and the information should be easily accessible, to the extent possible in electronic format with the Central Public Information Officer or State Public Information Officer, as the case may be, available free or at such cost of the medium or the print cost price as may be prescribed.

Explanation—For the purposes of Sub-sections (3) and (4), "disseminated" means making known or communicated the information of the public through notice boards, newspapers, public announcements, media broadcasts, the internet or any other means, including inspection of offices of any public authority.

5. Designation of Public Information officers- (1) Every public authority shall, within one hundred days the enactment of this Act, designate as many officers as the Central Public Information Officers of State Public Information Officers, as the case may be, in all administrative units or offices under it as may be necessary to provide information of persons requesting for the information under this Act.

(2) without Prejudice to the provisions of Sub-section (1), every public authority shall designated an officer, within one hundred days of the enactment of this Act, at each sub-divisional level or other sub-district level as a Central Assistant Public Information Officer or a State Assistance Public Information Officer, as the case may be, to receive the applications for information or appeals- under this Act for forwarding the same forthwith to the central public Information officer or the State Public Information Officer or senior officer specified under Sub-section (1) of Section 19 or the Central Information Commission or the State Information Commission, as the case may be:

Provided that where an application tor information or appeal is given to a Central Assistant public information Officer or a State Assistant Public Information Officer, as the case may be, a period of five days shall be added in computing the period for response specified under Sub-section (1) of Section 7.

(3) Every central Public Information Officer or State Public Information Officer, as the case may be , shall deal

with requests from persons seeking information and render reasonable assistance to the persons seeking such information.

(4) The Central Public Information Officer or State Public Information Officer, as the case may be, may seek the assistance of any other officer as he or she considers it necessary for the proper discharge of his or her duties.

(5) Any officer, whose assistance has been sought under Sub-section (4), shall render all assistance to the Central Public Information Officer or State Public Information Officer, as the case may be, seeking his or her assistance and for the purpose of any contravention of the provision of the Act, such other officer shall be treated as a central Public Information Officer or State Public Information Officer, as the case may be.

2. Respect for obtaining information-(l) A person, who desires to obtain any information under this Act, shall make a request in writing or through electronic means in English or Hindi or in official language of the area in which the application is being made, accompanying such free as may be prescribed, to-

(a) the Central Public information Officer or State Public Information Officer; as the case may be, of the concerned public authority;

(b) the Central Assistant Public Information Officer or State Assistant Public Information Officer, as the case may be, specifying the particulars of the information sought by him or her:

Provided that where such request cannot be made in writing, the Central Public Information Officer or State Public Information Officer, as the case may be, shall render all reasonable assistance to the person making the request orally to reduce the same in writing.

(2) An applicant making request for information shall not be required to give any reason for requesting the

information or any other personal details accept those that may be necessary for contacting him.

(3) Where an application is made to a public authority requesting for an information,-

(i) which is held by another public authority; or

(ii) the Subject matter of which is more closely connected with the functions of another public authority, the public authority, to which such application is made, shall transfer the application or such of it as may be appropriate to that other public authority and inform the applicant immediately about such transfer:

Provided that the transfer of an application pursuant to this sub-section shall be made as soon as practicable but in no case later than five days from the date of receipt of the application.

Comment

A person desirous to obtain any information has to make a request for obtaining such information under this Act either in writing or through electronic means in English of Hindi or any official language of the area with the prescribed fee, to the Central/State Public Information Officer of the concerned public authority or to the Central/ State Assistant Public Information Officer, as the case May be.

3. Disposal ofl request- (1) Subject to the Proviso to Sub-section (2) of Section 5 or the proviso to Sub-section (3) of Section 6, the Central Public Information Officer or State Public Information Officer, as the case may be, on receipt of a request under Section 6 shall, as expeditiously as possible, and in any case within third days of the receipt of the request, either provide the request for any of the reasons specified in Sections 8 and 9:

Provide that where the information sought for concerns the life or liberty of a person, the same shall be provided within forty-eight hours of the receipt of the request.

(2) If the Central Public Information Officer or State Public Information Officer, as the case may be, fails to give decision on the request for information within the period under Sub-section (1), the Central Public Information Officer or State Public. Information Officer, as the case may be, shall be deemed to have refused the request.

(3) Where a decision is taking to provide the information on payment of any further fee representing the cost of providing the information, the Central Public Information Officer or State Public Information Officer, as the case may be, shall send intimation to the person making the request, giving-

(a) The details of further fees responding the cost of providing the information as determined by him, together with the calculations made to arrive at the amount in accordance with fee prescribed under Sub-section (1), requesting him to deposit that fees, and the period intervening between the despatch of the said intimation and payment of fees shall be excluded for the porpose of calculating the period of thirty days referred to in that sub-section;

(b) Information concerning his or her right with respect to review the decision as to the amount of fees charged or the form of access provided, including the particulars of the appellate authority, time limit, process and any other forms.

(4) Where access to the record or a part thereof is required to be provided under this Act and the person to whom access is to be provided is sensorily disabled, the Central Public Officer or State Public Information Officer, as the case may be, shall provide assistance to enable access to the information, including providing such assistance as may be appropriate for the inspection.

(5) Where access to information is to be provided in the printed or in any electronic format, the applicant shall, subject to the provisions of Sub-section (6), pay such fee as may be prescribed: provided that the fee prescribed under

sub-sections (1) of Section 6 and Sub-sections (1) and (5) of Section 7 shall be reasonable and no such fee shall be charged from the persons who are of below poverty line as may be determined by the appropriate Government.

(6) Notwithstanding anything contained in Sub-section (5), the person making request for the information shall be provided the information free of charge where a public authority fails to comply with the time limits specified in sub-section (1).

(7) Before taking any decision under Sub-section (1), the Central Public Information Officer or State Public Information Officer, as the case may be, shall take into consideration the representation made by a third party under Section 11.

(8) Where a request has been rejected under Sub-section (1), the Central Public Information Officer or State Public Information Officer, as the Case may be, shall communicate to the person making the request,-

(i) The reasons for such rejection;

(ii) The period within which an appeal against such rejection may be preferred; and

(iii) The particulars of the appellate authority.

(9) An information shall ordinarily be provided in the form in which it is sought unless it would disproportionately divert the resources of the public authority or would be detrimental to the safety or preservation of the record in question.

4. Exemption from disclosure of information— (1) Notwithstanding anything contained in this Act, there shall be no obligation to give any citizen,-

(a) information disclosure of which would prejudicially affect the sovereignty and integrity of India, the Security, strategic, scientific or economic interests of the State, relation with foreign State or lead to incitement of an offence;

(b) information which has been expressly forbidden to be published by any Court of tribunal or the disclosure of which may constitute contempt of Court;

(c) information, the discloser of which would cause a beach of privilege of Parliament or the State Legislature;

(d) information including commercial confidence, trade secrets or intellectual property, the disclosure of which. would harm the competitive position of the third party, unless the competent authority is satisfied that large public interest warrants the disclosure of such information;

(e) information available to the person in his fiduciary relationship, unless the competent authority is satisfied that the larger public fnterest warrants the disclosure of such information;

(f) information received in confidence from foreign Government;

(g) information, the disclosure of which would endanger the life or physical safety of any person or identify the source of information or assistance given in confidence for law enforcement or security purposes;

(h) information which would impede the process of investigation or apprehension or prosecution of offenders;

(i) cabinet papers including records of deliberation of the Council of Ministers, Secretaries and other officers:

Provided that the decisions of Council of Ministers, the reasons thereof, and the material on the basis of which the decisions were taken shall be made public after the decision has been taken, and the matter is complete, or over:

Provided further that those matters which come under the exemptions specified in this section shall not be disclosed;

(j) information which relates to personal information the disclosure of which has no relationship to any public activity or interest, or which would cause unwarranted invasion of the privacy of the individual unless the Central Public

Information Officer or the State Information Officer or the appellate authority, as the case may be, is satisfied that the larger public interest justifies the disclosure of such information:

Provided that the information which cannot be denied to the Parliament or a State Legislature shall not be denied to any person.

(2) Notwithstanding anything in the Official Secrets Act. 1923 nor any of the exemptions permissible in accordance with Sub-section (1), a public authority may allow access to information, if public interests.

(3) Subject to the provisions of Clauses (a), (c), and (i) of Sub-section (1), any information relating to any occurrence, event or matter which has taken place, occurred or happened twenty years before the date on which any request is made under Section 6 shall be provided to any person making a request under that section:

Provided that where any question arises as to the date from which the said period of twenty years has to be computed, the decision of the Central Government shall be final, subject to the usual appeals provided for in this Act..

5. Grounds for rejection to access in certain cases- Without prejudice to the provisions of Section 8, a Central Public Information officer or a State Public Information Officer, as the case may be, may reject a request for information where such a request for providing access would involve an infringement of copyright subsisting in a person other than the State.

Comment

The request for any information involving infringement of copyright of any individual other than a State may be rejected by the Central/ State Public Information officer.

6. Severability- (1) Where a request for access to information is rejected on the ground that it is in relation to information which is exempt from discloser, then, notwithstanding anything contained in this Act, access may be provided to that part of the record which does not contain any information which is exempt from disclosure under this Act and which can reasonably be severed from any part that contains exempt information.

(2) Where access is granted to a part of the record under Sub-section (1), the Central Public Information Officer or State Public Information Officer, as the case may be, shall give a notice to the applicant, informing-

(a) that only part of the record requested, after severance of the record containing information which is exempt from disclosure, is being provided;

(b) the reasons for the decision, including any findings on any material question of fact, referring to the material on which those findings were based;

(c) the name and decision of the person giving the decision;

(d) the details of the fees calculated by him or her and the amount of fee which the applicant is required to deposit; and

(e) his or her rights with respect to review of the decision-regarding non-disclosure of part of the information, the amount of fee charged or the from of access provided, including the particulars of the senior officer specified under Sub-section (1) of Section 19 or the Central Information Commission or the State Information Commission, as the case may be, time limit, process and any other from of access.

Comment

Where a reqúest for access to information is rejected on the ground that such information is exempt from disclosure, than, access may be provided to that part of the record which is not exempted from disclosure under this Act and which can reasonable can reasonably be severed from any part which contains exemption information.

7. Third party information- (1) Where a Central Public Information Officer or a State public information Officer, as the case may be, intends to disclose any information or record, or part thereof on a request made under this Act, which relates to or has been supplied by third party and has been treated as confidential by that third party, the Central Public Information Officer or State Public Information Officer, as the case may be, shall, within five days from the receipt of the request, give a written notice to such third party of the request and of the fact that the Central Information Officer or State Public Information Officer, as the case may be, intends to disclose the information or record, or part thereof, and invite the third party to make a submission in writing or orally, regarding whether the information should be disclosed, and such submission of the third party shall be kept in view while taking a decision about disclosure of information:

Provided that except in the case of trade or commercial secrets protected by law, disclosure may be allowed if the public interest in disclosure outweighs in importance any possible harm or injury to the interests of such third party.

(2) Where a notice is served by the Central Public Information Officer or state Public Information Officer, as the case may be, under Sub-section (1) to a third party in respect of information or record or part thereof, the third party shall, within ten days from the date of receipt of such notice, be given the opportunity to make representation against the proposed disclosure.

(3) Notwithstanding anything contained in Section 7, the Central Public Information Officer or State Public Information Officer, as the case may be, shall, within forty days after receipt of the request under Section 6, if the third party has been given an opportunity to make representation-under Sub-section (2), make a decision as to whether or not

to disclose the information or record or part thereof and give writing the notice of his decision to the third party.

(4) A notice given under sub-section (3) shall include a statement that the third party to whom the notice is given is entitled to prefer an appeal under Section 19 against the decision.

Comment

If any information or record or part thereof, of a request made under this Act is related to or has been supplied by a third party and has been treated as confidential by that third party, the Central/State public Information Officer, as the case may be, shall, within five days from the receipt of the request serve a written notice on such third party of the request and of the fact that the central/state public information officer as the case may be, intends to disclose information or record, or part thereof and invite the third party to make a submission in writing or orally, with regard to whether information should be disclosed, and such submission of the third party shall be kept in view wtyle taking a decision about the disclosure of such information.

Chapter III

The central information commission

12. Constitution of central information commission—(1) The Central Government shall, by notification in the Official Gazette, constitute a body to be known as the central information commission to exercise the powers conferred on, and to perform the functions assigned to, it under this Act.

(2) The central information shall consist of -

1. the chief information commissioner; and

2. such number of central information commissioners, not exceeding ten, as may be deemed necessary.

(3) The chief information commissioner and information commissioners shall be appointed by the president on the

recommendation of a committee consisting of -(i) the prime Minister, who shall be the chairperson of the committee;

(ii) the Leader of opposition in the Lok Sabha; and (iii) a Union cabinet Minister to be nominated by the prime Minister.

Explanation- For the purposes of removal of doubts, it is hereby declared that where the Leader of opposition in the House of the people has not been recognised as such, the Leader of the single largest group in opposition of the Government in the House of the people shall be deemed to be the Leader of opposition.

(4) The general superintendence, direction and management of the affairs of the central information commission shall vest in the chief information commissioner who shall be assisted by the information commissioners and may exercise all such powers and do all such acts and things which may be exercised or done by the central information commission autonomously without being subjected to directions by any other authority under this Act.

(5) The chief information commissioner and information commissioners shall be persons of eminence in public life with wide knowledge and experience in law, science and technology, social service, management, journalism, mass media or administration and governance.

(6) The chief information commissioner or an information commissioner shall not be a Member of parliament or Member of the Legislature of any state or Union territory, as the case may be, or hold any other office of profit or connected with any political party or carrying on any business or pursuing any profession.

(7) The headquarters of the central information commission shall be at Delhi and the central information commission may, with the previous approval of the central Government, establish offices at other places in India.

13. Term of office of and conditions of service -(1) The chief information commissioner shall hold office for a term of five years from the date on which he enters upon his office and shall not be eligible for reappointment:

Provided that no chief information commissioner shall hold office as such after he has attained the age of sixty-five years.

(ii) Every infor.mation commissioner shall hold office for a term of five years from the date on which he enters upon his office or till he attains the age of sixty-five years, whichever is earlier, and shall not be eligible for reappointment as such information commissioner:

Provided that every information commissioner shal^on vacating his office under this sub-section be eligible for appointment as the chief information commissioner in the manner specified in sub-section (3) of section 12:

Provided further that where the information commissioner is appointed as the chief information commissioner, his term of office shall not be more than five years in aggregate as the information commissioner and the chief information commissioner.

(3) The chief information commissioner or an information commissioner shall before he enters upon his office make and subscribe before the president or some other person appointed by him in that behalf, an oath or affirmation according to the form set out for the purpose in the first schedule.

(4) The chief information commissioner or an information commissioner may, at any time, by writing under his hand addressed to the president, resign from his office: Provided that the chief information commissioner or an information commissioner may be removed in the manner specified under section 14.

(5) The salaries and allowances payable to and other terms and conditions of service of-

(a) the chief information commissioner shall be the same as that of the chief Election commissioner;

(b) an information commissioner shall be the same as that of an Election commissioner:

Provided that if the chief information commissioner or an information commissioner, at the time of his appointment is, in receipt of a pension, other than a disability or wound pension, in respect of any previous service under the Government of India or under the Government of a state, his salary in respect of the service as the chief information commissioner or an information commissioner shall be reduced by the amount of that pension including any portion of pension which was commuted and pension equivalent of other forms of retirement benefits excluding pension equivalent of retirement gratuity: Provided further that if the Chief Information Commission or an Information Commissioner if, at the time of his appointment is, in receipt of retirement benefits in respect of any previous service rendered in a Corporation established by or under any Central Act or State Act or a Government company owned or controlled by the Central Government or the State Government, his salary in respect of the service as the Chief Information Commissioner or an Information Commissioner shall be reduced by the amount of pension equivalent to the retirement benefits:

Provided also that the salaries, allowances and other conditions of service of the Chief Information Commissioner and the Information Commissioners shall not be varied to their disadvantage after their appointment.

(6) the Central Government shall provide the Chief Information Commissioner and the Information' Commissioners with such officers and employees as may be necessary for the efficient performance of their function under this Act, and the salaries and allowances payable to and the terms and conditions of service of the officers and other employees appointed for the purpose of this Act shall be such as may be prescribed.

14. Removal of Chief Information Commissioner or Information Commissioner- (1) Subject to the provisions of Sub-section (3), the Chief Information Commissioner or any Commissioner shall be removed from his office only by order of the President on the ground of proved misbehaviour or incapacity after the Supreme Court, on a reference made to it by the President, has, on inquiry, reported that the Chief Information Commissioner or any Information Commissioner, as the case may be, ought on such ground be removed.

(2) The President may suspend from office, and if deem necessary prohibit also from attending the office during inquiry, the Chief Information Commissioner or Information Commissioner in respect if whom a reference has bee made to the Supreme Court under Sub-section (1) until the President has passed orders on receipt of the report of the supreme Court on such reference.

(3) Notwithstanding anything contained in Sub-section (1), the president may by order remove from office the Chief Information Commissioner or any Information Commissioner if the Chief Information Commissioner or a Information Commissioner, as the Case may be,-

(a) is adjudged an insolvent; or

(b) has been convicted of an offence which, in the opinion of the President, involves moral turpitude; or

(c) engages during his term of office in any paid employment outside the duties of his office; or

(d) is, in the opinion of the President, unfit to continue in office by reason of infirmity of mind or body; or

(e) has acquired such financial or other interest as is likely to affect prejudicially his functions as the Chief Information Commissioner or a Information Commissioner.

(4) If the Chief Information Commissioner or an Information Commissioner in any way, concerned or interested in any contract or agreement made by or on

behalf of the Government of India or participates in any way in the profit thereof or in any benefit or emolument arising therefrom otherwise than as a member and in common with the other members of an incorporated company, he shall, for the purposes of Sub-section (1), be deemed to be guilty to be guilty of misbehaviour.

Chapter VI

The State Information Commission

15. Constitution of State Information Commission—(1) Every State Government shall, by notification in the ***Official Gazette,*** constitute, constitute a body to be know as the ....(name of the State) Information Commission to exercise the powers conferred on, and to perform the functions assigned to, it under this Act.

(2) The State Information Commission shall consist of-

(a) the State Chief Information Commissioner, and

(b) such number of State Information Commissioners, not exceeding ten, as may be deemed necessary.

(3) The State Chief Information Commissioner and the State Information Commissioners shall be appointed by the Governor on the recommendation of a committee consisting of-(i) the Chief Minister, who shall be the Chairperson of the committee;

(ii) the Leader of Opposition in the Legislative Assembly; and

(iii) a Cabinet Minister to be nominated by the Chief Minister.

Explanation- For the purposes of removal of doubts, it is hereby declared that where the Leader of Opposition in the Legislative Assembly has not been recognised as such, the leader of the single largest group in opposition of the Government in the Legislative Assembly shall be deemed to be the Leader of Opposition.

(4) The general superintendence, direction and management of the affairs of the State Information Commission shall vest in the State Chief Information Commissioner who shall be assisted by the State Information Commissioners and may exercise all such powers and do all such acts and things which may be exercised or done by the State Information Commission autonomously without being subjected to directions by any other authority under this Act.

(5) The State Chief Information Commissioner and State Information Commissioners shall be persons of eminence in public life with wide knowledge and experience in law, science and technology, social service, management, journalism, mass media or administration and governance.

(6) The State Chief Information Commissioner or a State Information Commissioner shall not be a Member of Parliament or Member of the Legislature of any State or Union territory, as the case may be, or hold any other office of profit or connected with any political party or carrying on any business or pursuing any profession.

(7) The Headquarters of the State Information Commission shall be at such place in the State as the State Government may, by notification in the ***Official Gazette,*** specify and State Information Commission may, with the previous approval of the State Government, establish offices at other places in the State Government, establish Offices at other places in the State.

Comment

Every state Government has to constitute State Information Communication to exercise the powers conferred on, and the performed functions assigned to it under this Act. The State Information Commission shall consists of - (i) the State Chief Information Commissioner, and (ii) State Information Commissioners, not exceeding ten. The State Chief Information Commissioners and the State Information

Commissioners shall be appointed by the Governor on the recommendation of a Committee consisting of: (i) The Chief Minister who shall be Chairperson of the Committee; (ii) The Leader of the opposition in the Legislative Assembly; and (iii) A Cabinet Minister to be nominated by the Chief Minister.

The Headquarters of the State Information Commissioner shall be at such place in the State as the State Government may specify.

16. Term of office and conditions of service—(1) The State Chief Information Commissioner shall hold office for a term of five years from the date on which he enters upon his office and shall not be eligible for reappointment:

Provided that no State Chief Information Commissioner shall hold office as such after he has attained the age of sixty-five years.

(2) Every State Information Commissioner shall hold office for a term of five years from the date on which he enters upon his office or till he attains the age of sixty-five years, whichever is earlier, and shall not be eligible for reappointment as such State Information Commissioner:

provided that every State Information Commissioner shall, on vacating his office under this sub-section, be eligible for appointment as the State Chief Information Commissioner in the manner specified in Sub-section (3) of Section 15:

Provided further that where the State Information Commissioner is appointed as the State Chief Information Commissioner, his term, of office shall not be more than five years in aggregate as the State Information Commissioner and the State Chief information Commissioner.

(3) The State Chief Information Commissioner or a State Information Commissioner shall before he enters upon his office make and subscribe before the Governor or some other person appointed by him in that behalf, an oath or

affirmation according to the form set out for the purpose in the First schedule.

(4) The State Chief Information Commissioner or a State Information Commissioner may, at any time, by writing under his hand addressed to the Governor, resign from his office: Provided that the State Chief Information Commissioner or a State Information Commissioner may be removed in the manner specified under Section 17.

(5) The salaries and allowances payable to and other terms and conditions of service of-

(a) the State Chief Information Commissioner shall be the same as that of an Election Commissioner;

(b) the State Information Commissioner shall be the same as that of the Chief Secretary to the State Government:

Provided that if the State Chief Information Commissioner or a State Information Commissioner, at the time of his appointment is, in receipt of a pension, other than a disability or would pension, in respect of any previous service under the Government of India or under the Government of a State, his salary in respect of the service as the State Chief Information Commissioner or a State Information Commissioner shall be reduced by the amount of that pension including any portion which was commuted and pension equivalent of other forms of retirement benefits excluding pension equivalent of retirement gratuity:

Provided further that where the State Chief Information Commissioner or State Information Commissioner if, at the time of his appointment is, in respect of retirement benefits in respect of any previous service rendered in a Corporation established by or under any Central Act or State Act or a Government Company owned or controlled by the Central Government or the State Government, his salary in respect of the service as the State Chief Information Commissioner or the State Information Commissioner shall be reduced by the amount of pension equivalent to the retirement benefits:

Provided also that the salaries, allowances and other conditions of service of the state Chief Information Commissioner and the State Information Commissioners shall not be varied to their disadvantage after their appointment.

(6) The State Government shall be provide the State Chief Information Commissioner and the State Information Commissioners with such officers and employees as may be necessary for the efficient performance of their function under this Act, and the salaries and allowances payable to and the terms and conditions of service of the officers and other employees appointed for the purpose of this Act shall be such as may be prescribed.

Comment

The State Chief Information Commissioner can hold office for a term of five years from the date which he enters upon his office and cannot be eligible for re-appointment.

17. Removal of State Chief information Commissioner or State Information Commissioner- (1) Subject to the provisions of Sub section (3), the State Chief Information Commissioner or a State Information Commissioner shaH be ramoved from his office only by order of the Governor on the ground of proved misbehaviour or incapacity after the Supreme Court, on a reference made to it by the Governor, has on inquiry, reported that the State Chief Information Commissioner or a State Information Commissioner, as the case may be, ought on such ground be removed.

(2) The Governor may suspend from office, and if deem necessary prohibit also from attending the office during inquiry, the State Chief Information Commissioner or a State Information Commissioner in respect of whom a reference has been made to the Supreme Court under Sub-section (1) until the Governor has passed orders on receipt of the report of the Supreme Court on Such reference.

(3) Notwithstanding anything contained in Sub-section (1), the Governor may by order remove from office the State Chief Information Commissioner or a State Information Commissioner if a State Chief Information Commissioner or a State Information Commissioner, as the case may be,-

(a) is adjudged an insolvent; or

(b) has been convicted of an offence which, in the opinion of the Governor, involve moral turpitude; or

(c) engages during his term of office in any paid employment outside the duties of his office; or

(d) is, in the opinion of the Governor, unfit to continue in office by reason of infirmity of mind or body; or

(e) has acquired such financial or other interest as is likely to affect prejudicially his functions as the State Chief Information Commissioner or a State Information Commissioner.

(4) If the State Chief Information Commissioner or any State Information Commissioner, is in anyway, concerned or interested in any contract or agreement made by or on behalf of the Government of the State or participates in any way in the profit thereof or in any benefit or emoluments arising there from otherwise than as a member and in common with the other members of an incorporated company, he shall, for the purposes of Subjection (1), be deemed to be guilty of misbehaviour.

Chapter V

Power and functions of the Information Commissions, appeal and penalties

18. Powers and functions of Information Commissions—(1) Subject to the provisions of this Act, it shall be the duty of the Central Information Commission or State Information Commission, as the case may be, to receive and inquire into a complaint from any person,-

(a) who has been unable to submit a request to a Central Public Information Officer or State Public Information

Officer, as the case may be, either by reason that no such officer has been appointed under this Act, or because the Central Assistant Public Information Officer or State Assistant Public Information Officer, as the case may be, has refused to accept his or her application for information or appeal under this Act for forwarding the same to the Central Public Information Officer, or State Public Information Officer or senior officer specified in Sub-section (1) of Section 19 or the Central Information Commissioner or the State Information Commission, as the case may be;

(b) who has been refused access to any information requested under this Act;

(c) who has not been given a respbnse to a request for information or access to information within the time limit specified under this Act;

(d) who has been required to pay an amount of fee which he or she considers unreasonable;

(e) who believes that he or she has been given incomplete, misleading or false information under this Act; and

(f) in respect of any other matter relating to requesting or obtaining access to records under this Act.

(2) Where the Central Information Commission or State Information Commission, as the case may be, is satisfied that there are reasonable grounds to inquire into the matter, it may initiate an inquiry in respect thereof.

(3) The Central Information Commission or State Information Commission, as the Case may be, shall, while inquiring into any matter under this Section, have the same powers as are vested in a Civil Court while trying a suit under the Code of Civil Procedure, 1908, in respect of the following matters, namely:

(a) summoning and enforcing the attendance of persons and compel them to give oral or written evidence on oath and to produce the documents or things;

(b) requiring the discovery and inspection of documents;

(c) receiving evidence on affidavit;

(d) requisitioning any public record or copies thereof from any Court or office;

(e) issuing summons for examination of witnesses or documents; and

(f) any other matter which may be prescribed.

(4) Notwithstanding anything inconsistent contained in any other Act of Parliament or State Legislature, as the case may be, the Central Information Commission or the State Information, as the case may be, the central Information Commission or the State Information Commission, as the case may be, may, during the inquiry of any complaint under this Act, examine any record to which this Act applies which is under the control of the public authority, and no such record may be withheld from it on any grounds.

19. Appeal—(1) Any person who, does not receive a decision within the time specified in Sub-section (1) or Clause (a) of Sub-section (3) of Section 7, or is aggrieved by a decision of the Central Public Information Officer or State Public Information Officer, as the case may be, may within thirty days from the expiry of such period or from the receipt of such a decision prefer an appeal to such officer who is senior in rank to the Central Public Information Officer or State Public Information Officer as the case may be, in each public authority:

provided that such officer may admit the appeal after the expiry of the period of thirty days if he or she is satisfied that the appellant was prevented by sufficient cause from filing the appeal in time.

(2) Where an appeal is preferred against an order made by a Central Public Information Officer or a State Public Information Officer, as the case may be, under Section 11 to disclose third party information, the appeal by the concerned third party shall be made within thirty days from the days from the date of the order.

(3) A secccnd appeal against the decision under Sub-section (1) shall lie within ninety days from the date on which the decision should have been made or was actually received, with the Central Information Commission or the State Information Commission: Provided that the Central Information Commission or the State Information Commission, as the case may be, may admit the appeal after the expiry of the period of ninety days if it is satisfied that the appellant was prevented by sufficient cause from filing the appeal in time.

(4) If the decision of the Central Public Information Officer or State Public Information Officer, as the case may be, against which an appeal is preferred relates to information of a third party, the Central Information Commission or State Information Commission, as the case may be, shall give a reasonable opportunity of being heard to that third party.

(5) In any appeal proceedings, the onus to prove that a denial of a request was justified shall be on the Central Public Information Officer or State Public Information Officer, as the case may be, who denied the request.

(6) An appeal uhder Sub-section (1) or Sub-section (2) shall be disposed of within thirty days of the receipt of the appeal or within such extended period not exceeding a total of forty-five days from the date of filing thereof, as the case may be, for reasons to be recorded in writing.

(7) The decision of the Central Information Commission or State Information Commission, as the case may be, shall be binding.

(8) In its decision, the Central Information Commission or State Information Commission, as the case may be, has the power to-

(a) require the public authority to take any such steps as may be necessary to secure compliance with the provisions of this Act, including-

(i) by providing access to information, if so requested, in a particular form;

(ii) by appointing a Central Public Information Officer or State Public Information Officer, as the case may be;

(iii) by publishing certain information or categories of information;

(iv) by making necessary changes to its practices in relation to the maintenance, management and destruction of records;

(v) by enhancing the provision of training on the right to information for its officials;

(vi) by providing it with an annual report in compliance with Clause (b) of Sub-section (1) of Section 4;

(b) require the public authority to compensate the complainant for any loss or other detriment suffered;

(c) impose any of the penalties provided under this Act;

(d) reject the application.

(9) The Central Information Commission or State Information Commission, as the case may be, shall give notice of its decision, including any right of appeal, to the complainant and the public authority.

The Central Information Commission or State Information Commission, as the case may be, shall decide the appeal in accordance with such procedure as may be prescribed.

Comment

An appeal can be preferred by any person who does not receive a decision within the specified time, or is aggrieved by decisions of the Central/State Public Information Officer as the case may be within 30 days to such Officer who is senior in rank.

20. Penalties- (1) Where the Central Information Commission or the State Information Commission, as the case may be, at the time of deciding any complaint or appeal is of the opinion that the Central Public Information Officer or the State Public Information Officer, as the case may be, has, without any reasonable cause, refused to receive an application for information or has not furnished information within the time specified under Sub-section (1) of Section 7 or ***malafidely*** denied the request for information or knowingly given incorrect, incomplete or misleading information or destroyed information which was the subject of the request or obstructed in any manner in furnishing the information, it shall impose a penalty of two hundred and fifty rupees each day till application is received or information is furnished, so however, the total amount of such penalty shall not exceed twenty-five thousand rupees: Provided that the Central Public Information Officer or the State Public Information Officer, as the case may be, shall be given a reasonable opportunity of being heard before any penalty is imposed on him:

Provided further that the burden of proving that he acted reasonably and diligently shall be on the Central Public Information Officer or the State Public Information Officer, as the case may be.

ii. Where the Central Information Commission or the State Information Commission, as the case may be, at the time of deciding any complaint or appeal is of the opinion that the Central Public Information Officer or the State Public Information'Officer, as the case may be, has, without any reasonable cause and persistently, failed to receive an application for formation or has not furnished information within the time specified under Sub-section (1) of section 7 or ***malafidely*** denied the request for information or knowingly given incorrect, incomplete or misleading information or destroyed information which was the subject of the request or obstructed in any manner in furnishing the information, it shall recommend for disciplinary action against the Central Public Information Officer or the State Public Information Officer, as the case may be, under the service rule applicable to him.

Comment

(i) No legal proceeding shall lie against any person or anything which is done in good faith,

(ii) If any Central/State Public Information Officer has, Without any reasonable cause,

refuses to receive an application for information or has not furnished information within the specified time or mala fidely deny the request for information knowingly given incorrect, incomplete or misleading information or destroyed information which was the subject of the request or obstructed in any manner in furnishing the information, a penalty of Rs.250/- each day till application is received or information is. furnished, so however, the total of such penalty shall not exceed Rs. 25,0007- shall be imposed on that officer.

Chapter-VI

Miscellaneous

21. Protection of action taken in good faith- No suit, prosecution or other legal proceeding shall lie against any person for anything which is in good faith done or intended to be done under this Act or any rule made thereunder.

22. Act to have overriding effect- The provisions of this Act shall have effect notwithstanding anything inconsistent therewith contained in the Official Secrets Act, 1923, and any other law for the time being in force or in any instrument having effect by virtue of any law other than this Act.

23. Bar of jurisdiction of Courts- No Court shall entertain any suit, application or other proceeding in respect of any order made under this Act and no such order shall be called in question otherwise than by way of an appeal under this Act.

24. Act not to apply to certain organisations- (1) Nothing contained in this Act shall apply to the intelligence and security organisations specified in the Second Schedule, being organisations established by the Central Government or any information furnished by such organisations to that Government.

Provided that the information pertaining to the allegations of corruption and human rights violations shall not be excluded under this sub-section:

Provided further that in the case of information sought for is in respect of allegations of violation of human rights, the information shall only be provided after the approval of the Central Information Commission, and notwithstanding anything contained Section 7, such information shall be provided within forty-five days from the date of the receipt of request.

(2) The Central Government may, by notification in the Official Gazetted, amend the Schedule by including therein any other intelligence or security organisation established by that Government or omitting therefrom any organisation already specified therin and on the publication of such notification, such organisation shall be deemed to be included in or, as the case may be, omitted from the Schedule.

(3) Every notification issued under Sub-section (2) shall be laid before each House of Parliament.

(4) Nothing contained in this Act shall apply to such intelligence and security organisation being organisations established by the State Government, as that Government may, from time, by notification in the Official Gazetted, specify:

Provided that information pertaining the allegations of corruption and human rights violations shall not be excluded under this sub-section;

Provided further that in the case of information sought for is in respect of allegations of violation of human rights, the information shall only be provided after the approval of the State Information Commission not notwithstanding anything contained in Section 7, such information shall be provided within forty-five days from the date of the receipt of request.

(5) Every notification issued under Sub-section (4) shall be laid before the State Legislature.

25. Monitoring and reporting- (1) The Central InfoOrmation Commission or State Information Commission as the case may be, shall as soon as practicable after the end of each year, prepare a report on the implementation of the provisions of this Act during that year and forward a copy thereof to the appropriate Government.

(2) Each Ministry or Development shall, in relation to the public authorities within their jurisdiction, collect and provide such information to the Central Information Commission or State Information Commission as the case may be, as is required to prepare the report under this Section and comply with requirements concerning the furnishing of that information and keeping of records for the purposes of this section.

(3) Each report shall state in respect of the year to which the report relates,-

(a) The number of requests made to each public authority;

(b) The number of decisions where applicants were not entitled to access to the documents pursuant to the requests, the provisions of this Act under which these decisions were made and the number of times such provisions were invoked;

(c) The number of appeals referred to the Central Information Commission or State Information Commission, as the case may be, for review, the nature of the appeals and the outcome of the appeals;

(d) Particulars of any disciplinary action taken against any ; officer in respect of the administration of this Act;

(e) The amount of changes collected by each public authority under this Act;

(f) Any facts which indicate an effort by the public authorities to administer and implement the spirit intention of this Act;

(g) Recommendations for reform, including recommendations in respect of the particular public authorities, for the development, improvement, modernisation, reform or amendment to this Act or other legislation or common law or any other matter relevant for operationalising the right to access information.

(4) The Central Government or the State Government, as the case may be, may, as soon as practicable after the end of each year, cause a copy of the report of the Central Information Commission or the State Information Commission, as the case may be, referred to in Sub-section (1) to be laid before each House of Parliament or, as the case may be, before each house of the State Legislature, where there are two Houses, and where there is one House of the State Legislature before that House.

(5) If it appears to the Central Information Commission or State Information Commission, as the case may be, that the practice of a public authority in relation to the exercise of its functions under this Act does not conform with the provisions or sprit of this Act, it may give to the authority a recommendation specifying the steps which ought in its opinion to be taken for promoting such conformity.

26. Appropriate Government to prepare programmes—(1) The appropriate Government may, to the extent of availability of financial and other resources,-

(a) Develop and organise educational programmes to advance the understanding of the public, in particular of disadvantaged communities as to how to exercise the rights contemplated under this Act;

(b) Encourage public authorities to participate in the

development and organisation of programmes referred to in clause (a) and to undertake such programmes themselves;

(c) Promote timely and effective dissemination of accurate information of accurate information by public authorities about their activities; and

(d) Train Central Public Information Officers or State Public Information Officers, as the case may be, of public authorities and produce relevant training materials for use by the public authorities themselves.

(2) The appropriate Government shall, within eighteen months from the commencement of this Act, compile in its official language a guide containing such information, in an easily comprehensible from and manner, as may reasonable be required by a person who wishes to exercise any rights specified in this Act.

(3) The appropriate Government Shall, if necessary, update and publish the guidelines referred to in Sub-section (2) at regular intervals which shall, in particular and without prejudice to the generality of Sub-section (2), include-

(a) The object of this Act;

(b) The postal and street address, the phone and fax number and, if available, electronic mail address of the Central Public Information Officer or State Public Information Officer as the case may be, of every public authority appointed under Sub-section (1) of Section 5;

(c) The manner and the form in which request for access to an information shall be made to a Central Public Information Officer or State Public Information Officer, as the case may be;

(d) The assistance available from and the duties of the Central Public Information Officer or State Public Information Officer, as the case may be, of a public authority under this Act;

(e) The assistance available from the Central Information - Commission or State Information Commission, as the case may be;

(f) All remedies in law available regarding an act or failure to act in respect of a right or duty conferred or imposed by this Act including the manner of filling an appeal to the Commission;

(g) The provisions providing for the voluntary disclosure of categories of records in accordance with Section4;

(h) The notice regarding fee to be paid in relation to requests for access to an information; and

(i) Any additional regulations or circulars made or issued in relation to obtaining access to an information in accordance with this Act.

(4) The appropriate Government must, if necessary, update and publish the guidelines at regular intervals.

27. Power to make rule by appropriate Government—(1) The appropriate Government may, by notification in the ***Official Gazette,*** make rules to carry out the provisions of this Act. (2) In particular, and without prejudice to the generality of the forgoing power, such rules may provide for all or any of the following ' matters, namely:

(a) The cost of medium or print cost price of the materials to be disseminated under Sub-section (4) of Section 4;

(b) The fee payable under Sub-section (1) of Section 6;

(c) The fee payable under Sub-sections (1) and (5) of Section 7;

(d) The salaries and allowances payable to and the terms and conditions of service of the officers and other employees under Sub-section (6) of Section 13 and Sub-section (6) of Section 16,

(e) The procedure to be adopted by the Central Information Commission or State Information Commission, as the case may be, in deciding the appeals under Sub-section (10) of Section 19; and

(f) Any other matter which is required to be, or may be, prescribed.

28. Power to make rules by competent authority- (1) The competent authority may, by notification in the official Gazette, make rules to carry out the provisions of this Act.

(2) In particular, and without prejudice to the generality of the foregoing power, such rules may provide for all or any of the following matters, namely:

(i) the cost of the medium or print cost price of the materials to be disseminated under sub-section (4) of section 4;

(ii) the fee payable under sub-section (1) of section 6;

(iii) the fee payable under sub-section (1) of section 7; and

(iv) any other matter which is required to be, or may be, prescribed

29. Laying of rules—(1) Every rule made by the central Government under this Act shall be laid, as soon as may be after it is made, before each house of parliament, while it is in session, for a total period of thirty days which may be comprised in one session or in two or more successive sessions, and if, before the expiry of the sessions immediately following the session or the successive ns atoresaid, both houses agree in making any von in the rule or both Houses agree that the rule should be, the rule shall thereafter have effect only in such i or be of no effect, as the case may be; so, however, modification or annulment shall be without prejudice to the validity of anything previously done under that rule.

(2) Every rule made under this Act by a state Government shall be laid, as soon as may be after it is notified, before the state Legislature.

30. Power to remove difficulties-(1) If any difficulty arises in giving effect to the provisions of this Act, the central Government may, by order published in the official Gazette, make such provisions not inconsistent with the provisions of this Act as appear to it to be necessary or expedient for removal of the difficulty: Provided that no such order shall be made after the expiry of a period of two years from the date of the commencement of this Act.

(2) Every order made under this section shall, as soon as may be after it is made, be laid before each house of parliament,

31. Repeal—The freedom of information Act, 2002 is hereby repealed.

THE FIRST SCHEDULE
[See sections 13 (3) and 16 (3)]

From of oath or affirmation to be made by the chief information commissioner/the information commissioner /the state chief information commissioner /the state information commissioner

"I...................... having been appointed chief information commissioner/information commissioner/state chief information commissioner/state information commissioner swear in the name of God/solemnly affirm that I will bear true faith and allegiance to the constitution of India as by law established, that I will uphold the sovereignty and integrity of India, that I will duly and faithfully and to the best of my ability, knowledge and judgment perform the duties of my office without fear or favour, affection or ill-will and that I will uphold the constitution and the laws."

Index

G

H

T

U